THE
WATSON DYNASTY

THE

WATSON DYNASTY

THE FIERY REIGN AND TROUBLED LEGACY OF IBM'S FOUNDING FATHER AND SON

Richard S. Tedlow

HarperBusiness

An Imprint of HarperCollins*Publishers*

HarperCollins books may be purchased for educational, business, or sales promotional use. For information, please write: Special Markets Department, HarperCollins Publishers Inc., 10 East 53rd Street, New York, NY 10022.

Designed by Nancy Singer Olaguera

Library of Congress Cataloging-in-Publication Data

Tedlow, Richard S.
    The Watson dynasty : the fiery reign and troubled legacy of IBM's founding father and son / Richard S. Tedlow.
        p. cm.
    Includes bibliographical references and index.
    ISBN 0-06-001405-9
    1. International Business Machines Corporation—History. 2. Family-owned business enterprises—United States—Case studies. 3. Fathers and sons—United States—Case studies. 4. Executives—United States—Biography. 5. Watson, Thomas John, 1874–1956. 6. Watson, Thomas J., 1914– I. Title.

HD9696.2.U64I258   2003
338.7'61004'0922—dc21
[B]

                                                                    2003051145

03 04 05 06 07 ❖/RRD 10 9 8 7 6 5 4 3 2 1

To my late beloved wife, Joyce R. Tedlow, M.D.

"Children have never been very good at listening to their elders, but they have never failed to imitate them."

—James Baldwin

"The problem with the family firm is growth. Either the family grows faster than the firm or the firm grows faster than the family."

—a well-known aphorism

Contents

Prologue

One day in April 1993, Lou Gerstner got into his car to drive from his home in Greenwich, Connecticut, to his office in Armonk, New York. On April 1, Gerstner had become the chief executive officer of the International Business Machines Corporation. IBM was on its way to losing $8.1 billion that year, more money than any other business had ever lost.

On this particular morning, Gerstner encountered a little surprise when he opened his car door. He had company. Thomas J. Watson Jr. was already there.

Watson, seventy-nine years old, was a man with a pedigree and a résumé. His father had taken the reins of a small struggling mess of a company in 1914 and turned it into a global powerhouse by the time he retired in 1956. Watson Jr. had taken an already great company and made it greater, introducing one of the most important products in the history of business, the System/360.

But now, Watson was "animated, agitated, and angry." He told Gerstner to save "my company." He urged bold action.

Many people thought IBM's chances for survival were not good. Many believed that Gerstner was not the man to save it. This book will help explain why the skeptics were wrong. The Watsons had built IBM to last. The process of creating the company took a heavy personal toll on many who were involved. The strength was there, however. The question was: Would Gerstner be able to build on it, or would IBM be sucked into the tar pit of oblivion?

CHAPTER 1

Defining Moments

The world's fair in New York City at the end of the depression decade was a big deal. Planning began in 1935. The fairgrounds covered 1,216.5 acres in what had been a garbage dump in Queens. By opening day, April 30, 1939, the moonscape that had been Flushing Meadows was transformed, in the perhaps pardonable hyperbole of the guidebook, into a "stupendous, gigantic, super-magnificent . . . greatest show on earth." *Time* magazine called it "the biggest, costliest, most ambitious undertaking ever attempted in the history of international exhibitions."

Over sixty nations had pavilions and exhibits clustered around the "Court of Peace" on the fairgrounds. Every major country was represented save Germany. New York's mayor, Fiorello H. La Guardia, had suggested in 1937 that a "Chamber of Horrors" be dedicated to Nazi Germany. The Nazis did not see the humor in the idea of the man they labeled "a dirty Talmud Jew," lodged a protest with the State Department, and refused to participate in the festivities.

Dozens of corporations saw the fair, with its theme of "Building the World of Tomorrow," as an ideal venue for institutional advertising and image making. This fair was to be more than merely a "showroom for the display of goods"; it was to be, according to historian Roland Marchand, a *"World Stage* upon which to dramatize the advantages of the American system of free enterprise."

Foremost among the more than forty company exhibitors was the nation's largest industrial corporation, General Motors. Still smarting from the disastrous sit-down strike in Flint in the winter of 1936–37, the result of which was the unionization of its plants and the creation of the United Automobile Workers, General Motors was anxious to turn the nation's attention to its ambitions for the future. This it attempted to do through "Futurama," a remarkable invitation to "share our world." It was the hit of the fair, with more attendees and rave reviews than any other exhibit. Other companies spending large amounts of money to educate the public about their greatness included Ford, Chrysler, AT&T, General Electric, and Westinghouse.

Also making their presence known at the fair were the International Business Machines Corporation and its indomitable leader, Thomas J. Watson Sr.

Watson was sixty-five years old when the fair opened, an age when many businessmen think about retirement. But Watson had the energy of a man in his thirties, and we can confidently assert that thoughts of retirement never entered his mind. For years he had been telling his troops, *"The IBM is not merely an organization of men; it is an institution that will go on forever."* He planned to accompany IBM on its journey—if not forever, then at least for a good many more years. And he had every intention of using the fair to tell the world that he and IBM—the two were inseparable in his mind—mattered.

On May 2, IBM held a huge meeting at the fair, with 2,200 employees in attendance. Watson told the listening throng that he wanted to keep the business session brief because the fair's educational opportunities "are so much broader than anything we could hope to give you that we are going to give you as much time as possible to visit these things." Nevertheless, there were eighteen speakers at the event.

May 2 was as nothing compared to Thursday, May 4—IBM

Day at the world's fair. May 4 was a busy day for Watson, but not a uniquely busy day. Indeed, one of the remarkable aspects of his long life was the number of days such as this which he arranged (and which those around him endured). Things were kicked off as Watson opened the fair for the day. He was accompanied by a mounted escort from Perylon Hall on the fairgrounds to the IBM exhibit at the Business Systems Building, where a precursor of a form of E-mail was displayed:

> As a demonstration of the latest device out of the I.B.M. research laboratories, a letter of congratulation was flashed through the air from San Francisco to New York on an I.B.M. radio-type. . . . It was offered as the high-speed substitute for mail service in the world of tomorrow.

Not only technology but art had a place in IBM Day. The company had commissioned the *IBM Symphony* by Vittorio Giannini, and the work was performed at this event and was broadcast. In a burst of understatement, *Fortune* magazine described the symphony as "somewhat programmatic in nature." The second movement contained a melodic reference to the most often sung of IBM's many songs, "Ever Onward."

Painting as well as music was part of IBM's artistic contribution to the fair. Watson was described in the *New York Times* as taking "a bold and potentially constructive step" by displaying works from seventy-nine countries in his Gallery of Science and Art in a large hall in the Business Systems Building at the fair. "Far-flung" would be the best way to describe the countries represented. They included French Indochina, Libya, Luxembourg, and the USSR. "Our endeavor," explained Watson,

> has been to increase the interest of business in art and of artists in business. . . . This step by an industrial organization is in recognition of the part played by art in industry and its

importance to industry in broadening the horizons of culture and influencing the needs and desires of the people of every country.

Whatever that might mean.

This collection traveled from one country to another after the fair. "To be sure," sniffed the *Times* reporter, "representation by one painter alone [from each country] is inclined to provoke a smile and must have caused prodigious head-scratching." Nevertheless, the plan was pronounced to "[work] well enough . . . upon the whole." This project generated a good deal of publicity for Watson and for IBM.

Watson made speeches during IBM Day ("As a businessman, I think of world peace as a sales problem"—what intelligent response, one wonders, could be made to such an assertion?), received compliments, and unveiled a statue of Peter Stuyvesant, the last colonial Dutch governor of what was New Amsterdam and became New York, at the Dutch pavilion.

But the day was still young. The IBM contingent headed back to Manhattan for more festivities at the Waldorf-Astoria. Over two thousand guests saw Watson inducted into the Quarter Century Club (he had joined IBM in 1914). He was presented with the Order of the Southern Cross of Brazil by a representative of its government and with innumerable other gifts from IBM's eleven thousand employees, among which was an oil portrait of himself. The evening concluded with a series of speeches, including one by Watson.

The world's fair ran from April 30 to October 31 in 1939 and again the following year from May 11 to October 27. The fair's second year took place in a context far different from its first. War was looming in the summer of 1939. It was reality in 1940. Some of the nations represented in the first year were gone by the second. The staff of the Polish pavilion did not go home after the fair closed in 1939. "Home was no longer on the map. They opened a Polish restaurant on Fifty-seventh Street. . . . Hitler destroyed Czechoslovakia even before its pavilion was complete." The fair's official theme was changed from "Building the World of Tomorrow" to "For Peace and Freedom."

Even though the war clouds of 1939 were generating torrential rain by 1940, the fair was still a splendid stage to tell the world about the glories of the International Business Machines Corporation and its peerless, fearless leader. But how was Watson to top the previous year's performance? That is the kind of question that never seemed to bother him.

For starters, this year IBM Day would be on the fair's opening day. And Watson would not be lonely in Flushing Meadows. He decided to bring ten thousand guests to New York, including all of the company's factory employees and sales and field-service men plus their wives, and put them up in Manhattan hotels for three days. He took out advertisements in the New York papers announcing "THEY ARE ALL COMING." "Nobody," observed Watson's eldest son, "had seen anything like it since the troop movements of World War I." Ten chartered trains would come from the factory and offices at Endicott, New York, in the "Valley of Opportunity" just north of the Pennsylvania border; one each would arrive from Rochester and from Washington, D.C.; and there would be "additional chartered Pullmans from all over." The cost for this extravaganza was $1 million, more than 10 percent of profits that year.

Everything was set. All the arrangements had been made. And then something went seriously wrong. The headline in the *New York Times* was:

250 HURT IN CRASH
OF TRAINS, JAMMED
FOR OUTING AT FAIR

———————

Two Specials Carrying I.B.M.
Staff Collide at Port Jervis
—Excessive Speed Blamed

———————

35 Remain in Hospitals

The trains involved were two of the ten specially chartered from the Erie Railroad to transport employees from the factories and administrative offices at Endicott. When one of these stopped at Port Jervis, another, which had been traveling too fast, ran into it. Said one passenger, "It felt like—you know how they do when they start off. You got a jolt like when they start a freight train. A suitcase fell on my head." Said another, "It felt as if we got an awfully hard bump. There was splitting and cracking and glass breaking. People were sitting on the floor. I don't know how I ever got out of my seat." She wound up sitting on the tracks waiting for first aid.

Word of the accident reached Watson in Manhattan at two o'clock on the morning of May 13. He hopped in a car with his oldest daughter, Jane, and headed for Port Jervis, about sixty-five miles northwest of New York City. Watson and Jane personally visited the injured in the hospitals. He mobilized IBM's executives in the city. He arranged for more doctors and nurses to be dispatched to Port Jervis. He hustled up another train to take those able to travel the rest of the way to Manhattan. A fully staffed hospital was set up at one of the hotels at which the IBM contingent was staying. Watson got back to New York City and immediately ordered flowers for all of the families who had been involved in the accident. His executives woke florists up to be sure that these bouquets were delivered to the hotel rooms before breakfast.

This sixty-six-year-old man then betook himself to the fair, where he delivered a speech alongside Mayor La Guardia and other personages. Lily Pons and Lawrence Tibbett of the Metropolitan Opera sang accessible opera as well as more modern pieces to "thrill" a crowd of twenty thousand. IBM Day was declared by one and all to be a success.

What did it all mean?

Compared to some of the other companies which chose the fair as a platform, IBM was tiny. Sales of General Motors in 1940 were $1.8 billion, profits $196 million, and assets $1.5 billion. The corresponding numbers for IBM were $46 million, $9.4 million, and $83 million. AT&T's assets were sixty-six times IBM's. Peter Drucker, at the time a correspondent for some British newspapers, suggested a story on IBM because of the size of its pavilion. He "thought a story on so small a frog behaving like a big shot might be amusing. 'Forget it,' my editor wrote back. 'We are not interested in a story on an unsuccessful company which as far as anyone can tell is never going to amount to much.'"

The editor was wrong, and the numbers did not matter. What mattered was the future. What mattered was the incident at Port Jervis. "Nobody ever forgot the way my father handled the Port Jervis wreck," recalled his eldest son. It was yet more proof of Watson's bulletproof leadership. What would have been a disaster for ninety-nine CEOs out of a hundred, he turned to advantage.

Doubtless "Ever Onward" was rendered with even greater gusto after Port Jervis:

> *There's a thrill in store for all,*
> *For we're about to toast*
> *The corporation in every land.*
> *We're here to cheer each pioneer*
> *And also proudly boast*
> *Of that "man of men," our friend and guiding hand.*
> *The name of T. J. Watson means a courage none can stem:*
> *And we feel honored to be here to toast the "IBM."*

Or, as the "IBM School Song" put it:

> *With Mr. Watson leading,*
> *To greater heights we'll rise*
> *And keep our IBM*
> *Respected in all eyes.*

CHAPTER 2

The Early Years of the "Man of Men"

Considering that Thomas J. Watson rose to the apex of the American business pyramid, it is surprising how little is known of his family's background and of his own childhood, boyhood, and youth. We know a lot about where he wound up but not so much about how he began.

Watson's grandfather, John, was from Clyde, Scotland. He and his two brothers emigrated to Castlederg, a small town in county Tyrone, Northern Ireland, to "engage in the linen business." In the 1840s, the three brothers and their families joined the hundreds of thousands of Britons (Andrew Carnegie and his family among them) to cross the seas to the United States. The port of entry was New York City. One brother, Samuel, remained in Brooklyn. Another, Andrew, settled in Orange Town, New York. The third, John, moved to Hornby Township in Steuben County, not far from Orange Town, and just over five miles north of the New York–Pennsylvania border about halfway between the Hudson River and Lake Erie.

John and his wife had six children, four boys and two girls. Two of the boys, Andrew and Thomas, went into the lumber business. Andrew became a sawyer while Thomas, in the words of author William Rodgers, "with a wider range of interest and, apparently, a more encompassing outlook on his job, became something of an expert in judging the value of timber stands and in various phases of milling, curing, and selling lumber." From about 1855 to 1870, he "worked and wandered" through timberlands from New York State to Ohio. He eventually returned to Steuben County to start his own lumber business, in which he was joined by brother Andrew.

The lumber industry had been a mainstay of the southern tier of New York State (i.e., the counties bordering Pennsylvania) since the 1790s, when settlers of European origin successfully broke the power of the Iroquois League during and after the Revolutionary War. Pioneers found in Steuben County a land rich in timber, with trees up to six feet in diameter and a hundred feet high. The county is drained by the Chemung River, which meets the Susquehanna in Pennsylvania. The Susquehanna flows south through Pennsylvania and Maryland and empties into the Chesapeake Bay (and eventually the Atlantic) at Baltimore.

The Erie Canal, linking Buffalo to Albany, was completed in 1825, changing the face of the state and the nation. By the mid-1830s, the Feeder Canal and the Chemung Canal had turned the commerce of Steuben County on its head. Commodities were moving north to the Erie Canal, east to Albany, and south down the Hudson to find the Atlantic at New York City, rather than down the Susquehanna to Baltimore. These canals were eventually superseded by the Erie Railroad, which for decades was the main artery linking the southern tier of New York counties with New York City and the Great Lakes. This is the same railroad on which the accident took place in 1940 while transporting IBM employees from Endicott (fifty-five miles east of the tiny town of Painted Post in Steuben County, which Watson considered his family's first home) to the world's fair.

Why did Thomas and Andrew Watson go into the lumber business? We do not know. The stands of giant trees were largely gone by the 1860s, cut down and uprooted, with the remaining stumps set on fire in what came to be known as the "Burned Over District" in western New York State. There is clear evidence that the lumber business in Steuben County had entered a long-term decline by the 1860s.

The industry of the future in Steuben County just after the Civil War was glassmaking. In 1868, a glassworks in Brooklyn was having a hard time because of labor troubles and difficulties in obtaining raw materials. The company was lured to the town of Corning with promises of easy access to coal and sand for glassmaking and also by a $50,000 subsidy. This was a small fortune for a town of four thousand citizens, but in the long run it proved an investment well worth making.

Corning lay just east of Painted Post, also on the Pennsylvania border in Steuben County. First settled by European-Americans in 1789, Corning was developed by nine "gentlemen . . . engaged in the building" of a railroad south to the Pennsylvania coalfields. One of those nine gentlemen was Erastus Corning. Born in Norwich, Connecticut, on December 14, 1794, Corning migrated with his family to the Albany area at an early age. He had a knack for business, and there was little with which he was not involved. His interests included iron manufacture, transportation, land speculation near and far, and politics. He was a key figure in the consolidation of the railroads which became the New York Central in 1853, a road to which he sold rails from his ironworks and of which he became the first president.

Corning was a nationally known entrepreneur in the nineteenth century. It is a bit ironic that in the twenty-first century his family name is primarily associated with a town in which he invested as one small sideline of his innumerable ventures. The eight other "gentlemen . . . engaged in the building" of a railroad and the development of the town which would be that railroad's terminus wanted to name the town after Erastus Corning because, even as early as 1838, they felt his name was prestigious.

At any rate, in 1868 Corning had its glassworks, whose president, Amory Houghton, was the founder of another famous New York family. Corning is, at this writing, a "new economy" company in the fiber-optics industry. In the late nineteenth century, it developed lightbulbs for Thomas Edison. Indeed, the town of Corning and its vicinity became famous for glass. A cluster of glass companies, some producing high-end, genuinely artistic artifacts, sprang up in the environs. The most well known of these was and remains Steuben Glass, founded by, among others, Arthur A. Houghton Jr., great-grandson of Amory. It was glass, not wood, for which this region became famous.

Amory Houghton's descendants became wealthy and prominent in business, politics, and high society. The most famous family member is Katharine Houghton Hepburn (1907–2003), whose mother, Katharine Houghton (1878–1951), was a prominent advocate of birth control in the United States. In this cause she was an ardent supporter of Margaret Sanger (1883–1966), also, as chance would have it, a native of Corning.

Thus there was some fame and even a touch of glamour attaching to Steuben County in the mid- and late nineteenth century. But precious little of either touched the Watson family. The upstate Watsons had entered into a feud with David Watson, who had remained in Brooklyn, because David married a Roman Catholic and converted. Thomas Watson may have lived in Ireland, but he was more identified with Scotland, where his family had originated.

To disassociate himself from the Catholic branch of the family, he changed his name to Wasson, as did his brother Andrew. Indeed, his son, T.J., was born "Wasson" on February 17, 1874. Soon thereafter, however, he changed his name back to Watson, in part, perhaps, because he had earlier had that name tattooed on his arm. (The previous sentence is tentative because there is more than one account of this family's genealogy, and there will never be an authoritative resolution to the discrepancies.) Watson's wife was Jane White Watson, from a family the Watsons had known in Ireland. The

couple had five children. T.J. was the first, and the next four were
girls: Effie, Jennie, Emma, and Louella.

It is much easier to list what we do not know about Watson's
early life than what we do. Take the matter of religion. Was the family Presbyterian or Methodist? In a state known for its evangelical
Protestantism prior to the Civil War and where the "fires of the
spirit" burned more brightly than any of the forest, such distinctions
mattered.

The Watsons are said to have been a churchgoing family, but we
do not know anything about the religious beliefs of Watson as a boy
(or, for that matter, as a man). This is a pity because secular analo-
gies to religious devotion abounded in the IBM that Watson built.
IBM was more than an employer to the tens of thousands of people
who worked for the company during Watson's tenure between 1914
and 1956. The degree of devotion encouraged and demanded
strongly suggests the kind of enthusiastic religious practices which
swept western New York State periodically during the first half of
the nineteenth century. The company's education program, in which
IBM classrooms were arranged to have the instructor appear as if he
spoke from an altar; the unending claims of immortality ("The IBM
is an institution that is going on forever"); the omnipresence of Watson, through the spoken and written word and through his picture
which was everywhere on the company's many premises—all these
practices suggest religiosity.

Perhaps in no other aspect of IBM's operations is the analogy to
religion more strongly present than in selling. During most of the
nineteenth century, selling was a vocation about which Americans
were of two minds. On the one hand, it was a necessity if the
imports and inventions of the great port cities were to be made
available in the hinterland. The United States is more like a conti-
nent than a country in the old-world sense. Without Alaska and
Hawaii, it still covers 3 million square miles. As late as 1850, there
was an average of only one family per square mile. Not until 1920
did the urban population exceed the rural, a good deal later than in

other economically advanced nations. For material progress to take place, selling and distribution were essential. That is why attached to the name "salesman" was so often the adjective "traveling."

There was a romance to the road for a young man starting out as a traveling salesman. The escape from the rural isolation which might otherwise have been his fate could be welcomed. For camaraderie, he had the squad of other traveling salesmen, swapping stories in railroad observation cars or hotel bars. What he did not have was a home. The word *travel* comes from the French word *travail,* meaning "work." For the traveling salesman, travel meant lugging his sample case from one place to another, never being quite comfortable, sleeping in one hotel room after the next. Worst of all, it meant encountering what William Rodgers calls the "ego-shattering" rejection with which any salesman has to cope. The temptation to drown his disappointments in alcohol was ever present and often given in to. For the family man, traveling meant weeks, perhaps months, separated from loved ones. The excitement a twenty-year-old might feel for the open road was often gone by thirty.

Keeping up the spirits of such men was vital if a company was going to compete effectively in the twentieth century. No one was better at this job than T. J. Watson. IBM boasted the most fervent sales force in the United States. It is, unfortunately, difficult indeed to find the roots of his unique ability in this field within the snippets of what we know of his early life.

We do know that Watson grew up surrounded by women. In a family of seven, he and his father were the only men. Watson's father was not a poor man; but, depending on economic conditions, business could be difficult. "The father's lumber business," writes Rodgers, "was constantly endangered by competition and diminishing stands of timber, and the Watsons moved to a new address at intervals, as the focus of the father's business opportunities changed from town to town." T.J. lived in four towns growing up, but they were all in Steuben County, pretty close to one another, so he probably did not spend his early years feeling like a stranger.

Discussions of young Watson's personality are contradictory. Biographers Thomas and Marva Belden describe him as "a lively, assertive boy, expressing his energy in a quick temper and pranks." However, they also observe that "there was always a suggestion of restraint in him. . . . [E]ven at parties he sometimes had a speculative look, strained and dissatisfied, as if he had drawn apart and was measuring himself."

Few people are all one thing or all another, so these contradictions should not surprise us. The dominant theme of Watson's youthful years does seem to be shyness and perhaps a touch of social phobia. "He did not go swimming with the other boys [of Painted Post]," reports Rodgers. Neither did he hunt and fish with them. There is no indication that he was a leader among his peers. And there are some reasons to think he was not very comfortable with his body.

Nothing that we know about T.J.'s father makes it likely that he would have been able to help an adolescent boy learn to become more at ease with himself and with others. The adjectives that are attached to the father by the Beldens and Rodgers include "brawny" and "brusque, stern, domineering, and fiercely attractive." He had a "black beard and dark, angry eyes," say the Beldens. He did not shrink from a fistfight. Probably not an easy man to confide in. As for T.J.'s siblings, it is not unreasonable to speculate that four younger sisters might have looked up to and perhaps competed for the affection of their sole older brother.

We do know two things about Thomas J. Watson as an adolescent. First, although he was a bit withdrawn in groups, he wanted to make his mark in the world. We know this because he did. According to Rodgers, he "loved to write his name repeatedly on things in a bold and heavy hand—on the village monument, in the stairwell of the local public hall, and on other sites convenient for graffiti."

Second, we know that he never considered using his father's lumber company as a way to make that mark. Neither the son nor the father expressed any interest in the son working for the father. The Houghtons built a dynasty in Corning. There was no discussion about the Watsons building a dynasty in Painted Post or some other nearby town.

This disposition of events should not be taken for granted. The Watson lumber company was a small business, and no financial records have survived. We must, however, assume that it was reasonably profitable. Poor people, as Andrew Carnegie once observed, go to work early in life. (Carnegie himself had his first full-time job as a bobbin boy in a cotton textile mill in Pittsburgh at the age of twelve.) T. J. Watson's first job was as a bookkeeper in Clarence Risley's butcher shop in Painted Post in May 1892 at $6 a week. He was eighteen years old. Not only had he completed high school, he had spent a year studying business at the Miller School of Commerce in Elmira.

When we put all this together with the fact that Watson's father had four other children, all daughters and all younger than his son, as well as his wife and himself to support, we have to assume that his business generated reasonable profits. Not only did Watson finish high school (which was very rare in 1890), his father urged him to go to Cornell or to read for the law. It was T.J. who elected the one-year post–high school course in Elmira. Watson's father did not need his son's earning power to make ends meet. In 1892, the family lived on High Street in Painted Post. Not, perhaps, equivalent to Fifth Avenue, but not a hand-to-mouth existence either.

The contrast with T. J.'s own attitudes toward his children could not have been more stark. His eldest son, Thomas J. Watson Jr., was destined in his father's eyes to work for IBM and eventually run it. His second son, Arthur (known as Dick), was slated to follow in the first son's footsteps. This future was foreordained—taken for granted without discussion. Yet there was never a breath of possibility that T.J. Sr. would follow in his father's footsteps.

While a young man, Watson had done some work on the family farm. It was hard, physical work, the kind of honest work conjured up in the American imagination as typifying nineteenth-century rural life. The Beldens tell us that he topped trees, harvested crops, trained horses, and managed teams to pull stoneboats through the waterways which drained Steuben County. Farm life had one thing in common with the lumber business. Young Tom did not like it. What was unclear was what he would like. Lumbering, farming, and teaching did not qualify. He wanted to go into business, whatever that vague term signified.

Compare young Watson's first seventeen years of life with that of a teenager in the early twenty-first century. In one sense, his life had been very narrow. When he went off to the Miller School of Commerce in 1891, that journey of twenty miles was as far as he had ever been from Painted Post. His life had been circumscribed by Steuben County.

Steuben County is large geographically. At 1,393 square miles, it is considerably larger than Rhode Island (1,045 square miles). There is some variety in topography as well, with elevation above sea level ranging from about 700 feet to about 2,500 feet.

The land is described in the Belden book as so poor "that you couldn't even raise a disturbance on it." Things were not that bad in the whole county. Some of the bottomlands near the rivers were fertile. However, as the nation's transportation infrastructure was built out, bringing midwestern farmlands within reach of the East Coast, the center of commercial farming was bound to shift.

Despite the growth of the glass industry, Steuben County's best days were behind it by the time T. J. Watson was considering how to make a living in the early 1890s. According to the New York State Census of 1875, the average value of dwellings ($914) placed it fiftieth out of the state's sixty counties. Steuben's population in 1890 (just before Watson was to launch himself on his life's journey) was 81,473. In 1920, it was 80,627. During the same period, the population of New York State more than doubled, from 5 million to 10 million.

If you visit Steuben County in May, you will find a countryside of quietly intense beauty. Flowering trees grace a landscape of meadows and rolling hills punctuated by rock-filled, rushing streams. The line between the picturesque and the seedy is indeed a thin one, and you don't have to search too far to see the rusting '58 Chevys between the country inns. Nevertheless, the general impression of

Steuben County in May is appealing. Nature is at hand. It is not overwhelming as it is in the Rockies or menacing as it is in the deserts of the Southwest. It is inviting.

Another impression is one of spaciousness. In a nation becoming ever more crowded, there is room in Steuben County. You can buy land by the acre at reasonable prices. Though larger than Rhode Island, there are fewer than a tenth as many residents.

Some things do not change. Steuben County was doubtless as beautiful in May of 1892, when T. J. Watson returned from studying in Elmira, as it is now. It is, however, one thing to drive through pretty countryside on a brief outing and quite another to live in that same place twelve months a year. Weather conditions differ because of the size of the county and because elevation above sea level varies as just noted. Speaking generally, however, we can say that the winters are long, cold, barren, and forbidding. Mean temperatures in January are well below freezing, and you can expect a good deal of precipitation through the season. With the exception of the belching smokestacks at the Corning Glass Works, the phrase "dead of winter" aptly describes the county in the 1890s. Life there without the climate control and plumbing which we take for granted today was wet and bleak.

Economically, with the exception of Corning Glass, the region had come to a stop. In the 1830s, after the completion of the Chemung and Feeder Canals, the town of Corning became an important inland port, supplying lumber, tobacco, grain, and whiskey from the Painted Post area as well as Pennsylvania soft coal to the Mohawk and Hudson River valleys and to New York City. At the height of this trade more than 1,100 canal boats passed through Corning annually. Steuben County's population increased by more than a third in the 1830s. By the time of Watson's return from Elmira, in contrast, Painted Post and Steuben County were an economic backwater, and they would remain so.

If there is no evidence in the forgotten village of Painted Post that T. J. Watson was a leader, neither is there any indication that he was a follower. This is true not only among his peers but in his family. Just before going off to Elmira, he took the measure of his father. "I was absolutely sure that I was a smarter man than my father," he later remarked about this period in his life, the Beldens tell us. "I was positive of that. I felt I could prove it, if I were called upon to prove it." This rather aggressive and hostile observation was another way of saying that his father could never be a role model for him. It is, moreover, a remark that neither of T.J.'s own sons would have made about him. If they had, it would have enraged him and wounded him deeply.

Watson's father doubtless was not the perfect parent; but gruff though he may have been, he wanted what was best for his boy, and he had some very good advice. First: Get an education beyond high school. Second, and even more important: Get out of Painted Post. T.J. could make a living there, but it was not the place to spend his life.

On both counts, father was spot on. Watson tried bookkeeping at the local butcher shop but quickly discovered that it was not for him. Nevertheless, he was at home with numbers, a prerequisite for success in business. He tried teaching. That lasted one day. It was while still in Painted Post that he discovered his true vocation—a vocation that he would transform into a profession, indeed into a calling. He began selling.

Here is how the Beldens describe T.J.'s early experiences. His first selling job was as an assistant to a man who sold pianos, organs, and sewing machines for a local merchant in Painted Post. He liked selling and apparently was pretty good at it. He was ambitious. He was making $12 a week but wanted more and asked for a raise. His boss countered by offering to sell the agency to him. Watson needed his father's financial backing but did not get it. We do not know whether his father doubted the outlook for the enterprise or whether he simply did not have the money at the time. Whatever the case, the lack of backing said more to T.J. about his father than about himself. "I guess my father was never meant to be a rich man," he later observed.

The time had come to leave Painted Post. T.J. had more faith in himself than those around him did. "His fellow villagers would be surprised at the man the boy grew up to be." He headed west to Buffalo. Why he chose that destination is another unknown. The city and its environs were booming in the 1890s. It was New York's gateway to the Midwest as well as the western terminus of both the Erie Canal and the New York Central Railroad. Although no one knew it at the time, the automobile revolution was about to bring undreamed of prosperity to the Great Lakes cities of Buffalo, Cleveland, Detroit, Chicago, and others. Steel, machine tools, and raw materials would, soon after the turn of the century, be sucked into Detroit in fantastic quantities as the United States leaped into the auto-industrial age. Buffalo, burned to the ground by the British during the War of 1812, would play its part.

That said, there were literally a dozen cities where T.J. could have sought his fortune. The country was mired in a miserable depression in 1894. By 1898 that was over, and the United States would embark on two decades of economic growth which would make it the richest nation in the world. T.J. had no family connections in Buffalo. It is as if he threw a dart at a map and decided to seek his fortune where it landed.

There were only six hundred people living in Painted Post when Watson left it. He had not made a striking impression even there. The biggest town he had ever seen was Elmira. There was nothing in his background to prepare him to deal with the "city slicker." He was a "rube," a "buckwheat." He would learn the hard way.

Buffalo in 1890 had a population of a quarter of a million, and it added another hundred thousand during the next ten years. Watson, with no connections in the midst of an environment the like of which he had never before seen, took a month and a half to find a job. He became a salesman for Wheeler and Wilcox, one of the principal competitors of Singer in the sewing machine business. By the time he got this job, he was almost broke; and when he lost it, which was distressingly soon after he got it, he was in the same predicament.

Young T.J. fell in with "a worldly fellow" named C. B. Barron; and in a couple of years as Barron's sidekick, T.J. learned a lot about how not to get ahead in business. Barron was a slick, hail-fellow long on blarney and short on substance. With Watson (and some money borrowed from Watson's father), the two engaged in a number of commercial ventures about which they knew nothing.

By the time Watson was twenty-one, Barron had disappeared and Watson was broke. The only place for him to rest his head at night was a pile of sponges in the basement of a store. Watson went from rags to riches, but he did not begin life in rags. He worked his way down before he worked his way up. Of money, he would say in later life: "They say money isn't everything. It isn't everything, but [it] is a great big something when you are trying to get started in the world and haven't anything. I speak feelingly."

Sleeping on sponges in the middle of an economic depression in a city in which he had no prospects, the twenty-one-year-old Watson gave precious little hint of transforming himself into the "man of men" who would become a business leader to be reckoned with. It would indeed have been difficult to single him out as really special among the thousands of other young men his age who had come to the big city to seek their fortune and found themselves on a bed of sponges.

The "man of men" was looking very much like just another man among many.

CHAPTER 3

Watson and National Cash

Since the beginning of commerce, most businesses have been small and family run. To this very day, that is still true. When one surveys economic activity around the world, the small family firm predominates. T.J.'s father's lumber company was the rule, not the exception.

Not until the mid-nineteenth century did the big company staffed by general managers begin to develop. The catalyst was the railroad revolution; and the leading nation was the nation in which railroads played the most vital role in economic development, the United States. There was no precedent for the size attained by the most important railroads. The Pennsylvania, for example, employed over 110,000 workers in 1891, or more than two and a half times the total of the soldiers, sailors, and marines in the American armed forces. In any terms—employees, sales, profits, assets—the railroads were large by modern measures.

The railroads placed a national market within the reach of hundreds of manufacturers who could sell their products not merely locally or regionally but across the whole of a country which, despite sharp periodic depressions, was growing very fast through the 1800s. The opportunity for these manufacturers to reach more customers meant the potential for greater sales. Greater sales justified

higher levels of investment in property, plant, and equipment to produce more merchandise.

When the scale of enterprise changed, the methods through
which businesses operated had to change as well. The number of
decisions to be made about production and distribution escalated
exponentially. A new economic actor was called into being to make
these decisions. There was never a family that could by itself run a
firm with a hundred thousand employees. What was needed were
professional managers: that is, men (and management ranks were
populated exclusively by men in the early years) who were not
related to the owners of the firm and who themselves owned little if
any equity in the company for which they worked. These men
needed training and direction, and they needed to be controlled.

This "managerial revolution in American business," to use
Alfred Chandler's well-known phrase, was in full swing by the
1890s. Until 1895, Watson had been almost untouched by the corporate reconfiguration of American enterprise. With the exception
of a couple of weeks as a sales agent for the Wheeler and Wilcox
sewing machine company, all his experience had been small-time.
Trundling pianos and organs in a horse-drawn wagon around the
countryside in the hope of a sale. Opening a butcher shop in the
hope of starting a chain. Experimenting in finance through a building and loan society.

In a word, the young Thomas J. Watson had proven himself a
jack-of-all-trades and a master of none. For a mentor, he had selected
C. B. Barron, a phony, lying in wait for a small-town sucker like T.J.

Thus, it was with an unimpressive résumé that Watson betook
himself to the Buffalo agency of a firm that was at the cutting edge of
the new world of big business, the National Cash Register Company.
Watson betook himself there not once or twice but at least three times.
He wanted a job. He needed one. He owed money to "the Cash" itself
for one of its machines, which he had purchased for his failed butcher
shop. He also owed money to his sixty-one-year-old father, an ailing
man who did not have a lot of money—or time—to spare.

It was in October 1895 that Watson convinced the manager of the Buffalo office of NCR, John J. Range, to take him on for a trial period. The trial was not, alas, very successful. In his first two weeks, Watson did not sell a single cash register. "I haven't got any orders," he told Range, "but I have some good business in sight."

Watson was then spoken to as he had never been spoken to before. "In sight?" asked Range. "How far away is it? Can I see it? Don't you ever waste my time by talking about business that's in sight. I am not interested until you can show it to me in the form of a signed order."

That was just the beginning. Range really teed off on this country bumpkin. Watson seemed mighty lazy. But even had the young salesman worked hard, Range had to doubt Watson would succeed.

Watson had old-fashioned, outmoded conceptions of what it meant to sell. The salesmen he had known and spent his time with were men who believed the key to selling was personality. They themselves rather than their wares were their real stock-in-trade. This was something Watson could understand. When he had wandered around Steuben County pushing pianos to farmers, his ability to chew the fat with them seemed a lot more important than the virtues of the particular pianos he happened to be selling.

In 1884, one George M. Hayes published *Twenty Years on the Road; or, The Trials and Tribulations of a Commercial Traveler by One of Them*, wherein he recounts, as reported by historian Timothy J. Spears, what his first employer told him: "Any general advice I consider useless; you must learn by experience; but one point I want to press particularly on your mind: In making a new customer, try to read him through and through, but don't let him read you. Follow this rule, and act honestly and conscientiously."

This is the sum total of sales training Hayes received. It could not have been terribly helpful. Look, for example, at the first phrase. General advice is useless. That statement is itself general advice, so it has a certain tautological character. Then we have one piece of specific advice: "read" the prospect but don't let him read you. What might that mean? one wonders. How do you learn to achieve that goal? If you are going to be honest and conscientious, why be hidden? Why not be transparent?

In a word, as advice for a young man setting out on the road, this is worthless; and this is about all that even the best salesmen knew at the time that Watson first encountered Range. Others, the C. B. Barrons of the world, fell into the long and unattractive tradition of the confidence man. These were the people who made a practice of victimizing the unsophisticated. Their methods are chronicled in such exposés as Bates Harrington's *How 'Tis Done: A Thorough Ventilation of the Numerous Schemes Conducted by Wandering Canvassers Together with the Various Advertising Dodges for the Swindle of the Public.*

Whatever self-esteem remained to Watson when he finally landed a job with Range could not easily survive the outburst to which he was subjected. He later said he was waiting for the storm to abate so he could resign. But he did not resign. He persevered.

Why?

One reason was that suddenly and unexpectedly, Range changed his tone. He began, the Beldens tell us, to comfort Watson. "Now, young man," he said,

I know what you're up against. I have been all through it. I know just what's happened to you. . . . Nearly everybody you have called on has said, "I don't want a cash register." Now, we all know that, because, if they decided they wanted a cash register, they would come down to the office and buy it. They wouldn't need any salesman. Now, let's take a different tack. . . . We'll put one on the rig and go out together and call on your best prospects. If we fall down, we'll fall down together, and then I can not find any fault with you.

One wonders what must have been racing through Watson's mind at this turn of events. One minute he is stripped naked and humiliated—facing again a bed of sponges and the financial debt to his father. The next minute the very man who was berating him wants to become his mentor. Watson never forgot this episode for the rest of his life, and he often spoke of it.

A more frightened man, a prouder man, a less ambitious man would have walked out of Range's office in the middle of the opening tirade. But Watson, in the words of William Rodgers, was "quite capable of extraordinary, even complete, subordination." Watson became famous during his career for his temper. He fell prey to anger attacks during which he really lost control of himself, rages which were sometimes followed by remorse equally intense. Before he began dishing it out, however, he learned to take it.

Watson could take abuse and frustration if there was a clear reason why, and there certainly was in this case. He wanted to learn how to sell. Range was no C. B. Barron. He was running an important office for "the Cash," a company that everyone knew was going places. By the turn of the century, four hundred salesmen worked for it. There were only six hundred people in Painted Post. Range knew what Watson wanted to learn. Range was willing to teach, and Watson was determined to be an apt pupil.

Watson's encounter with Range was meaningful in ways that Watson, not a psychologically-minded man, was probably unaware of. It is a not uncommon method of exercising power for a dominant individual (Range in this case) to generate anxiety in a subordinate (Watson) and then to hold himself out as a safe harbor for defense against that anxiety. For Watson, Range thus presented himself first as the problem and then as the solution. The problem is so acute and painful that the poor benighted subordinate binds himself to the solution with hoops of steel.

Break them down. Then build them up. Range was good at this. He was, however, an amateur compared to his own boss, the founder of the National Cash Register Company, John Henry Patterson. Patterson denuded a man of his ego. For him, Watson willingly violated federal law and walked to the gates of the penitentiary. But we anticipate ourselves.

Range took Watson out on the road. They sold a cash register to the first prospect they approached. They visited their second prospect, and the result was another sale. Third prospect; third sale. Fourth prospect; fourth sale. This was more like it. Everything Range did was a lesson to Watson. The special genius of John Patterson's approach to selling was to put the salesman and the prospect on the same side, never at odds with each other. Arguing with a customer makes as much sense as arguing with your wife.

When Range encountered a prospect who did not want to buy a cash register, he was not defensive; and therefore he was not offensive. He was not argumentative. With a smile, he would say, "I know you don't [want to make a purchase]. What I've come for is to find out why you don't want one."

Look at what was achieved by this approach. First, Range was not telling the prospect that he should want something that he had just said he did not want. That would only have generated tension and hostility. Second, by having such a response at the ready, Range did not have to hesitate. Third, he agreed with the prospect, thus putting him at his ease. Finally, he endorsed the prospect's point of view, thus paying him a compliment. Range seemed to be soliciting his opinion, nothing more. The result was that Range and the customer made contact on friendly turf. Conversation ensued. A sale resulted.

Business is a lot of fun when you're making money, and the Cash was generous with its sales force. All of a sudden Watson, a man who had just recently been experiencing real poverty, was making $100 a week or more—a far cry from the $6 weekly take at Risley's shop back in Painted Post. Watson may have been naturally shy in unstructured situations; but when given a role to play, he stepped into it impressively. In a matter of weeks he was as good as Range. In a matter of months, he may even have been better.

Unlike the small family firm, the big businesses of the Second Industrial Revolution were hierarchical. They were (and are) structured like pyramids, with salaried employees reporting to other salaried employees on the level above them and being reported to by salaried employees on the level below. There were, moreover, objective, quantitative indexes by which one's performance could be measured. If you generated sales and profits greater than expected, you could be rewarded not only by a raise in pay but by a promotion. This was true even if, as in Watson's case, you were not a relative of anyone in the firm.

This is not to say that politics exists in family firms and not in bureaucratic, professionally managed companies. Promotions and compensation are valuable, and everything valuable is political to some degree. The Cash itself hung a large poster in the entrance hall of its headquarters in Dayton, Ohio, touting "Eighty-two Reasons Why National Cash Register Is a Good Place to Work." Reason number five was: "No relatives employed in the business." Yet in 1922, when John Patterson died at the age of seventy-seven, he was succeeded by his unqualified son Frederick.

Quantitative measures did, however, unquestionably become more important as business grew big. They were more important in 1900 than they were in 1800. In a large firm with employees scattered all over the country and eventually the world, there was no way to know every employee personally. Patterson did not know Watson, but he apparently did know his record through the numbers. It was on that basis that he promoted him to the management of NCR's Rochester office.

Not long after Watson had moved to Buffalo, his family followed. We are not certain when they came, but it was probably in 1896 or 1897, after Watson began to achieve some success at the Cash. His father's health had been deteriorating, and he and the rest of the family began to spend only the summers back in Steuben County. It is a commentary on life there that they preferred to winter in Buffalo. Watson's four sisters, "strong-willed, competent women," took up teaching school.

Watson's father was about forty years older than he. Watson himself did not become a father until a month before he turned forty. Forty is not young to become a first-time parent, and it was relatively older a hundred years ago than it is today. It is an intriguing characteristic of Watson that he did not allow his life to be ruled by the clock or the calendar. This is true despite the fact that his whole life with IBM was devoted to products which measured time or speeded things up.

Watson was a man who had the capacity to wait. He was not the stereotypical "young man in a hurry." Unlike so many young people in recent years, whose career strategy has been to start at the top and work up, Watson was willing to serve an apprenticeship. He kept learning from John Range even as his own skills at selling came to equal Range's.

In 1899, Watson's numbers were speaking loudly enough that they could be heard clearly at the home office in Dayton. Time to move up. That is why on August 1, 1899, Watson was promoted to manager of NCR's Rochester office. By this time, he had become the de facto head of his family. They came with him to Rochester, and everybody moved into a house together. It must have been a pretty large house. When Effie married an NCR salesman, he moved in rather than her moving out. Jennie, meanwhile, served as Watson's assistant at the office. She made a couple of sales, too; and her brother, who always knew how to reward performance, bought her a diamond ring.

It was not sheer chance that brought young Watson to Rochester. Nobody else wanted to go there. The office was in disarray, and business was not good. Those sales Jennie made were much needed.

The problem was not only the kind of sales resistance which Watson had encountered along with Range in Buffalo. In Rochester he faced an additional problem: a viable competitor. The Hallwood Company also had an office there, and it was an obvious and irrefutable fact that every cash register Hallwood sold resulted in one less sale for NCR.

To understand what this meant from the point of view of the Cash, we have to say a word about the man who founded the company and developed the market for its product, the charismatic and more than slightly "touched" John H. Patterson.

Patterson was born in Dayton, Ohio, on December 13, 1844, the seventh of eleven children. His father was forty-three at the time. Patterson served in the Civil War and graduated from Dartmouth in 1867. He left behind no recollection of the Civil War. As far as college was concerned, "What I learned mostly was what not to do. They gave me Greek and Latin and higher mathematics and Edwards on the Will—all useless." Patterson didn't like anything useless. A less intellectual, less self-reflective man never lived. What he wanted was "small words and big ideas."

Patterson went to work directly after college as a toll collector on a canal in Dayton. It is fair to say that his career from 1868 to November 22, 1884, when he bought the National Cash Register Company, was undistinguished. When he bought the Cash, however, he was determined to use it as the vehicle to make his mark in the world. This was a goal he achieved.

Patterson has been called the "father of modern salesmanship," and there is some truth to the label. A cash register was a difficult item to sell in the 1880s. It was, first of all, new. Since the dawn of time, merchants had been running retail shops without it. Second, it cost money. A salesman could promise future savings, but the expense to acquire the cash register he was selling was incurred in the here and now. Third, the people who worked for the proprietor of the store hated cash registers. They were considered an aspersion on the honesty of a store's employees. They de-skilled the clerks. Originally, the clerks' job had been to make change from the drawer in which the cash was kept. Now, all they did was punch buttons on the register, and the results were there for all to see.

These matters may seem small today, but they were not in the 1880s. Clerks did not want to be de-skilled or untrusted. They did everything they could to keep a cash register salesman from the store's proprietor. They intercepted mail with "National Cash Register" on the envelope's return address. When the Cash stopped putting its name on the envelope, clerks began to destroy letters which were postmarked Dayton. More than one cash register salesman was thrown out of a store before seeing what came to be called the "pp"—the "prospective purchaser."

When the salesman did make it to the prospective purchaser, his task was only just beginning. What did the salesman do, for example, with a storekeeper such as the Kentuckian in the late nineteenth century who would have nothing in his store not referred to in the Bible? Having read the Bible myself, I can assure you that the term "cash register" does not appear therein. The NCR salesman knew that too. Nevertheless, the salesman sold that cash register to the grocer; and the story of his success became something of a legend in the company.

It was Patterson who taught American retailers that the cash register was an essential tool for them to take a step forward in their business. It recorded transactions by punching a paper tape, meaning the proprietor did not have to be on the premises every minute of every day to know how his store was doing. By displaying the amount of a transaction as soon as a sale was rung up, the cash register reassured the customer that he was being charged the correct amount. This display not only informed the customer, it did indeed act as a check on the occasional clerk who might have been tempted to make change incorrectly. Each time a sale was made, moreover, a loud but not unpleasant bell would ring. This rather cheery if somewhat startling sound periodically punctuated the day's activity in the shop, advertising to all that business was being done. It also called attention to the point of sale, making it less likely that the clerk would take some change for himself—that he would have "his hand in the till." No mere cash drawer could offer any of these features. It was not without reason that the cash register was called the "incorruptible cashier."

It was the monitoring—the "incorruptibility"—which made it possible for the NCR salesman mentioned earlier to sell a cash register to the Kentucky grocer who would not make a move without biblical sanction. He told the pp that he was not making a sales call but rather that he wanted to pray with him. The two began reciting the Lord's Prayer. (Note the similarity with Range's approach. The salesman begins his pitch by agreeing, not arguing, with the customer.)

Reciting the Lord's Prayer, the two reached "Lead us not into temptation," at which the salesman paused and observed that a Higher Power had brought them to this moment. Unlike the open cash drawer, the cash register recorded transactions publicly for all to see. It also generated a punched tape which kept track of every sale. What better way to lead a potentially wayward young salesclerk—and what youth in this world of sinners was not at least potentially wayward?—away from the very temptation mentioned in the Lord's Prayer than to install what might be thought of as an antitemptation machine? That is how this sale—or so the story goes, as recounted by Patterson biographer Samuel Crowther—was made.

This sounds a little too cute to be true, and perhaps it is apocryphal. But if it is more fable than fact, nevertheless the celebration of this tale says a lot about what NCR salesmen were expected to do. They were creating a market for an expensive mechanical device among people many of whom were unused to machines of any kind.

This was not an easy task; and in order to accomplish it, Patterson set about creating a school for selling. This school, the first of its kind in the industry and perhaps in American business as a whole, first met in 1894 in a cottage under an elm tree on Patterson's farm outside Dayton. There were thirty-seven students. The instructor was Patterson's brother-in-law, Joseph H. Crane, known as Ohio's leading wallpaper salesman. The text was Crane's "How I Sell National Cash Registers," a booklet which became known as the *Primer*. For years, NCR salesmen were expected to commit the *Primer* to memory. They deviated from it at their peril. It is notable that Patterson and Crane agreed that their salesmen should tell the truth. "Don't answer a question except with the truth" was a cardinal principle. Honesty bolstered self-respect. It was also good for business.

Perhaps because he put so much effort into developing the market, perhaps because he had done so much to transform selling from an exercise in trickery to an honest vocation guided by scientific rules, or perhaps because he simply thought without thinking about it too hard that anything he did was right because the definition of right was anything he did, Patterson believed with a fervor difficult to communicate with the frail and feeble tool of the mere written word that every cash register in the world should be manufactured and marketed by the National Cash Register Company. Competitors had no right in his market. They were sinners, and they could not be reformed. They had to be expunged.

Patterson, as we have noted, liked "small words and big ideas." Here's what he had to say about competitors: "The best way to kill a dog is to cut off his head." T. J. Watson set about eliminating the competition in Rochester in just this spirit.

Watson spied on the competition, posting spotters near their offices. He taught his team how to sabotage competitive products so they would malfunction. He intimidated prospective purchasers of competitive machines by threats. Once, according to the Beldens, he overheard a Hallwood salesman mention that he was going to pay a call on a prospect the next day. The salesman mentioned the prospect's name, which turned out to be a mistake. Watson got to the customer first and sold him one of his own machines. Watson had considered this Hallwood salesman a friend.

Watson did well in Rochester; he was nevertheless such an unknown in the company that when he was called to Dayton in October 1903, he himself was surprised. He had been tapped by Hugh Chalmers, the young, newly appointed NCR general sales manager, for a very special assignment. It would appear that the results he achieved in Rochester, his unrestrained methods, and the very fact that not too many people knew him all conspired to make him the right choice for the covert operation which Chalmers had in mind.

Accompanying competitors in the ninth circle of John Patterson's inferno was the used cash register. NCR's machines were rugged, so rugged that a market sprang up in used cash registers. These posed the same problem as competitors. Every sale of a used machine meant one less sale from the NCR factory. Used machines, moreover, put pressure on the prices the Cash could charge for new ones.

The used-goods market had to be stamped out. Chalmers, with Patterson's full support, devised a plan whereby this could be accomplished. The man chosen to captain this campaign was the twenty-nine-year-old Thomas J. Watson.

The plan Watson was to implement was simple and effective. He started in New York City, where the enemy was one Fred Brainin, proprietor of a secondhand cash register outlet at 124 East Fourteenth Street in Manhattan. Watson moved to the city and struck up a friendship with the unsuspecting Brainin. This must have been the first time Watson saw Gotham. At the time, the city was growing faster than all but a few places ever have. With its flood of immigrants from everywhere, it must have seemed like the center of the world. We do not know if this unique environment made any impression on Watson. If it did, he did not record it. Watson went to New York City with a job to do, and he set about it single-mindedly.

He opened a store of his own on Fourteenth Street—Watson's Cash Register and Second Hand Exchange. Watson could underprice Brainin because Brainin had one problem that Watson did not have. Brainin was in business to make money. Watson was in business to put Brainin out of business. No matter how low Brainin priced his cash registers, Watson would sell for less. If Brainin had put a used cash register on sale for a penny, Watson would have given his away free.

Eventually, Brainin realized that he could not stay in business against such an aggressive competitor. Watson offered to buy him out on the condition that he not reenter the business. Brainin agreed. The money Watson needed was laundered from Dayton through Rochester. In city after city, Watson put one secondhand dealer after another out of business in the same way. Watson's activities played an important part in Patterson's grand plan to monopolize the market. His success established him as a key member of the inner circle of top executives at the National Cash Register Company.

Watson did not seem to have much of a private life during the decade following October 1903, although he did date a number of women. He had his way to make, ascending the corporate ladder. After he was called to Dayton, he returned one more time to Rochester to tell his family about the big promotion. His father graciously told him how very pleased he was that his son was doing so well. That night, he died. Their uneasy relationship thus ended on a loving note. Watson dressed in silk top hat and tails for the funeral because he thought that is what his father would have wanted.

Having moved from New York, which was his headquarters for engrossing the cash register business in the East, to Chicago, where he did the same for the rest of the country, Watson finally relocated to Dayton in February 1907. His operations had been kept secret until 1906. Now everyone knew that Watson was managing the Cash's secondhand business. He had fifty-six people reporting to him, and he had become a man to conjure with in the company. He was also now in a position in which he saw on a daily basis the handful of men at the top, the men who made the decisions that ran the company. He grew close to the great man himself, John H. Patterson, a dangerous man to be close to.

Patterson contained within his personality a tangle of contradictions beyond any hope of unraveling. A great salesman himself, he was a sucker for the right sales pitch. The day after he bought NCR back in 1884, he realized how hard it would be to make a success of it. He tried to sell it back, at a greatly reduced price, to George Phillips, who had sold it to him. Phillips, according to biographer Samuel Crowther, replied to Patterson, "You have bought this stock. If you had paid for it and I had turned it over to you, then if you were to hand it back to me and say, '. . . I will make you a present of this stock,' I would not take it." That is just how bad Phillips thought this company was. And Patterson was stuck with it. Not good news.

Against the odds, Patterson turned the Cash into a powerhouse. His leadership combined opposite characteristics in a manner which was uniquely effective and difficult to decode. The key to the Cash's competitive advantage was its sales force. The key to the effectiveness of its sales force was meticulous study of what it took to sell a cash register and sustained, intense communication of that information to the salesmen. After Crane had developed the *Primer*, Patterson felt he knew the one best way to sell cash registers. Education in his view had nothing to do with the Latin root of the word: *educere*, "to lead out." To the contrary, it meant shoving into the brains of the salesmen the secrets of success.

Patterson was not only educating the brain; he was out to transform the whole person from a huckster to a smooth man of business. "When you go to a town," advised the *Primer*, "stop at the best hotel and get the best room you can [to demonstrate the cash register]." "You are representing a first-class concern—do it from the shine on your shoes to the room you occupy. Look it. Have the virtue, but assume the virtue if you have it not." In addition to these dos, there were plenty of don'ts in the Patterson system: "Don't do all the talking," "Don't remain idle," etc.

Role-playing occupied an important place in the educational program. Patterson himself would take the part of the prospect while the salesman made his pitch. The salesman would, by the time he reached this stage, have been thoroughly drilled in how to convince the customer that NCR's product was precisely what he needed. His training included seeing playlets of selling situations staged with professional actors. Drugstores, grocery stores, and other retail outlets were built at NCR's home office educational facility; and skits in these replicas were designed to illustrate how to sell.

The focus of sales training was unwaveringly on concreteness and detail. Thus, the salesman was expected to have precisely $7.16 with him in real cash. This was the amount needed to make change for each demonstration. The company even provided a purse to carry this amount in proper denominations. Patterson turned everything he had learned at college on its head. There was no theory, only practice. Practice in the one best way to sell.

Anecdotes about this regimen are legion. One of Joseph Crane's maxims, for example, was never to hesitate. But even the most experienced salesman encountered arguments and objections for which he was unprepared. What then? Crane's recommended response: "Why, that's just the very reason you should have one."

No wonder Crane was such a great salesman. This response was brilliant. It was always at the ready, thus satisfying the rule never to hesitate. Furthermore, it was quite confusing. A prospect has just advanced a reason why he should not buy a register. He encounters not hesitation, not argument, not refutation. Rather, he is told that his reason not to buy is actually the reverse of what he thought it was. Once again, the magic lay in putting the salesman on the same side as the customer. Crane put the customer in the position of arguing with himself while agreeing with the salesman.

Patterson himself was teaching aspiring salesmen in the early 1900s, and having him as an instructor must have been a pretty remarkable experience. It is said that no reading of Patterson's speeches could convey the impact of his message. In Rodgers's words:

> Standing before an easel, red chalk in hand, [Patterson] would be making some sales point when, crushing the chalk in his hands, he would rub it vigorously over his face and hair and throwing his arms up, looking like a tousled but well tailored Comanche, shout at the top of his lungs:
> "Dramatize, verbalize!"

His disquisitions on the competition had a similar tone: "Kill them . . . crush them!"

Thus, the salesmen and the executives at NCR at the turn of the century found themselves in a company which showed them two very different faces. On the one hand, it was a model of a Second Industrial Revolution big business. Its organization was designed to coordinate the production and distribution of a durable good. The product it sold was new to the market; so market creation through a highly rational, measurable, and bureaucratic selling system was essential.

The selling system featured the recruitment, training, deployment, and general management of salesmen in a manner which was unexcelled by any other company in the world. If you wanted to learn how to create a sales program in 1900, NCR was the place to be. A number of its top executives, such as chief operating officer Hugh Chalmers, went on to found companies of their own. Some became sales executives at other companies. Most notable among these was Richard H. Grant. Grant—who was known for such dicta as "Quote the price without a quiver"—became the head of marketing at General Motors during its glory days in the late 1920s.

Juxtaposed against these forces of sweet reason was Patterson himself. "He who overcomes others is strong," Patterson once said, "but he who overcomes himself is mightier." In search of this might, Patterson, not surprisingly, became a food faddist, a health nut, and an exercise fanatic. He once fasted for thirty-seven days (or so it is said), an impressive exhibition of overcoming oneself. Following this fast, he went in search of a physical trainer to restore his health and found in London, probably around 1906, a Cockney gymnast named Charles Palmer. To the alarm of everyone, Patterson brought Palmer back to Dayton and made him a member of NCR's board of directors.

Patterson's bizarre behavior was thus not confined to his personal life. It spilled over into the company. Palmer instituted a harsh physical regimen for executives and employees, and he came to have a say in personnel decisions because of his putative power to detect character by studying physiognomy.

If this were not enough—and it was plenty—Patterson got himself into a war with Dayton. By 1907, the local papers were accusing him and Palmer of ruining the Cash and the city with it. For his part, Patterson had no compunction in closing down the NCR plant and needlessly tossing two thousand workers out on the street just to display his power.

This background is important for understanding the situation facing Watson in Dayton. He was managing his career in what was at the same time the most rational and irrational of environments. Patterson owned the company. "Be present," it has been said, is the first rule of politics. It is also the first rule of corporate politics. But how do you run a rational bureaucracy when your boss is unpredictable and uncontrollable?

Recall how John Range would break a man down and then build him up. Patterson added a third step to that pattern. He would break you down, build you up, and then fire you. Why the third step? We can only guess.

The rational explanation would be that Patterson did not want any one man to become so important that the company could not do without him. This at least has a claim to being a sound management practice. In big bureaucratic firms, a man did not have a job as much as a job had a man. In other words, if, say, the sales manager for the Northeast should leave the company, he would be replaced by another person. That job—Northeast sales manager—needed a man. Any company which depended upon a particular man to hold a job was signing its own death warrant. No man lives forever; and the big, asset-intensive companies of the Second Industrial Revolution were designed to be immortal.

The problems with this explanation are unfortunately numerous. First, Patterson considered himself and probably Palmer as exceptions to the rule. Second, the way he went about dealing with executives who wanted nothing so much as to be loyal to him and to devote themselves to the advancement of the company had nothing of the rational about it.

It is not surprising that Patterson should be concerned with overcoming himself, for this was a battle he lost. His fiery temperament was characteristic not of bureaucratic management but of charismatic leadership. Indeed, Patterson's problem was that part of him believed in strict system and part of him rebelled against that system and insisted on the freedom to break free from the rules and from self-control. One foot was in the Second Industrial Revolution. The other was sailing the bounding main on a pirate ship. The wonder is that his deep ambivalence did not rip him apart.

If Patterson's combination of opposites was a problem for him, it was a much bigger problem for his executives. We are talking about a man who would take desks from people's offices and set them on fire. This was a man to whom you had to stay close if you wanted to learn the considerable amount he had to teach and if you wanted to protect your position in the political pecking order. But he was also the man who would fire you if you got too close. The moth and the flame.

In was in 1907 or 1908 that Watson's problems with Patterson first became acute. Hugh Chalmers, who acted as a buffer between Watson and Patterson and seems to have been something of a mentor to Watson (the relationship between the two men was later to sour), had been finding it progressively more difficult to bend the knee to the humiliating dictates of Charles Palmer. When Chalmers made this clear, he was immediately fired, igniting a lifelong mutual hatred. Watson was working in sales, closely associated with Chalmers. His neck seemed to be next in line for the chopping block.

One day, Watson came to work to discover his office occupied by someone else and his staff nowhere to be found. (A tip for ambitious executives: This is not a good sign.) Watson kept coming to work on succeeding days to face the same situation. He made no objection, not even a comment. He visited branch offices. When he encountered Patterson in Dayton, the two were cool but civil. Watson was shrewd enough never to ask why he had been publicly and deliberately slapped in the face by losing his office. This was real humiliation, but Watson took it without a peep of protest.

It was the Range treatment all over again, but this rendition was in a major key. Patterson talked about how the mightiest of men was capable of overcoming himself, and Watson is remembered as a man who, in his later years, could not control his temper. Yet Watson's progress in business would not have been possible without his ability to subordinate himself when the occasion demanded it. The situation certainly called for intense self-control at this moment, and Watson was capable of exercising it.

My own father was in business for almost a half century. After his retirement, he told me there was one lesson every executive had to learn: "Hammer strike. Anvil bear." Watson was the anvil, and that is how he acted. Many people put up with this unwarranted, irrational treatment. In a sane world, one should not have to. Sane or not, fair or not, Watson took the world as he found it.

One wonders what his innermost thoughts were during this crisis. He had no one in whom to confide. His father had died; and even if he had still been living, he could have offered little guidance. He was a man of the nineteenth century. His era had passed away. The rest of Watson's family was in Rochester, far from the action in Dayton. Even if they had all lived together as they had previously, there is no reason to think they could have made any sense out of what was happening. Watson was unmarried at this time. There was no one who loved him and understood him, who would be unreservedly on his side, who could be his teammate. Patterson, his surrogate father, was tormenting him. He simply had to take it. He had to be an anvil. Perhaps he understood that, with time, he would play the hammer.

Watson's perseverance paid off. In 1908, Patterson departed with Palmer for a two-year sojourn in Europe. Out of the blue, he promoted Watson to NCR sales manager. For two years, Watson had the NCR sales team to himself. No crazy boss to have to manage. Sales doubled. When Patterson returned in 1910, he was more than satisfied with Watson. He gave him an expensive automobile (a Pierce-Arrow) and a house. He took him around the country to visit NCR sales offices and agencies.

Things could not have looked better.

CHAPTER 4

Crime and Punishment

Tom Watson's career had in 1910 reached a peak with great swiftness from the trough in which it was wallowing when he had lost his office just a few short years previously. He was being squired about the country with the CEO of his company and one of the most successful businessmen of his era. He was a star that was in the ascendant.

We must reflect, however, on how this farm boy from Painted Post in Steuben County had come so far so fast. We should consider not just the remarkable self-control in the face of cruel provocation; we should also turn our attention to the ethics and legality of Watson's activities from the autumn of 1903, when he took over the Rochester office, to his rehabilitation in 1910.

Watson had engaged in corporate espionage, sabotage of competitive products, and predatory pricing, all for the purpose of monopolizing the cash register market.

Gathering competitive intelligence is a common practice today. If a salesman overhears a competitor speaking unguardedly about confidential matters, is he ethically obliged to alert the competitor to his presence or to move out of earshot? I have heard it said that there is not a salesman worth his pay who cannot read upside down.

That is to say, he can be seated across the desk from a customer and read papers which the customer has in front of himself. Is that unethical? It is not uncommon for companies to place spotters outside the offices of competitors to take note of comings and goings. Is that unethical? Issues such as these are as common in the business world today as they were a century ago.

Behavior on the border in the battle for competitive advantage makes us feel uneasy. Even if legal, sometimes it simply does not feel right, falling, as it does, so far short of the Golden Rule. To say that "everyone does it" is quite unsatisfying because, among other reasons, "everyone" was not doing "it" then (and does not do "it" now). Corporate wrongdoing was widely publicized during the first decade and a half of the twentieth century. Known as the Progressive Era, this period was marked by an outpouring of exposé journalism which appeared in newspapers, books, and especially magazine articles. Stories of corporations which handled themselves ethically were more difficult to find. Even today, the exploits of the buccaneers of the "Gilded Age" and of the "Robber Barons" are well known, while the history of proper conduct is relegated to footnotes.

Here is one example. In 1906, an executive from Sears named Louis E. Asher dispatched a subordinate named J. F. Jeffries into the field to report on the operations of what was at the time Sears's principal competitor, the now bankrupt Montgomery Ward. Jeffries let his enthusiasm run away with him. He actually got a job in Ward's Kansas City mail-order plant and reported back to Asher that "things are not running very well." Asher responded, "I don't like the idea of your working for these people and reporting to me. I don't think that it is high class either for you or for us. . . . I don't think you could continue in your employment without injuring your self-respect."

The Asher story is uplifting, but it is not what people were reading about business during the Progressive Era. The news of how the new rich had grown rich sparked popular criticism as well as a wave of government regulation. Antitrust enforcement became one of the most important issues of the age, perhaps the single most important economic issue of the presidential election of 1912. Patterson, like John D. Rockefeller, was a born monopolist. It was in his genetic code. He founded National Cash Register six years before the Sherman Antitrust Act was passed. Questioned before a congressional committee about antitrust, Andrew Carnegie is quoted by historian Edward C. Kirkland as saying: "Do you really expect men engaged in the active struggle to make a living at manufacturing to be posted about laws and their decisions, and what is applied here, there, and everywhere? . . . Nobody ever mentioned the Sherman Act to me, that I remember."

Back in the 1880s, when NCR was founded, the names on the lips of people in the know were those of the business titans of their times: Carnegie, Rockefeller, Morgan, and a few select others. But during the Progressive Era, these men were coming to the end of their careers. Some became semiretired board chairmen, others retired altogether, others passed away. For one reason or another, the great railroad barons and the founders of a dozen other industries which built the American economy were no longer directing the daily affairs of their corporations. They were fading into history.

As these men retired or died off, historian Martin J. Sklar has noted, it began to dawn on their contemporaries that they would have no real successors. The financier Otto H. Kahn of Kuhn, Loeb & Company said in 1911 of Edward H. Harriman, "His death coincided with what appears to be the ending of an epoch in our economic development. His career was the embodiment of unfettered individualism." Shortly before his death on March 31, 1913, J. P. Morgan observed that "American business must henceforth be done in glass pockets." When Morgan himself died, Frank A. Vanderlip, president of the National City Bank, wrote to his predecessor, James Stillman, himself one of the nation's wealthiest men, that "there will be no other king; . . . Mr. Morgan, typical of the time in which he lived, can have no successor, for we are facing other days."

Historians have generally agreed with Stillman's assessment. Robert H. Wiebe, for example, has written:

As the barons of nineteenth century business retired, their
successors appeared to have come from a smaller mold. No
one ranked William C. Brown of the New York Central
with the Vanderbilts, or George Gould and John D. Rockefeller, Jr., with their fathers; nor did the fastidious Elbert
Gary of U.S. Steel compare as a public personality with . . .
Andrew Carnegie. . . . The emphasis in business was shifting
from the man to the company, from ingenuity to training,
from an ideal of competition to a matter-of-fact belief in
cooperation and stabilized profits.

Writing in 1963, historian Richard Hofstadter observed that "Once
great men created fortunes; today a great system creates fortunate
men."

One must keep in mind that the transformation being here
described is a generalization not without exceptions. Henry Ford
was as much an advocate of slashing prices and cutthroat competition as Jay Gould, and he was as much an opponent of organized
labor in his plants as Carnegie. Ford, furthermore, had not made a
transition "from ingenuity to training." By the same token there
were salaried middle managers in the large companies in more
mature industries, especially railroads, by 1880.

Nevertheless, Ford must be regarded as what he was—an exception to the broad trend from charismatic business leadership in the
nineteenth century to systematic, bureaucratized business management in the twentieth. There were scores of great entrepreneurs in
the last century. But not even Sam Walton in 1990 or Bill Gates in
1999 occupied the center of national attention to the extent that
Rockefeller did in 1890 or Carnegie in 1899. No one has possessed
such great wealth in liquid form, "untrammeled and untaxed," when
compared to the economy as a whole since the moguls of the late
nineteenth century.

This point has been made at length because it deserves emphasis. In the 1880s, John Patterson fit right in with the business ethos

of the time. But by the 1900s, many of the people who had defined the Gilded Age had left the scene. Yet Patterson not only persisted, he became more eccentric with age and success. By 1910, he was a calcified relic of a bygone era, yet still all-powerful in his company. The insouciance of Andrew Carnegie toward antitrust was permitted in the 1890s. Patterson took that same devil-may-care attitude into the 1900s, when the White House was occupied not by Benjamin Harrison or William McKinley but by three serious people in succession who understood power: Theodore Roosevelt, William Howard Taft, and Woodrow Wilson.

The world had changed. Patterson had not. There would be hell to pay. Patterson boasted of his drive to monopolize the market. He gloried in it. He bragged not only of what he was doing but of the means he was using. No matter what one felt about the ethics of Patterson's methods, they were clearly illegal. Since early in Theodore Roosevelt's presidency (1901–9) and even more vigorously during William Howard Taft's (1909–13), the federal government was making it clear that the Sherman Antitrust Act was going to be vigorously enforced. The penalties for its violation were draconian.

As early as the *Northern Securities* case of 1904, the government shocked the business world by preventing the attempt by J. P. Morgan to arrange for joint ownership with another mover and shaker, James J. Hill, of the Great Northern Railroad. When the Supreme Court upheld the government's case, the decision made headlines all over the nation.

Creations of other great monopolists of the nineteenth century were also dismantled. The Supreme Court found for the government in 1911 against John D. Rockefeller's Standard Oil Company, which was broken up into numerous firms. Of all the robber barons, Rockefeller had probably been perceived as the most powerful and most devious. Although the actual damage done to his empire by the loss of this case was far less than was commonly supposed, the symbolic significance of the decision at the time can hardly be overstated. Also in 1911, James B. Duke's American Tobacco Company lost its antitrust case; and it, too, was dissolved.

On February 22, 1912, John H. Patterson, John J. Range, Thomas J. Watson, and more than two dozen other top executives of NCR were indicted for violating the Sherman Act. The opinion handed down by the federal district court is an extraordinarily complete review of the "flagrant . . . commercial piracy" in which NCR had engaged. If there was any doubt about either the legality or the ethics of the conduct of these executives and their company, such doubt must be dispelled by the findings of fact in this case. Patterson and his minions had offended the competition, the consumer, and the country.

The forthrightness of the company's monopolistic intentions, published in house organs and declared publicly in speeches, is remarkable:

May 1, 1892:   "We are receiving overtures to buy out competition. We will not buy them out. We do not buy out; we knock out."

August 1, 1895: "We are determined to absolutely control the cash register business."

March 25, 1897: Commenting on informing a competitor that the Cash intended to drive him out of business: "This, it is true, is what is called 'securing a monopoly'; but we think there can be no possible economic or other objection to it. Cash registers are not a necessity of life. Any one who chooses can do business without them, thus contributing nothing to the 'monopoly.'"

July 22, 1907:   Patterson speaking to a convention of district managers in Dayton: "[W]e are going to absolutely control the competition of the world. . . . [T]he first thing we aim to do is to keep down competition. . . .

"I asked the Standard Oil Company what was the secret of their success, and they said this question could be answered in a very few words. Men, nothing but men; men well organized; they will keep down competition and make things succeed."

These quotations provide a clear illustration of how, while the world was changing, Patterson remained the same. They also show that he defined what was right by what he wanted. For example, the March 25, 1897, definition of monopoly was clearly ridiculous. By these standards, the only three product markets to which the rules of antitrust could be applied were food, clothing, and shelter. One did not have to be a lawyer to explain that this view could not possibly be correct. But contradicting Patterson could be dangerous. So he sallied forward with this banner, his executive corps in tow, right off a cliff.

The court examined not only the monopolistic goals of NCR but also its means of achieving them. What it found can only be described as unvarnished. Earlier we discussed some difficult ethical dilemmas that are common in business both today and a century ago. But one does not have to be a moral philosopher to see that what the Cash was doing was just plain dirty. The bill of particulars included:

1. Bribing employees of competitors to reveal confidential information.
2. Bribing employees of common carriers such as railroads to obtain information on where competitive cash registers were shipped.
3. Lying to banks about the creditworthiness of competitors.

4. Making "false, libelous, and unwarranted" statements about the competition to prospective purchasers.
5. Predatory pricing.
6. Organizing dummy corporations, such as Watson did, to obtain information about and compete against other firms.

These are just some of the charges of which NCR was found guilty.

Was there actual physical violence by the Cash against its competitors' agents or products? This came up at the trial. Here is what Judge Howard C. Hollister of the Federal District Court, Southern District of Ohio, Western Division, had to say in his opinion:

> Of course, acts of violence by agents of National Cash Register Company upon agents of its competitors are not immediately involved in the question under discussion, because upon objection by the defendants to the introduction by the Government of testimony tending to show instances of fisticuffs between the agents of the National and the agents of competitors, the testimony was excluded from the consideration of the jury, for the reason, among others, that it might be difficult to determine who was immediately to blame for such occurrences, and it would be wandering from the issues to try incidental issues raised by charges of assault or assault and battery. There was, however, evidence tending to show that one of National's agents distributed small wires to other agents in his territory for the purpose of their surreptitious introduction into competitors' cash registers, if the customer gave opportunity to the National's agents for close examination of the competitors' cash register in the customer's possession.

It is difficult not to suspect that the distribution of those small wires took place more than once, and it is a pity that "fisticuffs" were ruled outside the court's purview. It would be interesting to know if there were a lot of fistfights over cash registers.

Life is lived on a slippery slope. If you are ambitious, you have to come to terms with what you are willing to do and what you will not do to succeed. Patterson and the other NCR defendants, including Watson, were revealed to have slid all the way down that slippery slope to the bottom of the pit. If the antitrust laws meant anything, surely they meant taking action against a concerted program to monopolize a market through fair means (we have to keep in mind that the product and the sales force were first rate) or foul.

That is the way Judge Hollister saw it when, at 10:30 in the morning of February 13, 1913, Mr. R. E. Morrow, the foreman of the jury, read the verdict to the defendants. Thirty were charged. Twenty-nine were found guilty. Judge Hollister did not mince his words in pronouncing sentence: "You men belong to the walk of life which should set the example. Yet you have lost the opportunity given you by the methods you pursued. In your desire for gain you forgot everything else." Patterson was fined $5,000 (the equivalent of almost $87,000 in 2000) and court costs. Watson was not fined, but he was assessed court costs.

Far more significant, Patterson, Watson, Range, and the others were sentenced to a year in the Miami County jail. (Dayton is located in Miami County.) This was the first antitrust prosecution in history that resulted in jail time for those convicted.

Daytonians were shocked. They should not have been. The case against the Cash was very strong, thanks in some important measure to the fact that Hugh Chalmers, who had said after Patterson fired him that "I will not be even with the old man till I put him behind bars," cooperated with the prosecution. Nevertheless, the thought that the most important businessman in a city of 130,000 would, at almost seventy years of age, be spending twelve months in the county slammer gave a lot of people pause. His two children cried openly at the verdict. Despite Patterson's numberless clashes with townsfolk, Dayton was proud of him and proud to be the headquarters of a leading firm with a global reach. The local economy depended upon the Cash's success. What had seemed eternal verities had now been called into question.

February 13, 1913, was hardly a red-letter day for Watson. Four days short of his thirty-ninth birthday, he had been branded a felon. How hard would the news be for his family back in Rochester? And what about Painted Post? Residents of his birthplace had watched his growing eminence in a world-famous company with pride. As one had observed, Watson's success was "only another illustration of what good old American grit and 'stick-to-itiveness' can accomplish."

Watson asked one of his friends back home to tell everyone that despite the verdict and sentence, "I do not consider myself a criminal. . . . I am absolutely innocent of any conspiracy such as we have been charged with, and I can state truthfully, that I have not committed a single act during my career of seventeen years with the NCR Company, that I am, in the least, ashamed of, or that I am not willing to have the whole world know about." To another he wrote, "I want to assure you and all my friends that I am not worried, in the least, about this matter; neither do I feel at all humiliated. My conscience is clear, and I am quietly waiting the action of the Court of Appeals." Thus began what was to be the most eventful year in Watson's long life.

During the year following the verdict, we can see in Watson's conduct many of the characteristics which were to enable him to rise to the heights of the American business world. The old phrase "bloodied but unbowed" fit him very well. Like other great tycoons, he was able to suffer defeats without being defeated. Like other great salesmen, he was deaf to certain words. Persistence in the face of disappointment is vital for the salesman. When a prospective customer says "no," the salesman must have the ability not to hear that word. When the foreman of a jury of his peers, Mr. Morrow, said, "We, the jury, herein do find the defendants guilty in the manner and form as charged . . . ," that word "guilty" had somehow to sail by Watson's ears without actually being heard.

Let us also consider the letters Watson wrote to his friends back in Painted Post. He maintained that he was "absolutely innocent," that he had done nothing of which to be ashamed, that his conscience was clear, and that all would come right on appeal. Why, then, had he been convicted? Watson never claimed that the jury was anything other than disinterested. Were they misled? He never said so, and it is hard to believe that Patterson was unable to afford competent counsel to prevent such a misunderstanding. Was his conscience clear because the real problem was the law rather than his breaking it?

Watson said none of these things. Nor did he bemoan his fate. Never complain, never explain. He did not express remorse because he insisted that he had nothing to be remorseful about. His faith in his pristine innocence deserves pause.

One could argue that Watson was more the brake than the locomotive on NCR's competitive practices. Though "known to be tough on competition," Watson was also said to have opposed the company's most obnoxious policies if for no other reason than that they would injure its reputation and eventually prove bad for business. Perhaps Watson had come to believe with Patterson that whatever Patterson did was right because the definition of "right" was whatever Patterson did.

The NCR executives were indicted on February 22, 1912 (about a year before the conviction). In 1912, the company these executives ran dominated the market, controlling 90 percent or more of unit sales. Its margins were high; its profits lavish. These men paid themselves well and lost no sleep about economies in their operations. Their expense accounts covered the finest hotels. Everything was first-class. For all his peculiarities, the man most responsible for creating this money machine was Patterson. There can be no question that Patterson was a key figure in the development of selling, the business function which interested Watson the most. Indeed, he seems to have turned NCR into a womb of important executives of other major corporations.

Perhaps Watson had taken a step further and come to believe that whatever he did was right because the definition of right was what he—Thomas J. Watson—did. After all, Watson had made more of a success out of the used cash register business than anyone had a right to expect. When Patterson, in his fit of pique at Dayton, closed the NCR factory, Watson, with his secondhand operation, was the only executive in the company making money, because for several months there was no new product to sell.

In 1908, when Patterson fired Chalmers and decamped to Europe with Palmer, Watson became acting sales manager. From its founding in 1884 to 1906, NCR sold about five hundred thousand cash registers. In the next two years, it sold fifty thousand per year. Under Watson's leadership, the company doubled its annual sales to one hundred thousand units. Patterson returned to the United States early in 1910. He was well pleased with Watson and on May 28, 1910, got rid of the "acting" in front of his title. He was now sales manager. He had set records at the company, which set records for American industry.

Watson's remarkable success resulted from a number of factors. General economic conditions were improving following the financial panic of 1907. The company's product was improving, thanks to the installation of an electric motor by a thirty-year-old inventor named Charles Kettering. Kettering was another of those remarkable people who found themselves in Dayton in the era of Patterson and the Wright brothers. He went on to establish the Dayton Engineering Laboratories (known as Delco); invent the electric self-starter, which was a major contribution toward turning the automobile into a mass-market product; and run the research arm of General Motors for more than two decades, from 1925 through 1947. Kettering was to invention what Patterson was to selling. When he died in 1958, he owned the largest block of stock in General Motors and was among the nation's richest men.

Watson deserves personal credit also for the outstanding sales performance under his leadership. Patterson may have been a genius at selling, but he has aptly been described by the Beldens as "immoderate even when right, and powerful even when wrong." What Watson did was to take a great sales force and make it greater.

He did not touch Patterson's innovations, such as quotas and guaranteed sales territories, which had proven themselves invaluable. Nor did he introduce economy into selling. Statistics do not survive to prove it; but anecdotal evidence suggests that, if anything, his salesmen's expense accounts increased. He "insisted," the Beldens report, "that his men go to the best hotels and take the best rooms, and be provided the large offices with a fleet of chauffeur-driven Buicks so that clients, riding off for a demonstration, would feel assured that they were dealing with a first class organization."

Parenthetically, it is worth noting that this approach was the polar opposite of Sam Walton's. Walton founded the largest retail company in history by focusing on keeping expenses down in every part of the business. When you traveled for Wal-Mart, you stayed in the least expensive motel you could find and you shared a room with another executive.

Both these approaches succeeded because both Watson and Walton understood that they were means to an end. The end was making sales, and the markets the two were serving were very different. Both men devised systems that were effective because of their internal consistency.

Watson's changes to the NCR sales force included loosening the grip of the iron laws which governed the salesman's conduct. He felt there was more to effective selling than the dictates of the *Primer*, memorized sales pitches, and rehearsed responses to often encountered questions. He wanted to give the salesman some latitude for whatever "lightning intuition and spontaneity" he might possess in order to meet the needs of the moment. He did not want to return to the days when the salesman was all blarney, selling himself rather than the product. But he seems to have believed that the pendulum had swung a little too far in the opposite direction, treating the salesman as if he were an automaton.

Another important change Watson introduced, also more one of emphasis than of innovation, was the increased attention to rectitude. A picture has survived of Watson making a presentation at NCR with flip charts on two large easels. At the bottom of one, he has written with chalk the words "Do Right." This photograph was taken the very year, 1913, in which Watson was convicted of doing wrong.

Certainty of rectitude in the face of proven wrongdoing. How can we make sense of this conundrum? We have already speculated about the self-definition of "Do Right," and perhaps the explanation goes no further than that. But perhaps it does. Watson came to see himself as more than a businessman. He was more than a man whose ambition ended with putting food on the table. He did not define success by money, although he was already well paid at the Cash and would make a fortune at IBM. Rather, he came to see himself as a force for good in the world. He was a force for fairness, for uprightness, for square dealing, for the highest ethical standards, for progress, for world peace. How do we square these lofty goals—some of which were actually in part achieved—with the man who lied to the secondhand cash register store owner Fred Brainin and put him out of business?

Part of the answer lies in Watson's connection with Patterson. Working for NCR was more than just another job. It was living in a special world defined by a charismatic leader. It was, after all, not only Watson who was convicted, but the whole executive team of one of the world's most successful companies.

If the problem was not with the antitrust law itself, there was room for reasonable people to question the fairness with which the law was being enforced. President William Howard Taft's administration was filing cases at a far greater rate than the administration of his predecessor in the White House, "Teddy the Trust Buster" Roosevelt. Taft's attorney general, George W. Wickersham, had once been an attorney for a company run by the prosecution's star witness, Hugh Chalmers. The prosecuting attorney, as the Beldens point out, was Taft's brother-in-law. The judge, Howard Hollister, had lost money in a company that had tried to compete against the Cash. Taft himself was from Cincinnati, which is forty-seven miles from Dayton and which is where this case was tried. The chances of the Cash sneaking by undetected were not terribly good.

It is also true that Watson's most egregious ethical and legal violations were well in the past by 1913. The Brainin incident took place a decade prior to the conviction. In more recent times he had, as we have just noted, been crusading to teach the sales force, among other things, to "Do Right."

All that said, one still feels one has not gotten a fully satisfactory explanation. After all, whether or not the government had a hidden agenda, Watson never disputed the facts. It is difficult to believe, especially in his later years, that he would have condoned in others the conduct in which he himself engaged. Yet he insisted he had done nothing shameful, and he came to encourage those who worked for him to regard him as a paragon.

Charles Revson, the founder of the Revlon cosmetics company, which was for many years the leading firm in its segment of the industry, once said to one of his top executives in the midst of a meeting: "Look, kiddie, I built this business by being a bastard. I run it by being a bastard. I'll always be a bastard, and don't you ever try to change me." One could say many things about Revson, but one could not accuse him of being a hypocrite.

Could one make that accusation about Watson? He talked one way but acted another, which is pretty close to the definition of hypocrisy. Yet it is also, one senses, too simple a formulation. Watson, rather, seems to have been able to compartmentalize his various endeavors and to work out a way to believe in his goodness and innocence within each compartment.

At the very moment when Watson was dealing day by day with the legal morass into which he had sunk, his situation was rendered more complicated by the fact that he had recently met the woman who was to become his life partner. Her name was Jeannette Kittredge, and she came from a wealthy family of strictly observant (no drinking) Presbyterians. He met her at a country club late in the spring of 1912. She was twenty-nine; he was thirty-eight. He had always been interested in women and had twice before been engaged. His career seemed to overwhelm sustained romantic attachments. This time, however, it was different.

Jeannette Kittredge was a woman of whom no one ever had anything bad to say. She was "a beautiful young woman with soft eyes and a shy manner." When her looks and her other fine qualities are considered together with her wealth, the wonder is that she reached her late twenties still single. She lived with her family in a Dayton town house across the street from Patterson's. When Watson told Patterson that he and Jeannette were engaged, Patterson said, "I was hoping you would marry that girl."

Then came the verdict and sentence of February 13, 1913. Watson offered to release Jeannette from their engagement, but she would not hear of it. She was going to stand by her man through hell and high water. As things turned out, it was to be through high water and hell.

CHAPTER 5

High Water and Hell

In the last half of March 1913, the weather in much of the United States was bad. Very bad. Three "great cyclonic storms" originated in the Far West and headed east. Unseasonable heat, tornadoes, and torrential rains blanketed the nation. People reported some fairly odd sights, including, according to historian Judith Sealander, "glowing wire fences along country roads and sparks flying from animals' ears." Rainfall in extraordinary amounts began in Indiana and Ohio on March 22. The storm hit the Dayton area the following day, Easter Sunday.

On Monday it rained hard and constantly. River levees began to give way. On Tuesday the twenty-fifth at 6:30 in the morning, Patterson got up on the roof of the NCR office building to take a look at the city. NCR's facilities covered twenty-three acres of floor space on high ground south of the city. For years, Patterson had complained that Dayton was insufficiently protected from potential flooding. After surveying the city from his property, he drove to the riverbank. He did not like what he saw. Upon his return to the Cash, he predicted that the flood he had long foreseen would come that very day and decreed that the company must prepare itself to care for displaced persons.

Shortly after this statement, Dayton was hit by a flood the likes of which it had never experienced. By noon, the business district was under five feet of water. Streets in various parts of town had become "roaring rivers over fourteen feet deep." Three hundred sixty-one people died, and more than $100 million in property was destroyed.

The miracle was that things were not worse. Much of the credit for saving what could be saved of Dayton accrued to Patterson, the head of the "Citizens' Relief Committee." NCR started building boats on Tuesday. Its headquarters, high and dry, housed thousands of refugees, who slept on cots with warm blankets, ate hot food three times a day, and sang hymns or listened to music played on pianos by musicians who appeared as if by magic. The man who in February was part felon, part lunatic, had been transmogrified in one month into Dayton's "man of the hour." The flood proved a godsend for Patterson's public standing. Addressing the throng at NCR during the flood, the commander of the Salvation Army said of Patterson's efforts, "It is a noble work and will be rewarded by One who recognizes good deeds." Patterson could not have put it better himself.

William Howard Taft's term in the White House expired on March 4. The new president, Woodrow Wilson, was the first Democrat in the White House since Grover Cleveland left it in 1897. Wilson was a vigorous advocate of antitrust, but he had no particular animus toward Patterson or the Cash. He was deluged with messages about Patterson's good works concerning the flood. Patterson wrote Wilson that such messages were sent "without my knowledge or consent. I am," said he, "guilty of no crime. I want no pardon. I only want justice."

Watson was in New York City when the flood struck Dayton. Like other top executives, he went into emergency mode. He organized three railroad trains to carry relief supplies to the stricken city. He worked so hard that he was hospitalized for exhaustion, but by then his mission had been a success. The 1940 Port Jervis train wreck was not the first disaster in which Watson had come to the rescue. He had learned how to act in an emergency at NCR.

Thomas J. Watson and Jeannette Kittredge were married on April 17, 1913, in her family's home, which only two weeks earlier had been partially flooded. After their honeymoon, the newlyweds moved into a summerhouse which Patterson gave them near his own home.

This was the pinnacle of Watson's career at the Cash. He began thereafter to have some trouble getting along with Patterson. Maybe his lifelong pattern of bending the knee when the knee had to be bent was fraying his trousers and getting on his nerves. Maybe he was, in other words, getting tired of being the anvil. Perhaps, on the other hand, Patterson had simply started acting the way he always did toward people who became too important in his company. Perhaps his instinct was to drive Watson out no matter what.

The climax was not long in coming. It fell to Watson to make preparations for the mammoth "Hundred Point Club" convention in July 1913. The Hundred Point Club was one of the keystones of Patterson's selling system at the Cash. The home office set strict quotas for the salesmen in the company's far-flung offices, and these quotas had to be met every year. Each salesman who met his quota was inducted into the Hundred Point Club, with the attendant economic and ego satisfaction. Patterson's biographer describes the club as the most famous of his innovations. Members were celebrated, and no expense was spared at the annual conventions.

The 1913 convention must have been a particularly emotional event. The top executives had just been excoriated by a federal judge and sentenced to prison. But their legendary leader, in a remarkable turn of events, had rescued his reputation by acting as his city's savior in the wake of the great flood which, by chance, happened to follow the trial's conclusion. An indication of what was at stake at the 1913 convention is that Watson's assistant, who was originally assigned to organize it, had a nervous breakdown. That was why Watson took charge.

Watson spoke at the plenary session; and, in the words of William Rodgers, "stammering a bit, but projecting sincerity and an affinity for the problems of a salesman, he evoked applause."

Then the ax fell. Hardly had Watson finished speaking when Patterson strode upon the podium for a few unscheduled remarks. He was lavish in his praise of Richard H. Grant (who had spoken before Watson). The language he used and his whole mode of presentation made clear that it was time for Grant's day in the sun and that Watson was finished. The internal exile that followed must have been dreadful. But Watson had survived an episode like this once before, and he was not one to give in easily. This time, however, things were different. Patterson and Watson engaged in shouting matches in the presence of other executives following the convention. Within two or three weeks, Patterson told him to leave. As was so often the case, being close to those who crossed Patterson was a death sentence. Watson's top assistant was also out. At the end of November, the "resignation" of the two was made public. As Rodgers put it, "After being systematically humiliated, after enduring it for many months, after having done so wonderfully well all that he was directed to do and having been convicted as a criminal for doing it, Thomas Watson was fired."

Watson, it is said, was "stunned" at the news. But why? He had spent a career at NCR watching fine men fired for no particular reason, "yet," according to Rodgers, "he could not seem to relate [that] knowledge to his own fate." It was that very inability which had probably made it possible for him to remain at NCR as long as he did.

Why suffer such shock at something so predictable? Perhaps it is the human condition. Here is a passage from Tolstoy's masterpiece, *The Death of Ivan Ilyich:*

In addition to the speculations aroused in each man's mind about the transfers and likely job changes this death might occasion, the very fact of a death of a close acquaintance evoked in them all the usual feeling that it was someone else, not they, who had died.

"Well, isn't that something—he's dead, but I'm not," was what each of them thought or felt.

Maybe that is what Watson felt. "He's fired, but I'm not." Now, however, it was Watson's turn.

Despite the pain of all this, Watson possessed the remarkable graciousness to write a letter of warm encouragement and support to his successor as sales manager, Richard H. Grant. He told Grant it was "a source of great satisfaction for me to leave knowing that you are to take up my work here." It was, he wrote, "my earnest desire to see you make a better record as sales manager than I made."

On January 8, 1914, almost precisely nine months after their marriage, Jeannette Watson gave birth to the couple's first child, Thomas J. Watson Jr. In the space of less than a year, Watson had gone from being the bachelor golden boy of a golden company to marriage, fatherhood, and unemployment. He was still facing one year in jail.

How would he come to terms with his career at NCR? What would be next?

When contemplating John Henry Patterson, the most lasting impression is not his sales methods, not his efforts to improve working conditions in his factory, not his version of welfare capitalism. Neither is it his peculiarities (to put it kindly)—the compulsion to fire those who got close to him professionally or personally, the imposition of the charlatan Palmer on hardworking people trying to make a living, the bizarre superstitions such as the belief in the special significance of the number "5." Not even the easy embrace of illegal business practices is what is uppermost in one's view.

Rather, the most lasting impression is of the extraordinary personal impact of the man. For all his idiosyncrasies—for all his undebatable idiocies—Patterson built a great company from nothing against extraordinary odds. If ever an institution were the lengthened shadow of a single man, it was the National Cash Register Company during the era of John H. Patterson.

The July 6, 1921, issue of *The NCR* published a banner headline: "96,756 Points in June." Patterson is pictured with his arms spread before a huge board (perhaps fifteen feet by ten feet) filled with cards from the 266 agents and salesmen who had reached or exceeded 125 percent of their quota. Everything on the cover is ordered and symmetrical, including Patterson himself, with his large, perfectly trimmed mustache. What is not in keeping with the symmetry of the print work and photograph is the message in the caption. In large, flowing script, as if it were written on one of Patterson's easel demonstrations, appears:

I am proud of you—
John H. Patterson

The effect is, even at this far remove, powerful. Patterson is not smiling. I have seen no picture of him smiling, nor have I seen a picture of any NCR function at which anyone was smiling. Business was business. Patterson's self-presentation in this picture was severe but satisfied—for now. If this is how he looked when he was satisfied, what was he like when he was unhappy? One would not want to find out. Patterson was a year short of his own death when this picture was taken. He was seventy-six. But he looks ageless. He appears utterly certain of himself.

It is a testimony to the magnetism of this grizzled old Civil War veteran that Watson eagerly subordinated himself to him. That is the last such relationship Watson would have for the rest of his life. Being fired by Patterson was a personal cataclysm for Watson. All that work. All that self-denial. All for nothing.

But not quite nothing. Watson had gotten a priceless education at NCR to assist him on his next venture. It was from Patterson that Watson learned to put selling in the driver's seat of the corporation. Like Patterson, Watson emphasized sales training. Patterson had his Hundred Point Club for salesmen who met quota. For Watson, it would be the "100% Club." The similarities could be pushed further, as William Rodgers noted. When the Watsons moved from their Manhattan apartment after the birth of their second child, Jane, they moved to the wealthy New Jersey suburb of Short Hills. Patterson's home in Dayton was named Far Hills. When Watson bought a thousand acres thirty miles away from Short Hills, he called the estate Hills and Dales. Back in Dayton, the NCR country club was called Hills and Dales.

At IBM, Watson's copyings from the Cash were everywhere to be seen, both in operations and in the more cosmetic aspects of business. Most important was that, purposefully or not, Watson the individual bore the same relation to the International Business Machines Corporation that Patterson did to the Cash. Both men dominated their organizations. Both were big spenders on themselves and on others. Both were born monopolists and were hounded by antitrust problems. Both demanded, explicitly or implicitly, so complete an allegiance to their own intensely personal views of how business should be done and how life should be lived that working for either made an employee subject to an imperialism of the soul.

Both were publicity hounds. Both had grandiose views about the impact they could have not only on their industries but on world politics. Both demanded and attracted sycophants. William Rodgers marveled that Watson required "but seemed often not to hear praise few other men would tolerate." This is less surprising when one realizes that the same could have been said of Patterson. Both had no compunction about striding to a podium unscheduled to upstage whoever was speaking. Watson, in other words, regularly did to others what Patterson had done to him at the disastrous NCR sales convention of 1913. Neither had a sense of humor. Neither had a sense of irony. Both were paternalistic. Both were extraordinarily successful. Both men were, in a sense, totalitarians.

Watson was not the lunatic Patterson was. He was not as bedeviled by superstitions as was Patterson. He had a successful, if often tempestuous, family life and did not need to rely on an *éminence grise* such as Charles Palmer for companionship.

Nor was Watson's policy toward executives as unerringly destructive of his company's future as was Patterson's. Like Henry

Ford, Patterson fired his best people. What might have happened had he not done so? In May 1914, after less than half a year of unemployment, Watson became the general manager of the Computing-Tabulating-Recording Company. He renamed the company International Business Machines in 1924. Under his leadership, IBM turned in a spectacular record.

Patterson had always justified his firing of top performers with the excuse that no business institution should be overly reliant on a single individual. But his worst violation of his principle was himself. He was the great motive force at the Cash; and when he died, that force left as well.

Just as John Patterson had set out to prove George Phillips (the man who had sold NCR to him) wrong for underestimating the cash register business back in 1884, so Watson, as Emerson W. Pugh reports, in 1914 "had vowed to build a larger and more successful company than Patterson." He succeeded.

Watson was the man Patterson could not afford to fire.

THE GREAT ANTITRUST CASE: FINAL ACT

Watson had expressed to his friends perfect confidence that the 1913 conviction would be reversed on appeal. There was no basis for that confidence. Watson had no background in the law. The case against him and his co-conspirators had been strong. The government had already fried bigger fish than he and his confreres in antitrust prosecutions.

But his prediction proved accurate. The case was appealed; and on March 13, 1915, twenty-five months after the federal district court had spoken, the Sixth Circuit Court of Appeals reversed the decision and remanded the case to the lower court for retrial.

The grounds for reversal are not easy to understand. The circuit court's opinion speaks strictly to legal technicalities and not to factual issues. Needless to say, it does not touch upon the ethics of the conduct of NCR's executives.

The government did not retry the case. The indictment was dismissed. The government settled for a consent decree in which NCR executives admitted to having done none of the things alleged, but promised that the Cash would never do them in the future.

Watson never signed the consent decree. He had departed the Cash prior to its being entered into, so the issue was moot. But there was more to Watson's not signing the decree than the fact that there was no legal requirement to do so. He refused to sign because to do so would have, in his view, constituted an acknowledgment that he had done something wrong. This was an admission he would never make.

What was the long-term impact of this prosecution on Watson? To part of this question we know the answer. As for the remainder, we can only guess.

Watson cherished a deep and abiding hatred of antitrust to the end of his life. He did not understand it. He refused to understand it. What is extraordinarily interesting is that Watson did not permit his feelings about antitrust to color his opinion of government in general. Unlike so many big business executives during the 1930s, Watson did not harbor doctrinaire views about the growth of government's size and regulatory power. He was a supporter of Franklin D. Roosevelt and the Democratic Party, quite a rarity among his peers.

The federal government became one of IBM's biggest customers, both because of the need to process information for the census and for Social Security. The Social Security Act was passed in 1935. That same year, the Justice Department won a suit against IBM for tying the sale of its punched cards to the leasing of its machines. It appeared that the federal government giveth with one hand and taketh with the other. Watson could deal with this reality because he could compartmentalize.

Over and above these practical matters looms the impact on Watson of the whole experience with the legal system from the indictment on February 22, 1912, to the conviction on February 13, 1913, to the reversal on March 13, 1915, to the final entry of the consent decree on February 1, 1916. Imagine, especially from the indictment to the reversal, his living with this Sword of Damocles over his head. Look at the earthquake that had taken place in his life with Patterson's firing of him in 1913. Look at the new responsibilities he had shouldered with marriage in 1913 and fatherhood in 1914.

Think about Watson's creation of himself . . . of his special self. He was not only a winner. In his own eyes, he was the man who won the right way. He was Mr. "Do Right." Yet in Patterson's eyes, he had done wrong enough so that he should be fired. In the eyes of the government of his nation, he had done wrong enough to deserve a year behind bars.

What must it have been like to live with this menace day after day, month after month? Everything—his very self—was at stake. Can you put this out of your mind? Even if you can, will there never be intrusive thoughts? What if things don't turn out for the best? What if . . . ? Watson had a lot of self-control. But the man who can control his dreams never lived. What kind of nightmares did he have?

If he lost sleep over these matters, he never let on. Hammer strike. Anvil bear. He was the anvil until this case was behind him. He would never be the anvil again.

CHAPTER 6

Down and Out

Fired.

In December 1913, Thomas J. Watson found himself without a job. His wife was seven and a half months pregnant. He was closing in on his fortieth birthday. He had no prospects for employment. He was facing a year in jail. He was separated—as things turned out the separation was to be permanent—from the strongest, most decisive man he had ever known: John Henry Patterson, the man who was sometimes wrong but never in doubt. To the best of our knowledge, Patterson never mentioned Watson again.

For Watson, the situation was quite the reverse. Under Patterson's aegis, Watson had taken some giant steps away from being just an average "man among many" toward his new status as a "man among men." He saw charismatic leadership in action. He learned how to focus the minds of others and unite them in pursuit of a common purpose. In a word, he saw firsthand the value of vision. According to Tom Jr., his father never complained about the way he was treated at the Cash "and revered Mr. Patterson until the day he died." Watson had to blame someone for his fate, and since both he and Patterson were ruled out, that blame fell on another NCR executive, Edward Deeds, for supposedly "whispering" to Patterson just before the disastrous 1913 sales convention that Watson was becoming very popular in the company. Their paths crossed several times in later life, but Watson never spoke to Deeds again. Chalmers, according to Watson's most recent biographer, Kevin Maney, fell upon hard times during the Great Depression and appealed to Watson for a job. Watson, generous to so many, "detested" Chalmers after the trial and offered him nothing.

Watson not only left Dayton with priceless knowledge about the creation of a company, he also left with a lot of money. Patterson, who was many things but never cheap, gave Watson a $50,000 cash severance, which was equal to over $900,000 in the year 2000. Thus, although he had new domestic responsibilities, he also had a considerable sum of money in the halcyon pretax America of 1913.

That money bought him precious time. He began to receive feelers from big, famous companies including Frigidaire, Montgomery Ward, Remington Arms, Electric Boat, and Dodge. It is a commentary on the growing importance of managerial ability as a discrete asset for firms of the Second Industrial Revolution that Watson received offers from companies in industries in which he had no prior experience. Perhaps the very number of these inquiries made it easier to turn each one down. It should also be said that we cannot be sure how solid each one of these inquiries was. There can be a lot of bumps in the road between talking about a job with a prospective employer and having a satisfactory offer placed firmly on the table.

Watson had compiled an impressive record at a profitable company that monopolized an important industry. NCR was famed for its sales force. Just as people like Andrew Carnegie learned the methods of big business working for a railroad (the Pennsylvania) and took these lessons to another industry (in this case, steel), Watson had the potential to take a key component of big business—the secrets of selling—to other industries as diverse as those represented by the companies just mentioned.

One of the oldest sayings in selling is "Know the territory."

Implicit in this dictum is the importance of knowing the product, because it is impossible to know the territory unless you know not only to whom you are selling but also what you are selling to them. Companies like Electric Boat (a shipbuilder in Groton, Connecticut, which eventually became part of General Dynamics and at this writing builds submarines for the United States Navy) and Montgomery Ward (at the time, along with Sears, one of the two great mail-order retailers in the country with a predominantly rural consumer base) sold very different products. Yet in the Second Industrial Revolution, selling came to be seen as a skill that could be taught rather than merely a knack which one either had or did not have. Watson Jr. said of this point in his father's life that he had "always been impressed with how picky [his father] was about what he'd do next." Watson Sr. "explained this by saying he was sure he'd find a job because he had a reputation for being able to sell almost anything."

At a time when others would have been disconsolate, Thomas J. Watson was a self-confident man (his stammer during public presentations notwithstanding). He had won one of the toughest battles of life. He had sold himself to himself. Watson's self-regard must also have been bolstered by friends who approached him with offers to back him in his next venture, whatever that might be.

Watson, however, did not have any idea about the industry in which he wanted to work. He did not have a passion for any product. As he looked for what would be his next and final job, he was more interested in the process by which the company would be run and what the definition of his role would be. He did not know what he wanted to do, but he did know how he wanted to do it.

Probably early in 1914, Watson met and entered into talks with a financier, international arms merchant, and high liver named Charles Ranlett Flint. In an era when the "trust" was widely reviled as a form of business organization, Flint became its apostle. He enjoyed being irreverent. The amalgamation of businesses in the same industry, he asserted, would generate economies of scale in numerous ways including both the basic functions of manufacturing and marketing and also fees for legal services and other staff activities which are necessary to running a large company.

Despite the public uproar against the coming of big business to the American economy, expressed in the press, at the ballot box, and in legislation, consolidation was the order of the day at the turn of the twentieth century. From 1897 to 1904, 4,227 firms disappeared into 257 combinations. This was the first great merger movement in American history. By 1904, 318 large businesses were said to control 40 percent of the nation's manufacturing assets. Flint was in the business of merging companies for a half century, from 1880 to his retirement in 1931. One of the driving forces behind the merger movement was the profits made by its promoters; and Flint made a lot of money acting, as he claimed in his memoirs, as the "organizer or industrial expert in the formation of twenty-four consolidations." One of these twenty-four was called Computing-Tabulating-Recording, known as CTR.

Flint advocated merging companies in the same industry; but in the case of CTR, the similarity of the businesses was more a product of Flint's imagination than of genuine operational efficiencies. In the 1880s, inventors began to tinker with mechanical and electrical means of weighing, counting, and measuring things and of keeping track of time. A number of these inventions were commercialized toward the end of the nineteenth century; and, among his many other activities, Flint busied himself with engineering mergers of these companies at the turn of the century. What eventually resulted was the International Time Recording Company, which manufactured and marketed machines that combined clocks and printers to keep track of time for such purposes as measuring the duration of a manufacturing process or documenting how long an employee worked during the day.

The second product of these mergers was the Computing Scale Company of America, whose products included scales for grocers and butchers, and cheese-cutting machines. The firm supplied the C of

CTR. (In no sense, it should be noted, was this the forerunner of the modern computer.) The International Time Recording Company provided the R (for "Recording"). The T was contributed by the Tabulating Machine Company, which Flint tossed into the mix at the last minute.

The Tabulating Machine Company was yet another "haphazard organization," to use the Beldens' phrase, that had grown up in the preceding decade or two. The company produced a device invented by Dr. Herman Hollerith for recording census data. Hollerith had gotten involved in tabulating back in 1880. At that time, it was realized that population increases were rendering the census so outdated that it was losing much of its value. The tenth census, begun in 1880, took a decade to compile. If ever necessity was the mother of invention, this was the moment. Hollerith developed his electrical tabulating system by 1889, making the tenth census the final one to be assembled manually. In 1896, the Tabulating Machine Company was established, with Hollerith the manager and principal stockholder.

With total assets of $17.5 million on December 31, 1911, Computing-Tabulating-Recording was probably one of the three hundred largest companies in the nation (in asset terms) at its formation. However, whipping these assets into shape so that the whole of this company would be greater than the sum of its parts—which is the point of a merger if it is to create genuine economic value rather than merely fees for the people who engineer it—was going to be extraordinarily difficult. From its formation in 1911 to 1914, CTR was not, in Flint's view, living up to its potential. That is why he wanted to talk to Watson about running it.

Flint played cat and mouse with Watson at first. His disquisitions were long on philosophizing but lacked any specifics about what role Watson might play in the numerous enterprises in which Flint had an interest. After a number of meetings, Flint at last got to the point. He wanted Watson to run Computing-Tabulating-Recording. Watson was interested; so Flint took the next step, the submission of his candidacy to the board of directors.

The board was not thrilled. The fact that Watson was, at the time he was being proposed for this position, a convicted felon did not pass unnoticed. "What are you trying to do?" one director asked Flint. "Ruin this business? Who is going to run this business while he serves his term in jail?"

When Watson met with the board, they were no less blunt. "Why did you leave the NCR Company?" barked one director. "Because Mr. Patterson asked for my resignation," was the reply. During a barrage of equally unfriendly inquiries, Watson gradually won the board over with his straightforward and undefensive replies.

After the board decided to approve Flint's recommendation, the question of remuneration arose. A committee of the board asked Watson what he was looking for. He responded that he wanted them to propose a compensation package to him, but the offer had to fall within certain bounds.

The result was a salary of $25,000, an option on 1,220 shares of stock, and a profit escalator to be negotiated in the future. Thus, he was paid a lot of money. Twenty-five thousand dollars in 1914 was the equivalent of more than $425,000 in 2000.

More important, however, was the upside potential if Watson succeeded. A salesman at heart, Watson liked commissions. He therefore asked for a percentage of the company's profits. In 1914, that did not look like much. Two decades later, this modern "pay-for-performance" arrangement made Watson the highest-salaried executive in the nation. But Watson had a very long way to go before reaching such heights.

CTR was in far worse shape than outside observers realized. Watson himself probably had no accurate idea of what he was getting himself into. CTR's bonded indebtedness was twenty-five times larger than its assets, many of which were little more than accounting fictions. The accounting system itself was so misleading that "Watson was spared having to face all the bad news at once."

CTR was a true conglomerate. The whole was worth less than the sum of its parts. It was not merely that the parts were not working together. Some were working at cross-purposes. Lawsuits were being pursued between what were supposed to be divisions of one corporation. There was, alas, little business logic behind the firm. It was created for the profit of the promoters who created it. It was, in a word, a formless mess.

From 1914 to the mid-1920s, Watson undertook the herculean effort of shaping this blob of a business into a corporate razor. He worked tirelessly to rationalize CTR, and in the process—unheralded in the press or by those who wrote so much about him in later years—he showed what a skilled manager he was. He got a big break, an essential boost, when his conviction for antitrust violations was reversed on appeal. Since Watson was no longer looking at jail time, a relieved board of directors elevated his title from general manager to president and general manager on March 15, 1915. The Ides of March were kind to him. He was at the helm of CTR, and he was there to stay. He was no longer marginal in his position. But the firm of which he was now the CEO was certainly marginal in the business world. During the tenure of Watson and his son, it moved from the margin to the center.

Slowly but steadily, the unglamorous work of rationalizing CTR began to bear fruit. The product line was whipped into shape. Sales and profits grew. These were the years when Watson was laboring in the vineyard. Watson's faith seemed unshakable that the grapes in that vineyard would mature and that after fermentation there would be vintage wine year after year.

On the home front, Watson's family was growing. Daughters Jane and Helen and son Arthur (known in the family and referred to hereafter as Dick) were born by 1920. Watson's ambitions for himself and his firm were limitless.

Nothing better symbolized that ambition than his changing the company's name in 1924 from the utterly prosaic Computing-Tabulating-Recording to the sky's-the-limit name it bears to this very day, the International Business Machines Corporation. What's in a name? The new IBM still employed the old CTR's "cigar-chomping guys selling coffee grinders and butcher scales." But one has to start somewhere. It turned out that there could be a great deal in a name.

Watson's overwhelming ambition created a lot of tension within him, and he brought that tension home. The target was his wife, Jeannette. It took years to whip IBM into shape; and during that time, "when Dad," Junior later wrote, "was most intense about his work, there was enormous tension in our household." Senior treated Jeannette like one of his staff at the office. At work, "he could press the button on his desk, a fellow would come in, Dad would say, 'Send a letter,' and boom, it would happen. When he wasn't thinking, he expected Mother to obey him in the same way."

It was not just Watson's peremptory bossiness that grated on his wife and wore her down. It was his attitude toward money. Watson was a confirmed social climber. He lived lavishly, well beyond his means. "The chances he took with money are amazing to me," recalled Junior. For the first eight years of his marriage, he was in debt to the tune of about a hundred thousand dollars, a fortune at the time. He took the family on business trips to Europe in 1922 and 1924 on borrowed money.

Senior managed CTR's finances the same way he ran the household—on the edge. One of the first things he did at CTR was ask for a $40,000 loan for research and development from the Guaranty Trust Company. CTR had already borrowed $4 million from this bank, and his banker told him the firm's books did not suggest that further loans would be prudent. Moreover, the banker could have rightly commented that money in this amount for a function with outcomes as unpredictable as research and development was really a stretch.

It was not for nothing, though, that Watson had worked at NCR for two decades. Summoning up the spirit of John Patterson ("Never hesitate," "Quote the price without a quiver"), Watson responded, "Balance sheets reveal the past. This loan is for the future." He made the sale.

In the years that followed, Watson sailed pretty close to the wind when it came to the finances of CTR/IBM. Rapid expansion brought CTR close to bankruptcy during the brief, sharp depression of 1921. During the early years of the Great Depression of the 1930s, IBM's stock dropped 200 points from its 1929 high to its 1932 low.

Senior brought the same almost devil-may-care attitude about finances to the family's business; and it drove his wife to distraction. Watson did not become a really rich man until the 1930s, but he started living like one almost from the time of his marriage. In Junior's words, Senior did not "worry about money. He wanted to rise in the world, so he knew he had to spend. . . . If it came in, it went out, and that was fine with him." He irresponsibly refused to hedge his bets, and his family was quite close to bankruptcy when IBM stock collapsed in the early 1930s. Jeannette, "strong on prairie virtues," found this way of living nothing short of "torture." "I remember incessant arguments," Junior would recall decades later. "The door to their bedroom would be closed but my brother and sisters and I would hear angry, muffled voices rising and falling."

Not a pretty picture.

CHAPTER 7

Terrible Tommy Watson

Jeannette Kittredge met Tom Watson Sr. late in the spring of 1912. They were married on April 17, 1913. As we have already mentioned, these were tumultuous times in Watson's life because of the trial and the conviction at NCR. On January 8, 1914, Thomas J. Watson Jr. was born. By then Patterson had fired Watson, and he was looking for a job. Jane Watson was born the next year, followed by Helen in 1917, and Dick in 1919. During these years, Watson Sr. took the position at CTR, and the family moved to an apartment on Eighty-fifth Street in Manhattan, and then to the exclusive suburb of Short Hills, New Jersey.

It is worth contemplating what a whirlwind this must have been for the bride. She had led a sheltered, privileged life for three decades. Now, in what must have seemed like an instant, she was the wife of a very ambitious man who was in the headlines and mother to his son and soon thereafter his three other children. From a lifetime as the daughter of a prominent Daytonian, she found herself living in an undistinguished apartment on Eighty-fifth Street in Manhattan.

The first year of marriage and the first year of parenthood are often not easy. For the Watsons, there was a three-month overlap in these life events. Jeannette's husband was ten years her senior. He was a tall, physically prepossessing man. She was five feet four inches in height. His childhood and youth were far different from hers, with her boarding-school background. These two people needed some "downtime," some time to get to know each other. They did not have it. All of a sudden, Jeannette found herself playing multiple roles—wife, mother, maid, butler, and executive secretary—not all of which were equally congenial.

For the first decade and a half of his life, Thomas J. Watson Jr.'s mother "was the biggest presence" in his life. It was not a happy childhood. Things did not come easily to Junior. He was so mischievous that he came to be known as "Terrible Tommy Watson." "Whenever there was trouble, I seemed to be involved." Most of the other kids his age stayed away from him. His grades at Short Hills Country Day School "were always a jumble of Ds and Fs with an occasional A or B." "[W]ords on a page seemed to swim around whenever I tried to read." He indulged in more than his share of childhood pranks. And he was beyond punishment, which merely drove him to greater misbehavior.

Young Tom Watson was the original poor little rich boy, but the pain he experienced was real enough. At the age of thirteen, he began to suffer recurring clinical depressions. The heralding event for the first was an attack of asthma. This depression lasted for a month. Then it disappeared, but it came back six months later and kept coming back every six months for six years. "Unless you've had such a depression," he recalled more than a half a century later, "you can't imagine what you go through. The fear is totally irrational, your whole thinking process goes awry, everything you see seems unreal."

Junior's mother must have found it difficult to understand his behavior and mood disorder. Nevertheless, she made him and her other children "feel protected and loved and wanted. I think she understood that at the root of my odd and mischievous behavior was a lack of self-esteem." By contrast to her warmth and love, Tommy's father seemed inaccessible. The two could not connect. "All sons," Junior later wrote,

> at some point have the idea that their father is the most important man in the world. But that impression is hard to outgrow when your old man's photograph is in every office and everybody around is bowing and scraping and trying to ingratiate themselves with him. Everything he did left me feeling inconsequential by comparison. The worst was when he was doing something that he thought would make me happy.

Junior had no recollection of his father's telling him that he wanted him to follow in Dad's footsteps and run IBM someday. Yet, for reasons which he did not understand, he came to believe that his father had anointed him as his successor. "The very idea made me miserable," wrote Junior.

Junior remembered one instance when he was about twelve years old sitting "on a curb thinking about my father. . . . [B]y the time I got home, I was in tears. . . . I can't do it," he said to his mother. "I can't go to work at IBM." His mother not unreasonably replied that no one had asked him to. "Yeah, but I know Dad wants me to," he said. "And I just can't do it." For some reason, it was as natural for Junior to assume he would follow in his father's footsteps as it was for Senior to assume that he would not follow in those of his own father. IBM's offices seemed "gloomy" to young Tom. His father had already begun to accumulate the pictures, medals, and mementos commemorating his interactions with the famous and powerful, and these adorned his office walls. The oriental rug, the mahogany desk, the lack of natural light, and the stench of cigars all combined to make IBM, as represented by Senior's office, a not very appealing place. Junior did not like it, and he did not feel worthy of it.

Junior's feelings of unworthiness could not have been ameliorated by the knowledge that he was not his father's favorite child. That distinction belonged to his sister Jane. Jane appears to have played to perfection the role of daddy's little girl. Junior just could not figure out how to please Dad. When he looked at himself from what he imagined to be his father's point of view, he saw himself as a profoundly unworthy son.

The person who made everything all right was his mother; and as we saw in the previous chapter, Mom and Dad were having their share of troubles making their marriage work. The "angry, muffled voices" kept rising and falling. Mostly rising.

This discord lasted for a decade. Senior was quite an oppressor. "Father would be rude to her [Mother], and then half an hour later he'd give us a lecture about how we ought to be good to our mother. I never had the guts to say, 'Then why aren't you?'"

One does not need psychiatric training to see that we have here all the fixings for serious emotional problems. The son, with an Olympian father whom he cannot please, feels miserable about himself. The mother builds up the son's self-esteem, thus protecting him from the ill effects of his father's temperament and temper. The father attacks the mother. The son cannot protect her.

At the onset of puberty, young Tom finds himself sitting on a curb thinking about his father. Soon thereafter, the depressions begin. No wonder.

But after a decade of strife, harmony suddenly came to characterize the marriage of Jeannette and Tom Sr. The picture they imparted to the world became that of a perfectly matched team. William Rodgers, who published a shrewdly critical book about the Watsons in 1969 when IBM was at flood tide, wrote that

> Jeannette Kittredge was a full and true partner in Watson's life, and they made a formidable pair for forty-two years [i.e., from their wedding day until Watson's death]. . . . They praised and paid court to each other—with the IBM family looking on, approving and applauding—at public affairs of honor, adulation, and dedication. . . . They were, in fact, the epitome of marital and corporate togetherness.

The picture of the two in Rodgers's book shows a serene and peacefully impressive couple.

Had Rodgers been fooled? Clearly neither he nor anyone else prior to the publication of Junior's autobiography in 1990 knew of the *agon* that had characterized the first quarter of this marriage. What had happened?

As just noted, the strife between the two disappeared suddenly. Junior himself did not know what had happened. Indeed, he was shocked. "I thought she'd stopped standing up for herself." Years later, she told Junior what had really happened. Wife, mother, maid, butler, and executive secretary—she had had enough. She told Senior she wanted a divorce. The depth of her unhappiness had never entered his thick skull, and he was thunderstruck. He was "so shocked, so upset," said Jeannette, that she realized how much he loved her. That was the last mention of divorce in the Watson family. Jeannette realized that the marriage ought to be preserved, and she made the "conscious decision" to play the role that she knew she had to play to make the marriage a success. That is the face the world saw. But it became more than that. With firmly accepted ground rules, these two people loved one another.

If all this was understandably confusing to the firstborn son, the confusion did not end there. During Junior's childhood, despite the tension just described, his father "knew how to loosen up and have fun with us. . . . When I was little I thought I had the liveliest father imaginable." He even knew how to poke fun at himself:

Dad loved to ham it up when our aunts and uncles and cousins visited for Sunday dinner. Sometimes he'd disappear with Mother and she'd help him struggle into one of her dresses. He'd come tottering down the stairs all decked out in a hat and veil and high-heeled shoes, clinging to the banister on one side with Mother steadying him on the other.

This playfulness and lightheartedness faded away. We do not know why. Perhaps it was the combined strain of the pressures of work and domestic discord. Perhaps it was the growing sense that a man of destiny should act in an aloof, distant, seignorial manner. Perhaps, as Junior speculated, it was the simple fact of age. In 1924, when CTR became IBM, Junior was ten; Senior was fifty. He was not palling around with the fathers of the other boys, nor was he spending his weekends coaching soccer. Poor Junior must have wondered where the enjoyable father went and how to get him back.

The family got along better when they left Short Hills. When father and son traveled by train together, Junior received lessons in how to act in the great world outside. Senior showed his son how to shave, wash up, and then clean up afterward in the men's room. Dad would leave the shaving basin "clean as a whistle." That way, his father explained, "the next fellow has the same chance you had."

Senior was a big tipper. On one trip, he tipped the Pullman porter $10, a good deal of money in the mid-1920s. His son asked why.

I do this for two reasons, Tom. First, that fellow has been up all night in his little cubicle and I feel sorry for him.

The second reason is that there is a whole class of people in the world who are in a position to poor-mouth you unless you are sensitive to them. They are the headwaiters, Pullman car conductors, porters, and chauffeurs. They see you in an intimate fashion and can really knock off your reputation.

Thus, Tom Jr. saw his father in more than one guise. He could be a fun-loving "cutup." Or he could be a man of the world instructing his protégé on how to act. The son yearned for these connections. But they were evanescent. The fun would end. The trip would be completed. They would be back home in Short Hills, and father would transform himself into the aloof, distant man he was most of the time. The glimpse of companionship could not have made the return to cold formality easy.

Terrible Tommy did not do terribly well at school. He did not set the world on fire at Short Hills Country Day School, although he did manage to ruin a leather jacket by burning it when he was eleven years old ("[I]t's fascinating to make fires when you're young," he later remarked). The next step was Carteret Academy, twelve miles away from home, to which Junior commuted. He failed academically there as well.

Junior's academic problems brought out a "warmth and gentleness" as well as a tolerance in his father which young Tom probably did not expect. Tom Sr. tried to console his son by telling him that youth could be difficult. When he discussed Junior's grades, he said: "I wish you were better in school, and I'm sure you do, but at some point, something will catch hold of you and you are going to be a great man." Such talk produced only incredulity in young Watson.

After Carteret came a year in a school called Morristown, noteworthy because at the age of fifteen this was Tom's first year boarding away from home. The following year, Tom enrolled at the Hun School in Princeton, New Jersey. A lot of Hun graduates went to Princeton University, which is where Junior wanted to go to college. "I figured I was as good as in."

> Hun was filled with playboys. . . . It was a style of life to which I felt to some degree qualified. It meant that studies were not particularly important, that you had a little more money than the average fellow, that you were always out with the girls, and that you owned a car.

Young Tom did not drink at Hun, which showed the influence of his father, who prohibited alcohol at IBM. This was an influence that would not survive college. Junior was not altogether without precocity at Hun. He smoked marijuana once.

With the exception of some bright spots, Junior's academic record both in prep school and on standardized college entry examinations ranged from mediocre to miserable. As he put it, "[A]cademically I was still a zero." Zero or not, Senior was determined that

Junior attend Princeton. It was the spring of 1933, the depths of the Great Depression. Personal fortunes had been lost. Companies had gone bankrupt. Institutional endowments had plummeted in value. The whole nation was far less wealthy than could have been imagined just a few years earlier. Real gross national product had declined by about 25 percent.

Against this backdrop, Watson Sr. pulled every string he could to get his eldest son accepted into Princeton. IBM in 1933 was not an exception to the trends of the Great Depression. Sales tumbled and the price of the stock, in which Senior was heavily invested, declined almost 80 percent from 1929 to 1932. Nevertheless, despite his remark to Junior that 1932 was a grim year financially, Senior continued to live well. Very well. When he approached the director of admissions at Princeton on behalf of his son, he presented himself as a successful man of the world with connections.

One does not have to spend too much time in a university in 2003 to learn that money talks. It did not talk during the 1930s; it shouted. Nevertheless, Princeton was not interested in Terrible Tommy Watson. The school was blunt about its views. "Mr. Watson," said Admissions Dean Radcliffe Heermance, "I am looking at your son's record and he is a predetermined failure." Even Senior had to accept the inevitable. One wonders whether anybody at the university was regretting that decision three years later, when Senior was widely publicized for pulling in a salary of $365,000.

Nothing daunted, the family decamped to the spacious summer home which Senior had purchased in the wealthy resort town of Camden, Maine. One day Senior got out his big Packard touring car and announced to his son that the time had come to find him a college willing to accept him despite his less than stellar grades. Junior suggested they try Brown for two reasons. First, he happened to know someone who went there. Second, Providence was not that far away, and he wanted to return to Camden as quickly as possible because he had a crush on a rich, beautiful socialite. Brown University in 1933 was not the Brown of seven decades later. It was feeling the depression. "The campus looked run down," said Junior, "and a good number of students seemed undernourished. Many of them commuted by bus from places like Pawtucket, because they couldn't afford to live at school."

Watson marched into the admissions office, son in tow. "I'm Thomas Watson, I run the IBM company, and my son would like to consider coming to Brown. By the way, who is the President of Brown?" One would have thought that if Watson wanted to know who Brown's president was, he could and should have found out from someone other than the director of admissions. There is, indeed, a tinge of disrespect in the question because it carries with it the unstated assumption that whoever the president might be, he was not someone whose name a man like Watson would be expected to know.

Watson would not have spoken this way at, for example, Columbia. He had met Columbia's president, Nicholas Murray Butler, and a picture of the two hung on his office wall.

At any rate, the president of Brown University in 1933 was Clarence Barbour. Barbour happened to have been the pastor of the church to which the Watsons had belonged in Rochester three decades previously. Next stop, President Barbour's office. When the Watsons returned to the admissions office, the dean said, "He's not very good, but we'll take him." So at last young Watson, deficient in so many ways though he may have been, had a place to go to college.

CHAPTER 8

Thomas J. Watson Sr. in 1893 and Thomas J. Watson Jr. in 1933

In 1893, Tom Watson Sr. was nineteen years old. In 1933, Tom Watson Jr. was also nineteen. As father and son, these two men obviously shared a lot of genes. However, the differences in their life experiences are more striking than the similarities.

Tom Watson Sr. was born and brought up on the wrong side of history. The growing nation had passed Steuben County by. His father, while not a failure as a breadwinner, was not a great success. There was never a thought of Watson's going into his father's business or following in his footsteps in any other regard.

By the time he was nineteen, Watson Sr. had weighed his father in the balance and found him wanting. He was "absolutely sure" he was a smarter man and could prove it if he had to do so. There was a note of contempt in his judgment that "my father was never meant to be a rich man."

As a boy and as an adolescent, Watson Sr. showed few of those traits that were to mark him as a "man of men." With the exception of his year studying at the Miller School of Commerce, Watson Sr. had spent his whole life within the confines of Steuben County. He seemed not to get much out of his environment. He left no recollections of being touched by its natural beauty.

He returned to Painted Post and got his first job, as a bookkeeper at Clarence Risley's butcher shop at $6 a week. He did not like that very much and soon became a salesman. He drove a team of horses which pulled what was called, quoting the Beldens, an "organ wagon . . . , a great long wagon with a high seat in front and the top over it. On a stormy day there was a rubber curtain I could hang up in front and put the reins through a slot, fill my pipe, and I was in command, at least of that outfit."

Watson liked having a job—"I had the sense to know that was a pretty important thing for a young man to have"—and he liked the job he had. Tom Watson liked selling. Be it organs, pianos, cash registers, tabulating machines, a whole company, or himself, he liked selling. Selling solved problems. World peace, he came to believe, was a sales problem.

In a world which still held the "drummer" in contempt, Watson respected selling. He came to revere it and the people who did it well. This honest, forthright respect was something the legions of men and women who would sell under his leadership for NCR and IBM cherished.

When he left Painted Post on his wagon selling organs and pianos, the great journey of Watson's life had begun.

Tom Watson Jr.'s youth was in sharp contrast to his father's on almost every dimension. Whenever he compared himself to his father, it was he who appeared the lesser figure. "Terrible Tommy" failed at most of the things he tried. Brought up not in a backwater but in the lap of luxury in the nation's metropolis, Tommy had very little he could call his own. Beset by uncontrollably severe depressions, he could not even call his mood his own. When young Tom looked in the mirror, he saw a pale imitation of the "man of men" his father was fast becoming.

Watson Jr. did not appreciate the extent to which—in terms of possessions and of experiences, if not of paternal guidance and nurturing—he was a spoiled boy. When he was seventeen, his parents gave him a car, "a really hot-looking black and red Chrysler." His father, "convinced that Europe was going to be a big deal one day," made frequent trips there. Not once, not twice, but five times during his youth Watson took extended European tours, the kind of luxury vouchsafed to very few Americans during the 1920s.

The privileged upbringing included not only money, but connections and influence. Young Tom's lifelong love affair with flight began "before I was even old enough to ride a bicycle." Dayton was the home not only of the National Cash Register Company but also of the Wright brothers, whom, needless to say, Tom's father had met. Young Tom's first ride in an airplane was at Le Bourget, the Paris airfield, in 1924, when he was only ten years old. Three years later, Senior bought tickets to a banquet in honor of Charles Lindbergh, who had just flown the Atlantic. At the banquet, Senior introduced young Tom to Lindbergh. Senior did not even know Lindbergh at the time. He simply marched up to the dais with his thirteen-year-old son in tow, introduced himself as the head of IBM (of which it is doubtful Lindbergh had ever heard), and then introduced his son. "He had such astonishing brass," commented the son, who was rendered almost speechless by his introduction to the world-famous pioneer in aviation.

Young Tom spent his summer vacations in the watering places of the rich. His father was a social climber who "married up" late in life. Junior had already socially climbed; and when he married, it would be his bride who was marrying up. When Senior finished high school, he spent a year in vocational school and then began the lengthy process of turning the vocation he chose—selling—into a profession. When Junior finished prep school, his father used his influence and his "brass" to get him into a brand-name four-year college. It took a shoehorn, but he managed.

Once matriculated at Brown, there was no question of Junior's being among the down-at-the-heels commuters from Pawtucket. He joined the Psi Upsilon fraternity, full of rich boys "who had the money to behave as if the 1920s had never stopped roaring." His dad gave him $300 a month for his clothes and other bills. Three hundred dollars was the equivalent of just under $4,000 in the year 2000. Perhaps a better comparison would be to the income of the average American family, which was about half that figure. "Dad never asked for an accounting," young Tom explained. "When we saw each other he'd say, 'you're probably a little short, son,' and pass me an extra hundred dollars. I spent every nickel."

I once asked a member of the Rockefeller family what it was like to be a member of the Rockefeller family. He said that when he was young, it seemed to him that he was like everyone else. He would walk past Rockefeller Center and assume without thinking about it that lots of people had centers . . . a Smith Center, a Jones Center, a Rockefeller Center. That is the mark of the genuinely privileged. When they are young, they are unaware of their special standing in this world. We see the same lack of awareness in young Tom when he was nineteen. "[O]ddly, I never knew if I was really rich." A lot of average Americans could have told him.

Thus, the Watsons, Senior and Junior, came from the same family. But they did not come from the same world. Their experiences of life in their formative years were fundamentally different. Senior graduated from the school of hard knocks. He drove a wagon through the woods selling organs and pianos. Whenever Junior graduated from anywhere, it was because standards were low. He had the devil's own time staying on a road that was paved just for him.

Senior had sold himself to himself. Junior had done precious little to build self-confidence. Senior had become, in a sense, his own parents as he began the task of inventing the "man of men." Junior had been not so much parented as patronized, especially as his father grew more important than his mother in his life.

Would these men ever be able to work together harmoniously in a business? The odds, one would think, were against it.

CHAPTER 9

The Searing Insight

As these words are being written in 2003, terms such as "vision" and "mission" have fallen on hard times. The business world was bloated with "visionaries" during the late 1990s. Many of these people turned out to have cataracts. Some were simply criminal. Enron, Adelphia, WorldCom, and Global Crossing are only a few of the spectacular failures that have been visited upon the investing public. As for "mission," there probably is not a major company in the country that does not have a mission statement. With very few exceptions, most notably Johnson & Johnson, these mission statements could not be more completely ignored. Mere hot air.

That said, when one looks at the true giants of enterprise in the history of business in the United States—a category into which Thomas J. Watson Sr. unquestionably falls—one sees repeatedly the central role played by visionary leadership with a crystal clear commitment to a corporate mission. Just as often, this vision and mission can be expressed in a few words understandable to everyone, even if the product being sold is technical in nature.

Perhaps words like "vision" and "mission" have been discredited because the soaring boom turned into the thud of a bust characterized by cheating to a degree shocking to everyone but the cheaters.

Nevertheless, the phenomenon which these two words represent has historically resided at the core of human greatness. A new label for this phenomenon may be in order. I suggest "searing insight," and I would like to offer a few examples of how a searing insight has served to organize a business venture and martial its resources toward a clear goal.

Andrew Carnegie has often been used as the exemplar of social and economic mobility in nineteenth-century America. It is rarely noted that before Carnegie became an entrepreneur, he was an organization man. With the help of a mentor's guiding hand, Carnegie was hired as a telegrapher at the Pennsylvania Railroad in 1853. He became the superintendent of the Western Division a mere six years later.

Carnegie worked for the Pennsylvania Railroad for twelve years; and by the time he resigned in 1865, he had learned something very important: Railroads were destined to change the face of the nation. To run efficiently, they needed steel, not iron, rails. Steel could also serve as the skeleton for all kinds of structures, from bridges to buildings. Steel, indeed, was destined to transform the material basis of civilization. That was his searing insight.

Carnegie entered the steel business in 1873; and he realized that to satisfy his overweening ambition to become the world's richest and most powerful businessman, he had to dominate the steel industry. To do that, he had to invest a fortune to construct the largest, most efficient mills. To make those mills with their huge fixed costs pay, he had to keep them running full and steady. His watchwords became: "Cut the prices; scoop the market; run the mills full." In a sense, Carnegie's immense fortune can be reduced to the searing insight represented by that phrase.

Carnegie was the rule, not the exception. In the case of photography, George Eastman understood—not through research but through gut instinct—that the great mass market would embrace photography if it was made simple and inexpensive. When he bought his first camera on November 13, 1877, it cost him $49.58.

It was not easy to use. One needed not inconsiderable chemical knowledge and mechanical ability, and Eastman had to spend an extra $5 on lessons. In 1900, his company brought out the Kodak Brownie. Price: $1. The key that unlocked the mass market was a slogan that became world famous: "You press the button. We do the rest."

In the face of a doubting world, Henry Ford was convinced there was a market for personal, mechanical transportation. That was his searing insight. The key was to build a car that was reliable. It had to be inexpensive, not cheap. The dream was realized with the creation of the Model T Ford. "It takes you there, and it brings you back" was Ford's analogue to the phrases that paid for Carnegie and Eastman.

"The Pause That Refreshes," "Always the Low Price, Always," "Doctors Recommend Tylenol," "Intel Inside"—one could make a lengthy list of such phrases because they so often accompany and encapsulate the success of a product or of a company by focusing on the searing insight which engrossed a market.

Now let's take a look at Watson Sr.

For most businesspeople, the problem posed by CTR in 1914, three years after its founding and the year Watson was hired, would have been insuperable. Managing products as unrelated as butcher scales, time clocks, coffee grinders, and tabulating machines would have presented the proverbial dilemma of herding cats. Yet Watson transformed this motley group of unexciting products manufactured and sold by a collection of second raters into one of the most effective, highly focused profit machines of the twentieth century. From formless blob to a razor. Not easy.

How did he do it?

Like Carnegie, Eastman, Ford, and a handful of others, he was possessed of a searing insight about his business and the role it could play not only in its industry but in society. Business, Watson came to believe, was about information. As the Second Industrial Revolution matured, an ever larger number of people were going to be needed to process that information—to transmit it from where it was generated to where it was needed, to analyze it, to store it, and to retrieve it. These people cost money. Any machine that could do their work more expeditiously than they would save money.

So when Watson surveyed the dozens of products CTR sold, what caught his eye was that T—for Tabulating Machine—which had been thrown into the conglomerate as an afterthought at the last minute. Charles R. Flint, the man who, it may be recalled, put CTR together in 1911, asserted that there were synergies (to use the modern word) between the measurement of time (thus the time clocks made by the Recording Division), the measurement of weight (thus the scales made by the Computing Division), and the counting of any number of items (thus the punched card machines made by the Tabulating Division). Any such synergies unfortunately were far more apparent in Flint's egotistical imagination than in reality. These products were made by different processes in different factories and sold to different purchasers by different sales forces. The various component parts of CTR eyed each other jealously and were more than a little suspicious that Watson would play favorites.

The Tabulating Machine Company was the smallest and least profitable unit of CTR when Watson took over in 1914. It had been founded by Herman Hollerith, who had done graduate work in statistics and worked for the U.S. Census. The Census Bureau was encountering a big problem during the 1880s. The United States was growing fast, and the census was being forced to record more information than its capacity would permit. During the 1880s, Hollerith developed an electromechanical tabulator capable of recording information by "reading" (i.e., by completing an electrical circuit) through a hole punched in a specially treated cardboardlike card. In a sense, it could also read the absence of information because if no hole was punched in a particular row in a particular column, no circuit would be completed.

The inspiration for this device came from various sources. One was as simple as seeing a conductor on a railroad train punch a hole in a passenger's ticket. The placement of that hole communicated how far the passenger would ride. There was no need to discuss the question each time passenger and conductor encountered one another.

Other sources were more complex. One of Hollerith's supervisors asked him to look into the Jacquard loom for possible clues. Joseph-Marie Jacquard was a French silk weaver who developed a loom which used punched cards to determine which threads in the warp would be depressed prior to the passage of the shuttle with the weft thread. Patterns woven on Jacquard looms could be detailed and complex; but because they were repetitive, they could be "programmed" by a set of punched cards. The Jacquard loom thus saved labor.

Jacquard's innovation was influential. The English mathematician Charles Babbage used it in his efforts to develop an automatic calculator. This line of mechanical investigation was the ancestor of the modern computer. Like the tabulating machines which Hollerith developed late in the nineteenth century, devices such as the Jacquard loom were binary. Either a hole was present or it was not. Zero or one.

Hollerith took the advice of his mentors at the Census Bureau and developed a tabulating machine based on punched cards that proved valuable for collecting information about the American population. Using Hollerith Tabulating Machines, the eleventh census was able to collect 235 discrete pieces of information about each American citizen, an increase by two orders of magnitude over the 1870 census despite the fact that there were many millions more people to count.

There was real business potential here, potential that meat slicers and coffee grinders could never match. This potential extended far beyond automating the census—which, by the way, Hollerith's machines were so successful at doing that they have been credited with saving two years' time and $5 million in the compilation of the 1890 census.

The hallmark of the Second Industrial Revolution was the

growth of big business. The coordination and control of all kinds of information—accounting, financial, operational—was essential for these firms to function. Hollerith's machines could save big firms time and money. They could also contribute to accuracy. Every time a clerk reentered a number, a mistake was possible. A hole in a card, on the other hand, always stayed where it was punched.

Understanding that tabulating was the future of his company was the sine qua non of Watson's business greatness. It was the beginning, the essential beginning, but only the beginning—and nothing more. We all learned during the course of the bubble that has just burst that technology alone does not a business make. Watson's experiences with Hollerith and his company illustrate the point.

Hollerith did not go away when Flint bought his company. He remained with the firm; and although doubtless an exceptionally talented inventor, he was a business idiot. Pompous and as sensitive to his own prejudices as he was insensitive to the legitimate needs of others, Hollerith was a pain in the neck for Watson to manage. He needlessly turned away potential customers who had heard about his machines and approached him. He was cast in the mold of the lone inventor rather than someone who could work with a team in a corporate setting.

Watson knew that other companies were developing tabulating machines, some of which, by the middle of the second decade of the century, had important features that his lacked. He knew that money needed to be spent to develop a superior product. He was shrewd enough to understand that Hollerith could not be a part of the corporate research and development effort that he had in mind for tabulating. Despite his inventive genius, Hollerith had allowed his tabulators to fall technically behind the machines of the principal competitor, the Powers Company. Add to this the fact that Hollerith was charging 30 percent more than Powers to rent his machine, and you have the picture of a company facing serious problems.

Watson was always known as the salesman's salesman, and not without reason. It was, however, his very appreciation of the difficulties of selling that prompted his constant push for better products and his support for engineers and the inherent risks of research and development. It is a great deal easier to sell a quality product than one with shortcomings. It took a long time, five years, for Watson to be able to manufacture a tabulating machine of a quality high enough to make his salesmen stand up and cheer—which they did, literally, on their chairs at the 1919 convention.

The essence of capitalism is an orientation toward the future—vision, mission, searing insight, call it what you will—combined with an intense, obsessive attention to the "blocking and tackling" necessary to turn that future into a reality. A business is nothing if it is not inflamed by imagination; but if all it has is imagination, it will surely go down in flames. The essence of what made Watson a giant of enterprise was not that he made marketing the center of his business. He did do that, thus practicing the "marketing concept" decades before it was enunciated by marketing professors. What made Watson great was his understanding that in order for marketing to succeed, the marketers needed a product to sell which the market would accept. Watson understood that selling was not the art of convincing a customer to buy something that he neither needed nor wanted. Good salesmanship had nothing to do with fooling, tricking, or putting anything over on anybody. Selling was the art of helping the customer to understand that he did indeed both need and want what you were selling to him.

Watson had not wasted his almost two decades at NCR. John Patterson knew that business was about the future. That is why he established his Future Demands Department around the turn of the century. Watson was a member. So was the great inventor Charles F. Kettering. From the Wright brothers to Kettering to Hugh Chalmers (whose motor car company eventually became part of Chrysler) to Patterson, an awful lot was going on in Dayton in 1900. Watson drank it all in.

Embracing the future meant improving current products and introducing new ones. Moreover, this effort could not wait. It could not be put off until finances were in better shape, morale was stronger, or the firm was consolidated or better organized. You could not wait for things to be "all set" before you invested in the future. Things were never "all set."

James E. Burke, the chief executive of Johnson & Johnson from 1976 through 1989 and the man responsible for rescuing Tylenol from the poisonings of 1982 and 1986, once said that it is easy to live with and forgive the shortcomings of a colleague or employee. Living with and making the most of his or her strengths is more difficult. To know that someone else is more able than you in certain areas and to make use of that ability for the good of the company requires a lot of self-confidence. It is a rare boss who can put aside the accolades with which courtiers shower him and admit his own ignorance. But that is essential for business greatness for the simple reason that no one can know everything.

Andrew Carnegie was without technical knowledge of steel-making. He cheerfully admitted to "no shadow of a claim to rank as an inventor, chemist, investigator, or mechanician." However, no one was more astute in knowing what he did not know but what his organization needed. Carnegie did not know anything about chemistry; but he knew how to hire a chemist, "a learned German, Dr. Fricke, and great secrets did the doctor open up to us. . . . What fools we had been! . . . [but] not as great fools as our competitors." They said they could not afford a chemist, while the truth was "they could not afford to be without one." A similar story can be told about Rockefeller, Standard Oil, and the Frasch process (which removed sulfur from crude oil and thus commercialized new oil fields).

This same requisite for greatness Watson possessed in full measure. He could make "no shadow of a claim" to inventiveness or to knowledge of engineering. He held not one patent. Herman Hollerith held more than thirty. Watson privileged engineers not despite his ignorance of their technical abilities but because of it. During the depths of the Great Depression, in July 1932, Watson opened a new engineering laboratory by declaring, "We have realized from experience that the future of our business largely depends on the efforts, brain, and ability of our engineers."

CTR's sales increased sharply from 1911 to 1920, and the increase was just as sharply halted by the depression of 1921. The company weathered that crisis, however, and proceeded to an impressive decade during the 1920s. In 1919, before-tax income reached $2.1 million, a fourfold increase in five years. The Tabulating Machine Company, despite having caught Watson's eye, was still last in sales and profits. There was a lot of work to be done in every aspect of this business before it achieved the potential Watson sensed within it. In 1924, the year CTR became IBM, profits climbed to $2.4 million. By 1929, profits jumped to $7.4 million. In 1933, profits sank to $6.5 million from a high of $8.2 million in 1930. In 1934, however, they rebounded to $7.5 million. The Great Depression was over for IBM, and the firm never looked back.

The first year of the New York World's Fair, 1939, IBM made $11.3 million. By 1940, IBM was outpacing its old rival, the National Cash Register Company, in sales as well as profits: $46.3 million to $39.9 million.

From the standpoint of profitability, the story was far more dramatic. From 1930 to 1940 inclusive, a dreadful period in the history of American business and a time that was particularly hard on business-to-business durable goods (which covered everything IBM sold—the company did no business directly with consumers), IBM racked up a total of $83.5 million in profits. NCR made a mere $16.1 million. Back in 1914, when Watson was fired from NCR, he "vowed to build a larger and more successful company than Patterson." He succeeded.

Not only was he vindicated, he was very rich. The value of the stock he held increased by the minute from 1933 onward. And his salary . . . Because he received 5 percent of IBM's profits in addition to a base salary of $100,000 each year, Watson was among the highest-paid executives in the nation in the latter half of the 1930s. He made, for example, $419,938 in 1937, which was "top for ordinary businessmen (outside of the amusement industries and W. R. Hearst)."

This was a very long way from a bed of sponges. How had it come to pass?

A lot of things had to go right. All were necessary conditions for this outstanding performance. None was sufficient.

First, Watson chose the product to bet on. The Tabulating Machine Division, which was last in sales and profits in the early 1920s, was first by the early 1930s. The most important decision any company makes is what markets it elects to serve with what products. Not only business in the twentieth century, but government too was about information. The Tabulating Machine Company was founded in response to the needs of the census. It is no accident that its headquarters were in Washington, D.C., when that was still a backwater, certainly compared to New York City, Chicago, or a dozen other cities in the United States.

Second, there was luck. The Social Security Act was signed into law in 1935; and all of a sudden, the stroke of Franklin D. Roosevelt's pen created a huge new market for the processing of information. Watson was one of the few big-business executives who supported Roosevelt, the Democratic Party, and the New Deal. Watson did some favors for Roosevelt when foreign dignitaries visited New York City. Roosevelt, in turn, made his face to shine upon Watson.

Third, there was IBM's culture. There have been in American business history a number of companies whose culture was so firmly embedded in their texture that employees found themselves viewing not only their jobs but their lives through the prism of their place of work. This is most commonly found in small family-owned businesses, but occasionally one finds this cultural glue in big companies as well. A good example would be Wal-Mart in, say, 1985. But there has probably never been anything quite like IBM under the aegis of Thomas J. Watson Sr.

CHAPTER 10

The Watson Way

If you had told Tom Watson Sr. that a corporation was an organization of property, plants, and people the purpose of which was to generate a return on the investment the shareholders had made in it, you would have been dismissed with a look of stark incredulity. He probably would not have bothered even to get angry. In his eyes, you would not have been worth it. Watson was the longest of long-term thinkers.

"This business of ours has a future," he said in a speech to his top salesmen in 1925.

> It has a past of which we are all proud, but it has a future that will extend beyond your lifetime and mine. This business has a future for your sons and your grandsons because it is going on forever. Nothing in the world will ever stop it. *The IBM is not merely an organization of men; it is an institution that will go on forever.*

One is tempted to say: "World without end. Amen."

From the beginning, Watson wanted to build a business that would prove immortal. The touchstone of this immortality was customer service. IBM would serve its customers better than any competitor. It would help them make money and thus win their loyalty. Not only customers but employees would be served by the company as they served it.

Without using the phrase, Watson subscribed to the "leader-servant" model. In his mind (and doubtless only his mind), IBM was organized as a pyramid. He was at the tip, but the tip was not at the heights. It was at the bottom. The top executive—the leader—bore the weight. Every promotion, in a sense, moved a man in two directions. One direction was upward in terms of salary, title, and responsibility. The other was further down the inverted pyramid. He served more IBMers. He carried more weight.

What holds a company together? Watson would have answered by saying its shared sense of purpose. How is that shared sense of purpose developed? At IBM, the answer was through a comprehensive program of indoctrination that began with hiring and proceeded through training to the job itself. This was the "Watson Way." It is doubtful that any single aspect of the Watson Way was new. Some companies—Carnegie Steel, for example, or Standard Oil—had no use for this sort of thing. In the words of top Standard Oil executive Henry Huttleston Rogers, "We are not in business for our health but are out for the dollars." But there was plenty of bonding and team building which was about more than only "the dollars" at other companies.

We have already seen it at Patterson's National Cash, where Watson learned so much of what he put into practice at IBM. There was song singing at Coca-Cola, where the song sung at conventions was "Onward Christian Soldiers." You were doing God's work by selling the beverage that provided the pause that refreshed. By no means did Watson invent the "rah-rah" culture. There are, however, few if any other executives in the history of American business who went to the lengths Watson did to turn a company into a way of life.

When talking about IBM, which he did incessantly, Watson often used the metaphor of family. He expected IBMers to regard themselves as members of a close family; and although he would not have agreed, this was a family over which he presided as a father out of the Old Testament. He was sometimes loving, sometimes vindictive, sometimes generous, sometimes cruel, and always unpredictable. Watson had a lot more freedom to run the IBM family than he did his own. He could hire, and he could fire.

IBM had an unwritten but nonetheless strict code of conduct, many elements of which are admirable and all too uncommon in the business world today. Rectitude would reign at IBM. Not only was tampering with a competitor's products out of the question, but even talking them down was frowned upon. IBM was to tell the world what was great about its products, not what was wrong with competitors'. This was a far cry from Patterson's preaching and Watson's practice back at NCR. Why the change? It is possible that Watson learned his lesson through his encounter with the law. He never admitted that, because he never admitted guilt for his actions at NCR. At any rate, it may be said that there were three ways of doing things: the right way, the wrong way, and the Watson Way. At IBM things would be done the Watson Way until he stepped down from leadership of the firm in May 1956.

THINK. The word became synonymous with IBM and the Watson Way. Other companies may have boasted a "phrase that paid." Watson got it down to a word: THINK. The word was everywhere in the company. On the walls of offices. On desks. Always in plain view. Watson expected to see it during his visits to IBM facilities. He would be very unhappy if he did not.

The origins of the word—should it be called a "slogan," a "mantra," or some other term?—date back to Watson's career at the Cash. Bored by an uninspired presentation on a dismal December morning, he blurted out, "The trouble with everyone is that we don't think enough. We don't get paid for working with our feet—we get paid for working with our heads." The next day Watson put the word on a sign with huge letters on the stage of the auditorium at which presentations were being made. Patterson happened by, liked what he saw, and directed that THINK be plastered all over the company. THINK migrated to CTR with Watson and took its place on the top stairs of the "Steps of Learning" at IBM's staged playlets in its school building. (The other four stairs were labeled, in descending order, OBSERVE, DISCUSS, LISTEN, and READ.)

THINK is a puzzling battle cry for a business. What did the word really mean? How was it supposed to guide the THINKer? Watson refused to elaborate very much. "By THINK," he said, "I mean take everything into consideration. I refuse to make the sign more specific. If a man just sees THINK, he'll find out what I mean. We're not interested in a logic course."

But how was a man to "find out what I mean" merely by seeing THINK? Business is more about action than cognition. Whatever THINK may have meant, what it did not mean was "think for yourself." It may have meant "think like me." Watson was no "organization man" in a "grey flannel suit." He was the leader with the answers. What IBM employees were supposed to think about were the views and attitudes of President Thomas J. These were easy to learn. Watson was not one to keep his opinions a secret.

As IBM grew and as its products became ubiquitous in offices in the United States and around the world, THINK came in for its share of satire in cartoons in magazines and newspapers. One would see captions such as "THIMK," "PLAN AHEAd," or "SCHEME." Watson did not mind. Mockery "died down abruptly on the financial pages of the press."

We are still left with the puzzle of what THINK meant to Watson, what he thought it meant to others, and what it did in fact mean to others. Watson's own explanation is delphic. One can speculate that it was a word which united the company. Who, after all, could be opposed to thinking? My own guess is that having that word everywhere in the company was part of the territorial imperative that this man, in whom there was always a touch of the primitive, felt. THINK was everywhere because everyone who worked for Watson knew it better be. In his youth back in Painted Post, Watson carved his name on trees and buildings. He made his mark everywhere. He had graduated. Now others would make his mark for him.

Hallmarks of the Watson Way included frequent meetings and conventions, equally frequent awards and celebrations, speech making, song singing, a dress code, and the prohibition of alcohol at any company event. There was no company manual which codified all these practices, some of which made good sense, and others of which made good sense in moderation. All of these practices served to define a corporate culture in which the pull was very strong if you threw yourself into it and the expulsion swift indeed if you did not. Watson and the world he built were both stimulating and stifling, inspiring and intimidating. To succeed at IBM, you had to be good at your job. Very good. But your performance had to be achieved the Watson Way.

Proper business dress meant dark suits (usually blue) and white shirts. Precisely how this dress code originated is not clear. It is said that Watson encountered a group of men so attired and remarked, according to Rodgers, "My, but those men look nice; I am proud to have them represent the company." He wanted his salesmen to dress like their customers.

As for alcohol, Watson never forgot that as a young man first starting out on the road, he allowed himself to have a drink following a sale. He was happy enough to have another; and however many followed, it was too many. When he staggered out of the friendly tavern, his wagon had been robbed of his samples. Success had turned into disaster because of demon rum. At IBM, this was one incident that was not to be repeated. No alcohol at company functions. Ever. That was the rule. Men were known to be fired for violating it.

We should note that Watson was not a doctrinaire teetotaler. He opposed the Eighteenth Amendment (which established Prohibition) and sent a note congratulating President Roosevelt when it was repealed in 1933. He simply thought it was bad to mix booze with business.

Even at this far remove, Watson's views on dress and decorum are understandable. That is not to say that they were right for every one of the thousands of IBM employees around the world, but the idea that you dress as your customers do is not unreasonable, nor does it call for an invasion of what businesspeople today would consider private space.

When it comes to Watson's addiction to song singing, the Watson Way becomes a bit more difficult to understand. We immediately apply the usual caveats. Singing songs in corporations was far more common a century ago, when Watson was a young man, than it is today. Even today, singing is not unknown in corporations in the United States and abroad. At college reunions or football games, a tear will often come to the eye of an alumnus singing his school's alma mater.

At IBM, however, the songs, all of which Watson was "vitally interested" in, were remarkable for their lavish praise of none other than that "man of men." It was as if everyone in the company were required to chant at each day's beginning and end songs that celebrated T. J. Watson not merely as a fine human being but as a sort of superman—faster than a speeding bullet, more powerful than a locomotive, and able to leap tall buildings in a single bound. By praising so effusively the man to whom these songs were dedicated, the singers diminished themselves. Some sample lyrics:

T. J. Watson—you're a leader fine, the greatest in the land,
We sing your praises from our hearts, we're here to shake your hand,
You're IBM's bright guiding star, you're big and square and true.
No matter what the future brings, we all will follow you.

or

"He's a real father and a friend so true."
Say all we boys.
Ever he thinks of things to say and do,
To increase our joys.

Watson is a "father." The singers are "boys." There are dozens of such songs. You can find them on the Web at http://homepage.ntl-world.com/barryf/songbook.html (as of January 31, 2003). You can download and play the IBM anthem and most well known song, "Ever Onward." But be warned. You do so at your peril. Once you hear it, it takes days to get it out of your head.

There was a benevolent side to Watson that sometimes was publicly known—as with his immediate and unstinting assistance to all who were injured in the train wreck described in the first chapter—and sometimes less well known—such as the pensions he granted to some of the old-timers from Painted Post or the funds he would provide to IBM employees who through no fault of their own had fallen on hard times. Some of these gestures, perhaps many, will never be known because of their nature.

When it came to the Watson Way, however, deviations from the true path were not permitted. It is in this regard that one can see how, though a strong culture can grant membership in an organization that seems far larger than oneself and though it can give meaning to the mundane tasks which are a part of any business, it also exacts a price.

The awards ceremonies over which Watson presided were not occasions for merriment as a reward for work well done. They were carefully choreographed events at which everyone was expected to play his part. Deviation was punished with the kind of cruelty which was the other side of Watson's benevolence.

An awards banquet might stretch five hours into the night. It began with the ceremonial entrance of Watson and his wife accompanied by "a sustained outbreak of applause" as an orchestra played "Ever Onward." A benediction, perhaps delivered by the Reverend John V. Cooper, who had left a profitable IBM sales territory for the ministry, would precede dinner. Following dessert came two hours of three-minute speeches by men whose achievements were deemed worthy of recognition.

After all this, a presentation would be made to Tom or Jeannette

Watson, or to both; and it is at this point that we move into the realm of the genuinely odd. Watson would sometimes be overcome with emotion at these presentations. Tears would come to his eyes. This happened even though he would previously have approved the engraving on the plaque or similar token that he was given.

I find this sufficiently strange that it bears emphasis. Watson knew what was to be said. He had heard whatever was said innumerable times. Yet he acted as if the presentation were a genuine and spontaneous expression of affection on the part of all in attendance and all who wished they could have been. Why?

I believe Watson's stage management prior to the molasses of praise and then his emotion when it was ladled onto him are not contradictory. They are consistent with his belief in his own myth. By the late 1930s, when he was one of the nation's richest men, running a very successful company in the middle of the depression, he had already gone a lot further than he or anyone who had known him back in Painted Post had a right to expect. When he had come to CTR, the company was in bad shape, and he was facing jail time. Watson, it will be remembered, was then forty years of age, which was about the life expectancy of the average American man in the year Watson was born. If this remarkable ascent had already happened, what was not possible in the future? World without end. Amen. We should probably be no more surprised at Watson's conduct than we should be that tears are often shed at weddings but rarely at dress rehearsals.

The evening did not conclude with the presentation to Watson. Having received his plaque, Watson would deliver a speech. We are now well into the fifth hour of this marathon. Watson would talk of the old days and how tough they were at times. He would speak of a future which was without limit in the good things it had to offer if everyone worked hard enough and smart enough. Yet another benediction followed, and the evening staggered to a conclusion with all joining in to sing "Ever Onward."

What would happen if a couple of attendees forgot themselves and allowed single-minded attention momentarily to wander from the proceedings at the dais? On one such occasion, which William Rodgers described, Watson "stopped speaking, and coldly, at length, addressed himself" to the men at the back of the ballroom who were in private conversation. He spoke directly to them, as if there were no one else in the crowded hall:

> Now, you men there; I don't know what you're talking about, but you can't be listening. You are employees of this company, being paid to come here and listen and learn what your colleagues, and perhaps even I, have to teach you. I am not concerned whether you respect me or think I can tell you anything or not. I would be more concerned if you insult the speakers I am going to introduce to you. I can't understand how you could allow yourselves to do what you've been doing, even when I'm speaking. To men who follow me, it would be outrageous. I want you to understand that this company is going on forever. Unless you realize this, you do not belong in this company.
>
> As long as you gabble as you have done here, or if it occurs again, just remember the implications of what I've told you. You do not belong in a company that is a world institution that is going on forever.

This dressing-down, this public humiliation, was, sad to relate, very much part of the Watson Way. Why would Watson verbally brutalize his own people as he did at this banquet? These putative miscreants were not throwing rotten eggs at the speaker. They were merely carrying on a quiet, private conversation in an out-of-the-way corner of a large banquet hall. They were trying to pass the time because whoever was speaking was probably recounting war stories they had heard ten dozen times.

From Watson's point of view, however, anyone not sitting in rapt attention, cheering on cue, and singing along was breaking the frame. In Watson's mind, he had set up a communal experience in which everyone was sharing equally in his enthusiasm. Banquets such as this, which Watson would have been happy to have every night, fed his spirit as much as his stomach. Even though he was the boss and he did most of the talking, his experience was of putting himself out and giving something to the audience. He felt he deserved some reciprocity. The thought that some if not many people would have found such an event stultifying doubtless never entered his mind.

Watson was giving to the audience, but he was getting a lot in return. His idea of this banquet and indeed of IBM as a whole was that everyone was giving and getting as he was. That is why I take him literally when he expressed incredulity at that private conversation. The men chatting were not only depriving themselves of the joy that they should have been feeling, they were also stealing his pleasure. They were breaking a pact that he imagined he had with them.

They were betraying him.

So the Watson Way exacted a high price. However, there was also a big payoff, as we will see in the next chapter.

CHAPTER 11

The Big Payoff

Thomas J. Watson Sr. ran IBM for forty-two years and one week, from May 1, 1914, to May 8, 1956. This is among the longest careers running a single company in American business history. The duration of Watson's tenure in office is made more remarkable by the fact that he did not go to work at IBM until he was forty and that IBM stood at the center of one of the world's fastest-changing, most technology-intensive industries.

Few indeed are the CEOs currently serving in the world's large publicly held companies who will hold their positions for four decades. Indeed, turnover at the top has been increasing in recent years. Fewer still are those who, after such lengthy service, will be able to choose their son as their successor with no questions asked from stockholders or employees. An added fact rendering this transition of power noteworthy is that the Watson family owned but a small percentage of IBM shares. What accounts for Watson's longevity in power and for his freedom to make Tom Jr. his successor?

A look at some numbers will help us understand. What if you had purchased 100 shares of CTR when Watson took over in 1914? They would have cost you $2,750. If you had exercised the rights attached to those shares through 1925, you would have in that year owned 153 shares at a total cash cost to you of $6,364. When Watson stepped down in 1956, you would have held 3,990 shares of IBM with a market value of $2,164,000, and you would have enjoyed $209,000 in dividends. Your investment (calculated from 1925) would have increased at a compound annual rate of growth of 21 percent for a period of more than three decades ($2,164,000 and $209,000 are the equivalent of $13,700,000 and $1,323,000 respectively in 2000).

People invest for a return, and these are numbers which would make any investor feel really great about life. Stockholders must have hoped that Watson would live to be as old as Methuselah. As far as successors were concerned, investors were likely to trust his judgment.

For employees, IBM was the place to be. There was, of course, the problem of the obeisance to the revered leader. There was his unchecked power, his anger attacks, his unpredictability, his infantilization of those who worked for him, his surrounding himself with sycophants. . . . I could make this list longer.

All this aside, Watson was without question a great businessman; and he was both willing and able to help those who worked for him fulfill their destiny. Thomas and Marva Belden describe the trade-off this way:

> Working for such a man was not easy; and IBM executives had a high turnover rate. . . . But the men who stuck it out, survived his jealousy if they lived too well, his contempt if they lived too poorly, his desire for fellowship, his suspicion of cliques, his need for ability, and his mistrust of too much of it—if they stuck it out, they had one of the most rewarding careers in American business. The tabulating machine business was one of the most challenging of [its] times; the company was growing at an astounding rate, offering dazzling prizes to its men; and above all, almost everyone who came into contact with Watson surpassed his expectations of himself.

No question about it. If you were going to work for Watson, you had to know how to "manage up." But if you were able and willing to do so, you could do great things.

When Watson first hit the road in the 1890s as a young fellow peddling pianos, organs, and sewing machines around the countryside of western New York, the job was as unscientific as it had been since selling began. Watson came to believe, however, that selling could be systematized. There were good and bad ways to do it. There were rules which, if followed, would generate results. Persuasion was the first job of successful business executives. It could prove "the most heartbreaking and in the end the most rewarding part of their careers."

Selling was a skill that could be taught. Salesmen were made, not born. Any good salesman could sell any good product. Perhaps it was this line of thinking that brought Watson in his later years to the belief that, as he announced at the New York World's Fair, nothing less than "world peace" was a "sales problem." It was not such a great leap from the belief that any good man could sell a good product to the view that any good product (such as world peace) could be sold by a good man (such as himself).

Watson saw how John Patterson transformed what was once a sleazy aspect of business into a clear, fair, quantifiable assignment. He believed he could do better, and he was right.

In Endicott, New York, not far from Painted Post on the Pennsylvania border in what Watson called the "Valley of Opportunity," IBM built a gleaming complex on a seven-hundred-acre industrial estate. The IBM schoolhouse in Endicott graduated ten thousand people from its inception in 1927 to World War II. Among the graduates were machinists and technicians, but the salesmen were the elite.

The creation of an IBM salesman began literally before the train pulled into the station. Future salesmen were recruited on college campuses: the main selection criteria were, reportedly, "good looks and manners." (True, Watson believed that salesmen were made, not born. But some things are more difficult to change than others, and it was perhaps concluded that even a course at Endicott could not make an ugly man handsome.) Like George Eastman, Watson never attended a college (other than a vocational school); but also like Eastman, he came to see colleges and universities as abodes of the elect which could be of great benefit to his firm. He gave some of his most advanced machinery to Harvard and Columbia free of charge.

Describing the curriculum at Endicott in 1941, journalist Gerald Breckenridge noted that it included visits to the plant,

> where engineers explain the electric accounting machine, a complicated maze of some seventy-five miles of wire and 55,000 separate parts, surmounted by a sort of typewriter which prints the results of the machine's calculations. . . . [T]he instructors show the boys how to plug up a sort of telephone switchboard connecting the wires in many different combinations.

The "boys" were tested on their ability to plug up a board, even though they would rarely be called upon to do so, such work being consigned to maintenance men under normal circumstances.

As for the actual selling process, there were three basic steps: the approach, the demonstration, and the closing. By the time the salesman made the approach, his first call, he was expected to know more about the prospect's accounting than the prospect himself. This knowledge was acquired "by talking to friendly minor employees of the prospect, examining his available records, and sometimes by discussing him with business rivals who already are using IBM installations." Here we see an example of the advantages of market share. Far more firms used IBM than anything else, so far more such opportunities for information gathering were available.

After investigating the decision-making process in the firm to see how and by whom decisions to spend money on the type of equipment IBM marketed were made, the salesman sent his card to the appropriate party along with a letter from a satisfied customer in a similar business. Usually the salesman got the interview he requested, because IBM had the reputation for sending people "to serve," not "to sell." Once inside the organization, the salesman was expected to learn every aspect of the prospect's accounting system and to present persuasively any deviations from best practice to the boss.

The next step was to speak with the chief accountant or head bookkeeper. This required exquisite tact, and "many hours at Endicott [were] spent in rehearsing 'delicate situations.'" The delicacy resulted from the fact that the top accountant often feared that the size of his staff would be diminished if machines replaced human labor. This fear was justified. That was the point of installing them.

Watson had encountered a similar dilemma back at NCR in the 1890s. The people closest to the cash registers—bartenders or soda jerks who actually handled cash—hated the machines. They might not be able to prevent their bosses from purchasing them, but they were adept at sabotage once the cash registers were in place.

Greater than the chief accountant's fear that his staff might shrink was the terror, also quite reasonable, that IBM's machines placed even him in danger of being "downsized." The salesman was trained to explain that mastery of the new machinery could increase his importance in his company. Encomiums to IBM from former bookkeepers who had risen in the ranks, some all the way to CEO, were standard weapons in the selling arsenal. Once again, market share helped here. The more companies that used IBM, the more such examples there were.

This was not all. The salesman was authorized to offer the top accountant a course for customer administrators at Endicott, where he would be treated as an "honored guest, . . . meeting coming executives from other companies, bowling and playing golf at [IBM's own] country club, and generally accumulating facts and social background which will make the boss sit up and take notice when he gets home."

Once the chief accountant was on board, the salesman undertook "the survey." It was this aspect of the selling process which, according to Breckenridge, "takes the IBM salesman out of the knocker-on-doors class; they are efficiency engineers." The survey took up to a half a year to complete. Its goal was to show how IBM's equipment could provide more accurate information at greater speed and lower cost than was otherwise possible.

The simple fact was that this was true. All the puffery which so often has surrounded selling, all the exaggeration which stopped ever so short of the outright lie, was not necessary. It is not clear whether IBM's product was superior to Remington Rand's. Its market share would suggest it was. But it was without question superior to the person-intensive manual methods of information gathering and retrieval that preceded it.

Management information, the IBM salesman understood, extended well beyond accounting. Its importance reached into all the corners of the business. Take, for example, the sales force and the issue of inventory management. As Breckenridge put it,

> The great argument . . . is that the head of a sales organiza-
> tion . . . may know at any moment the state of his inventory
> —or may check up on his individual salesmen. Using hand
> methods, he might not know his business was on the down-
> grade till months after the inventory was overstocked or the
> sales force became lax.

Rosser Reeves, a famous advertising agent of the 1950s and 1960s, used to describe the toughest problem he faced as follows. A prospective client walks into your office and puts two identical silver dollars on your desk. The prospect says: "Mine is the one on the left. Tell me why it's better." This is precisely the problem the IBM salesman did *not* have. He was pushing no "me too" product. IBM had genuine advantages over the manual methods it was replacing.

With the survey completed, the IBM salesman went back to management. "Already the battle [was] more than half won" because the salesman had thoroughly examined the prospect's information systems. The salesman accompanied management to the local IBM branch office to demonstrate his wares. The demonstration thus took place on home turf.

If one can picture the scene, one can envision how by this time the salesman had the prospective customer in his grip. He knew (or should have known) as much about the customer's business as the customer himself. He probably knew a lot more about the latest systems in the customer's industry and in other industries as well. We are not speaking now of a "drummer" or a "Willy Loman" figure. We are speaking of an expert selling an expert system to a man who had the option of buying it or being left behind by the rest of the business world.

Here is where all the training at Endicott was brought to bear. The customer might buy—or, rather, lease—one or two machines of the type IBM was selling during the course of his career. The salesman, by contrast, leased them every day. He was trained in what by World War II was the finest school of its kind in the world. At that school, all these salesmen pooled their experiences. They prepared themselves for every contingency.

Closing—that moment of truth so famous in sales lore—was not a moment of which most IBM salesmen stood in dread. An often asked question was "Why do we have to sign a one-year lease?" This was the only time the prospect asked that question, but the salesman heard it every day. He was prepared. "We'll send our customer service men around to inspect them [i.e., IBM's products] regularly; we're selling service, not machines."

Watson was loved not only by his investors but by his employees. The narrative of the creation of a salesman helps us understand why. The trainees arriving at Endicott were presentable and reasonably talented. They were not, however, geniuses, and they did not have to be. If we remember Patterson's trilogy—tear them down, build them up, fire them—we see that Watson chopped off the first and third steps and concentrated mightily on the second.

Watson's IBM, year after year, including right through the teeth of the Great Depression, took ordinary people and showed them how to capitalize on the extraordinary opportunity of working for a company that wanted them to succeed, would support them in their effort, would pay them if they performed well, and would celebrate their performance. Watson transformed the "seller as supplicant" to the "seller as consultant." By the time that IBM salesman's card appeared on your desk, you knew you needed his products as much as he needed your business. If self-esteem was the central psychological dilemma facing the salesman, IBM had devised a system that solved it.

Let us imagine that you are graduating from college in the spring of 1933, and IBM's recruiter on your campus has offered you a job. The fact that you have gotten a job offer at all has brightened your day considerably. When you enrolled in college in September 1929, the nation was enjoying close to full employment, and optimistic economic forecasts were on everybody's lips. By your graduation, economic activity had almost ground to a halt; and unemployment was at epidemic proportions. IBM had not escaped unscathed. Sales and earnings, which peaked at $19 million and $7 million respectively in 1930, were down to $17 million and $6 million in 1933. At IBM, however, employment had increased in 1933 to about 8,200, almost 30 percent higher than 1932. Part of this increase was probably due to an acquisition (of Electromatics Typewriters, Inc., of Rochester, New York); but part can be explained by Watson's willingness to build, as did Andrew Carnegie, during times when others could not.

Tom Jr. recalled the following exchange between his father and James Rand, the head of Remington Rand, IBM's chief rival in tabulating machines. "This was in the very depths of the Depression, 1933," recalled Junior, and

Rand must have thought Dad was losing his grip.

He said to my father, "Well, Tom, are you still hiring salesmen?"

Dad said, "Yes, I am."

"That's amazing!" Rand said, shaking his head. "Businesses are laying people off all over, and you're hiring salesmen. That's something."

"Jim, I'm getting along in years," [replied Watson]. "You know I'm almost sixty now. A lot of things happen to men at that critical age. Some of them get to drinking too much. Some of them are interested in girls. But my weakness is hiring salesmen, and I'm just going to keep doing that."

Jim Rand, like almost everybody, was not hiring in 1933. Tom Watson was. If he had hired you, you might be feeling a little nervous, but basically that first trip to Endicott was a very happy one.

Let us assume that you complete the training successfully and join the field sales force. Let us further assume that you stay with the company through 1941 and then join the army. Sales and profits in 1941 were $60 million and $10 million respectively. Employment exceeded fourteen thousand. If you have done your job well, the odds are that you have risen considerably at the company and in the world.

You would have probably made the 100% Club on a couple of occasions. You would not have been involved in furtive chatter in the back of the hall but would have sung "Ever Onward" lustily on cue. As your performance improved over the years, so did your pay. Like Patterson back at the Cash, Watson was not stingy. You were making more money than you dreamed possible in 1933 when you joined the firm. You may, although not yet thirty years old, have been making more money than your father ever did.

There were about 75 percent more people working for IBM in 1941 than when you joined. Six thousand additional employees had to be schooled in the Watson Way. That meant plenty of promotion opportunities for you, and along with your increased pay may have come management responsibility.

When the war came and your country called, you enlisted. You then discovered that IBM decided to pay you 25 percent of your salary—in addition, that is, to what you were receiving from the armed forces—for the duration of your service, with no quid pro quo about whether you would return to the firm. As one executive later observed, "I could have survived without it, I suppose, but the thought behind it impressed me. This was Mr. Watson's policy. I thought it was pretty unusual and pretty good."

Outsiders could make jokes about the Watson Way if it gave them pleasure. Investors, employees, and, perhaps most important, customers were agreed that it was "pretty unusual and pretty good."

The IBM training program was an important part of what made the company as unusually good as it was. The prospective salesman had to have a reasonable amount of talent, but only a reasonable amount. What you did with that talent was more important than merely having it. In other words, you had to make an effort. You had to try. If you did, you had a uniquely powerful system behind you that would help you succeed. The greatest business machine that IBM ever built was the IBM corporation itself.

Think of what our young college graduate had going for him when he joined IBM in 1933. First and foremost, he had Thomas J. Watson Sr. Despite his idiosyncrasies he was, it cannot be said often enough, a great businessman. He always had his eye on the future, perhaps the single most important trait for long-term success in business and an aspect of the Watson Way which simply cannot be overemphasized. Watson was thinking of the future from the beginning and he was thinking of the future when the average executive would be worried about making it through the day.

Now place yourself in the mid-1920s. Watson's investment of a decade previously was paying off for you in the present, in the here and now. You were able to lease a better product than the competition. This had not been true when Watson had taken over.

No theme in Watson's career was more assertive than this orientation toward the future. He broke ground for a large new research facility in July 1932, the lowest point in IBM's fortunes since its founding. During World War II, he understood that everything was going to change as a result of the great convulsions in the world. He was already in his seventies, but he knew that preparing for a changing future was the key to the success of a business.

When you work for a future-oriented company, that approach to business changes everything in the present. You are already ahead of the game this minute because this very minute you are benefiting from all the thousands of person-hours that your predecessors have invested in where you are now. That investment cannot be replicated. No start-up can benefit from the legacy that has muscle-built your organization. (It is essential, of course, that a legacy "muscle-build" a company rather than permitting it to become muscle-bound—which is what happened to IBM after the Watsons left.) An orientation toward the future is also a competitive advantage against incumbent rivals for the same reason.

Watson often used the metaphor of family for IBM, but the metaphor of team is equally appropriate. Watson was not only your boss, he was your coach. He wanted you to succeed and gladly put the resources of IBM at your disposal to help you. You had an exclusive sales territory and a quota, just as Patterson had established for salesmen at the Cash. Patterson told his salesmen, "We want you to make money and don't want you to fail." This was Watson's attitude precisely. Nothing would have made him happier than to welcome every single man in his sales force to the annual 100% Club Award Convention.

One final aspect of selling at IBM deserves our attention because it played an important role in the success of the efforts of the sales force. That is leasing.

All the products of the Electric Accounting Machine Division (which is what the old Tabulating Machine Company was renamed), with the single exception of the punched cards that ran through those machines, were leased, not purchased. The practice of leasing was instituted by happenstance before the turn of the century. The government wanted Hollerith's tabulators for the census but for nothing else. It cost a lot less to rent than to buy, so that was what the government did.

What happened by accident turned into a valuable marketing tool. A lower price for a government rental was also a lower price for rental to a private company. That lower price was a form of penetration pricing which increased the size of the market and led to economies of scale and the learning curve just as it did with the Model T Ford.

All marketers know that understanding the customer is a critical part of their job. This is true whether they sell a product with a service contract or they lease the product. Yet the desire to understand the customer might increase if the product the customer was using was still owned by the marketer's company. You are going to work a little harder to help the customer maintain the machine properly.

Flowing directly from leasing was IBM's insistence that only punched cards which it manufactured and marketed be used in its machines. The cards were fabulously profitable. In the late 1930s, the company was selling 4 billion of them a year. In 1938, the sale of cards was equal to one-fifth the rental income from electric accounting machines. In the 1930s, the card business was said to account for a third of IBM's profits.

The federal government was not only one of IBM's biggest customers, it was also the nation's principal antitrust enforcement institution. Tying the sale of IBM cards to the sale (as opposed to the lease) of an IBM machine would have constituted a violation of the Clayton Antitrust Act. If, on the other hand, IBM owned the machines being used by others, it could plausibly argue that it had a right to see that they were well maintained. Poorly made punched cards might damage IBM property. IBM in fact made this argument and charged higher rentals for any customer using other cards. The government brought suit, and in 1936 the Supreme Court decided that IBM's right to protect the machinery it owned did not give it the right to demand that renters use its cards. The Court did, however, grant the company the right to establish the specifications for the cards used in its machines.

The net result of all this maneuvering seems not to have been very detrimental to the company. Although the federal government was a major customer of IBM not only for the census but, after 1935, for the management of the Social Security system, and although it did make some of its own cards, IBM's dominance in this market was never seriously threatened. The manufacture of these cards was more difficult than one might suspect. If exacting specifications were not met, incorrect calculations might result or machines might jam altogether. These hurdles helped keep competition from entering this burgeoning market. The relationship with the customers which leasing facilitated helped smooth IBM's earnings.

By the beginning of the war, new product ideas, resulting in part from heavy research expenditures, began to bubble up and held out the promise of profit for the future. A remarkable variety of new applications were being developed for government, indeed for any institution—public or private, profit or nonprofit—for which sorting and tabulating mattered. The need to count, to file, to calculate, was everywhere, not just in large organizations but in small ones, not just in the United States but all over the world.

IBM's machinery cut costs so dramatically that if one competitor in an industry invested in it, others could not afford to be without it. The work it eliminated was boring, repetitive, and mind-numbing, yet very important. The cost of an accounting or an actuarial mistake is potentially very high indeed. Organizations get little credit for accuracy in those areas. It is expected. But they catch a lot of grief for mistakes. Of IBM's products, *Fortune* magazine observed in 1940 that their "historic function, like that of the most memorable inventions, is to allow men to invest less manpower in drudgery, to save labor." Or, as an IBM slogan decades later put it, "Machines should work. People should think."

When Alfred P. Sloan Jr., the man who made General Motors a great company, was starting out in business at the turn of the century, John Wesley Hyatt, the founder of the ball bearing firm Sloan's father bought for him, said that he "should find a market for antifriction bearings anywhere there was a turning wheel." At the dawn of the automobile age, that meant everywhere. The same kind of limitless expanse of possibility spread out before Watson in 1940. What was needed was to develop the market, to engross it, to defend it. Of all the initiatives Watson pursued to achieve that goal, none was more important than building what became the greatest sales force in the business world.

CHAPTER 12

High Time to Grow Up

While Tom Watson Sr. was creating himself as the man of men and building IBM into a very important company in a very important industry (i.e., information processing), his eldest son was working—or, better put, playing—his way through Brown. He continued to live as the super rich live. His youthful passion for flying had stayed with him. In his first term, he soloed following a mere five and a half hours of instruction. As a flier and later as a yachtsman, Watson was fearless to the point, at times, of imprudence.

Watson became quite well known around campus for partying with pretty girls and for drinking. Absent from his lengthy autobiography is any remark about a memorable course or professor. He apparently was not much of a reader. He mentions no book that made an impression. No one could have accused him of possessing intellectual curiosity. One infers from his autobiography that he did not earn his degree but rather was allowed to receive it by a dean who thought he was a nice fellow. Perhaps the dean also had Brown's financial future in mind. If so, he was not disappointed.

During and after his college years, Junior continued to wrestle with the issues of dependence, competitiveness, and self-esteem around which his life had always been centered. His mother may have been his most important companion in his early years, but his father had begun to take that place as Junior approached his twenties. He "exercise[d] a profound influence on me, something like the way religion affects some people. . . . Maybe he was four thousand miles away, but I'd feel him like the keel of a boat, pulling me back upright again." It is fortunate that Junior could feel Dad's presence when he was far away, because Dad was on the road a lot.

The Watson family had moved back to New York City from Short Hills; and when his parents were in town during the season, "their lives became a regular round-robin: Monday night at the opera with a few other couples, maybe two dinner parties and a charity banquet during the week, and then, every few weeks, an IBM dinner." Dad came to know everybody who was anybody.

Senior was also afoot abroad. In June 1937, he attended the first morning reception given by the newly crowned King George VI at Buckingham Palace. He became the head of the International Chamber of Commerce and endowed the organization with a handy slogan: "World Peace through World Trade." This organization had its convention in Berlin; and shortly after meeting King George VI, Watson had a private meeting with Adolf Hitler. The German government also gave Watson a medal, the Merit Cross of the German Eagle.

"Dad's optimism," according to his son, "blinded him to what was going on in Germany. . . . Hitler fooled him completely." (Jeannette Watson seemed to be a bit less taken in.) A good deal has recently been made of Watson's and IBM's dealings with the Nazis. Unlike Henry Ford, Watson was not an anti-Semite. He was, in fact, one of the founders of the National Conference of Christians and Jews. In my view, IBM's dealings with Nazi Germany were like other businesses'. The list of corporations which cost themselves sales and profits in order to put distance between themselves and the horrors of Hitler from the time he became chancellor in 1933 to the outbreak of World War II is short indeed, if there are any names on it at all.

When it comes to Watson and world affairs, we have a case (there have been many in American business history) of shoemaker stick to your last. Despite his world travels and his innumerable awards, Watson was quite ignorant about affairs of state. No one with the slightest knowledge of world history could have declared, as Watson did at the 1939 world's fair, that world peace was fundamentally a sales problem. Tribal hatreds dating back centuries cannot be whisked away by a clever sales pitch. His happy phrase "World Peace through World Trade" also gives one pause. The history of the world shows that the battle for trade has caused armed conflict as often as it has resulted in its avoidance. Watson's attraction to Mussolini (also shared by other American businessmen) resulted from a simpleminded equation of his posturing with dynamic leadership.

With regard to world affairs, both Watsons were afflicted with "IBM Think." To anticipate our story, President Jimmy Carter appointed Tom Jr. to be ambassador to the Soviet Union in 1979, probably the most important ambassadorship in the world during the cold war. Late that year, the Soviet Union invaded Afghanistan; and Watson was called back to Washington for consultation with the president. In his autobiography, published in 1990 when he was seventy-six years old, Watson Jr. reports that in conversations about the most effective response available to the United States, he objected to certain proposed sanctions. American companies were being prohibited from shipping spare parts for manufactured goods they had sold to the Soviets even though the goods were still warrantied. "I told the president," reported Watson, "this didn't make sense: if you want to declare war or have a boycott [of the 1980 Moscow Olympics], fine, but breaking a commitment to a customer is always wrong."

Again, one is at a loss for words. A war is one thing; but "breaking a commitment to a customer"—unthinkable. Watson Jr. was a rich and celebrated man of the world when he wrote these words (or had them written for him). Watson Sr. had not attended college.

Junior had; but by his own testimony, he did not receive a college education. His education took place at IBM, and the power of its corporate culture is well illustrated by Watson's remark about the invasion of Afghanistan. Without understanding the total immersion that was IBM in the Watson years, his observations stagger the imagination. If one read it in a novel, one would interpret it as a cheap satire of small-time American business.

Like so many American businessmen, both Watsons blithely believed that selling and business as a whole were for professionals but that any amateur could master public affairs. In the late 1930s, Watson was at the peak of his powers in building IBM. In the great big world outside the world he created, he was a babe in the woods. As for Tom Jr., he was a babe in all regards between his graduation from Brown in the spring of 1937 to mid-1940, when he enlisted in the armed forces.

During these years, the central theme of Junior's life to this time was intensified. Upon graduation from college, he was offered a job to take a world tour as a secretary for a journalist friend of Senior's whose assignment was to sell pavilion space for the upcoming New York World's Fair in 1939. "I was delighted by this offer and flattered" to be chosen for a job requiring, as he was told, "hard travel and hard work." The result was a world tour, during which Junior observed that "I love to buy things." He was so popular with the shopkeepers of Beijing that when he left, some of them sent small gifts to him at the train station.

A couple of weeks after Junior had gotten this job, he discovered that it was "make work," arranged and paid for by Dad. "This was a terrible blow to my pride. I would never have taken the job if I had known that my father created it. I was angry with myself for not seeing through it sooner." He had reason for his self-reproach. He had never asked how or why he came to be offered a job which amounted to an all-expense-paid global junket on the basis of his miserable college record or anything he had achieved. The man who "employed" him was a friend of his father's. How shrewd do you

have to be to piece this together? At any rate, after this rude awakening he decided to spend the trip "fooling around on Dad's money."
He made a discovery which has often been made before and since.
Your father's money can make you very popular with merchants, but
it cannot buy self-respect.

Discovering that the world was a not wholly uninteresting place
and that spending your father's money was not a bad way to spend
your time, Junior wrote Dad from Japan that he wanted to go to
India. Dad, in his Old Testament incarnation, ordered Junior back
to America. The decision had been made that he was to start IBM
sales school in the fall.

We do not know how this decision was arrived at, which is a
great pity. Sitting on a curb in Short Hills, New Jersey, when he was
twelve years old, Junior had expressed a tearful horror at the
prospect of running IBM. His mother, it will be recalled, responded
that no one had asked him to. That evening his mother talked to
Senior about this event; and Senior, apparently with kindness, said
that he had not followed the path his own father had had in mind
for him and that Junior should do whatever he wanted.

Junior knew, however, that his father wanted him to go to work
at IBM. From Junior's first encounter with the company (a plant
tour with Dad in 1919) if not from before that, IBM suffused his
life. It was everywhere . . . at the dinner table or far from home. It
made his father and therefore his family rich. It was beside him in
the hot Chrysler he owned at the Hun School. It was with him on
his five youthful trips to Europe. It accompanied the family to its
Camden, Maine, summer home. It spent four years with him at
Brown. It was with him in Moscow, in Beijing, in Tokyo. It accompanied him on dates.

When little Tommy visited that Dayton CTR scales plant in 1919,
the company was next to nothing, its very survival in doubt. By the fall
of 1937, it was still small compared to the largest companies in the
nation; but it was growing fast. It had a franchise it was developing and
a formula for success with a track record hard to dispute.

As IBM grew, Senior's ambition for the company and for himself grew even faster. That is a fundamental fact. "We must never feel satisfied," he told his men. Time and again he exhorted the troops by saying, "The IBM is not merely an organization of men; it is an institution that will go on forever." His son was amazed at Dad's "brass," and it is true that Senior's sense of entitlement sometimes takes one's breath away. But that sense arose because he saw himself as far more than a businessman making money for stockholders. IBM was a cause. It was his sacred mission and his family's to advance that cause for the good of everyone. He was a man with a mission that expanded with each success.

Following early English defeats during the Seven Years War, William Pitt the Elder took the reins of government in 1756 after declaring, "I am sure I can save this country, and nobody else can." He may have been right. Winston Churchill said that when he took office in perhaps Britain's darkest hour on June 10, 1940, "I felt as if I were walking with destiny and that all of my past life had been but a preparation for this hour and this trial." What could be denied men who conceived of themselves in such situations? Would anyone be astonished at their brass? Thomas J. Watson Sr. felt himself to be "walking with destiny" as well. Surely—surely—his eldest son would eagerly be of service in this great endeavor. That was his destiny, the fulfillment of which he began in the autumn of 1937. That was when Junior joined IBM.

The decision of a son or, these days, a daughter to join the family firm can be a complicated one. There is often a good deal of discussion among the family as a whole. No one in the family is disinterested. Other siblings may also want to join. Birth order has nothing to do with business talent. Perhaps the younger son is more capable of managing the firm than someone who, as chance had it, was born before him. What if more than two children (and perhaps a cousin or two) want to work for the family firm? Do they all get a chance? If the family grows faster than the firm, there is not going to be room for everyone. Who will have a chance? What if the child who is clearly the most able is not the one the father likes the most?

Selection and promotion in the ideal world are based on merit. If this principle is ignored, the firm will eventually fail. In the ideal (perhaps one should say "idealized") family, each child is entitled to expect to be equally loved by the parents. This is true at least in American culture. How well does that expectation compare with the selection of one child as the father's successor?

In not all instances does the family grow faster than the firm. Sometimes the opposite takes place. Then you have to hire professional managers to keep the firm moving forward. How are they going to feel about their own careers if they know that no matter how vital their contribution, they are going to wind up working for the founder's son? Are you going to be able to hire the most talented people if they know in advance that their own ambition will be blocked prior to the top spot, if they know that they will never be CEO, if they feel that managing up means not only managing your boss but managing the father of the man who will be your boss? Are you going to feel like a family retainer or a professional manager? What do you do if father and son disagree on a business issue? How honest can you be in expressing your views? Why put up with all this aggravation? Life and business are sufficiently difficult without it. If you are talented, you will find plenty of other places to work.

Let us consider the Watsons specifically. The job of any son is to differentiate himself from his father and establish himself as an independent individual with desires and goals which have their own integrity and toward which he has the right to strive. When your father is as rich, powerful, overbearing, and globally omnipresent as Tom Watson Sr., the job is tough enough. How do you escape this man of men whose unique Watson Way had put him on a first-name basis with what seemed like everyone on earth? He was the man who had already chained you to him not only with bonds of affection but with the "golden handcuffs" of cold, hard cash. It was his money which had enabled you to live an irresponsible life, devoid of accomplishment, in high style. By the fall of 1937, Junior, at the age of twenty-three, had seen the world. He had partied with the elite. But look at what he had not done. Never feeling the stern whip of necessity, financial or otherwise, he had never had to try at anything. He had never had to concentrate. He had never done a real day's work. He had no accomplishment to which he could point.

Remember our brief narrative about the college graduate recruited in 1933 for a career at IBM. Imagine an IBM recruiter on college campuses in 1937. It is quite out of the question that he would have tapped anyone of Watson Jr.'s description for a job. Junior knew it. He himself wondered why his father wanted him at the company.

Your father, who in every way seemed your superior and whose shadow you had to get out from under, was about to become your employer. Does this commend itself to common sense as a good idea? Would it not have been better to tell Junior to go out on his own, find himself a job, and then return to IBM? (This is, by the way, a common career path these days.) If there was any discussion along these lines, no record of it has survived. In October 1937, Junior found himself on a train for Endicott and the IBM sales school.

What was a giant step for everyone else in young Tom's class was nothing at all for him. All the shops in Beijing were stocked out because of his recent visit. None of his classmates could say the same. He was now completely in his father's world. Endicott, New York, was dominated by George F. Johnson's Endicott-Johnson Shoe Company and by IBM. Young Tom had imagined that he would be treated like any other enthusiastic, aspiring young student, but things did not turn out quite that way. He would walk to a class and perfect strangers would spot him and remark that this was "Mr. Watson's son." Needless to say, one of his final stops was at a local saloon, where the barkeeper reminded him about his father's views on liquor. So things did not get off to a great start for a young fellow who was in desperate need of something of which to feel proud.

Things went from bad to worse. The man who ran IBM's Endicott school had been the headmaster of the Hun School when Junior was a student there. So he knew, and Junior knew he knew, that Junior was not a world-beater intellectually. Watson's performance lived down to expectations.

Here is an example. Young Tom was as enchanted as his father by IBM's electromechanical accounting machines. Their potential for saving labor, saving money, and increasing accuracy captivated him. However, sales trainees had to do more than admire these machines. They had to understand thoroughly how they worked. This involved, among other things, "programming" an accounting machine by "plugging-up a board" (i.e., by connecting certain wires to certain outlets). This was not uncomplicated, but it was sufficiently manageable that every member of the class could master the task except one. Guess who that one was. "After only two weeks," Watson later recalled, "I had to be assigned a tutor" to teach him how the task was performed. "I spent many nights with that guy in the deserted schoolhouse, trying to hook up those little wires."

Petrified of Watson Sr., everyone at the Endicott school was in a tizzy about how to handle his son. Having shown the world from Short Hills Country Day through Brown that he was either of only modest intelligence academically or unable effectively to marshal whatever native talent he did possess, he had proceeded at Endicott in only two weeks to show that when it came to hands-on work with machines, he was not any good at that either. No one else needed a tutor. Odds are no one else would have been provided one. Anyone else so inept would have washed out of the program.

Nothing daunted by this display of limited acumen, the school's director thought it would please Senior if Junior was elected president of the class. He arranged to have this happen, even though everyone knew that Junior was the only trainee who had required tutoring. "Unfortunately for me," said Junior, "I lacked the force of character to say, 'I won't have this.'"

During "two miserable winters" in 1937 and 1938 Junior studied at Endicott. The weather was "perpetually cold and damp," and it was accompanied by precious little to brighten the spirit. For the rest of these two years, Junior assisted experienced salesmen in the field. During this time and after graduation—at which Junior and Dad were inducted into the IBM Father-Son Club, which Dad had founded in the 1920s because of Dad's "firm belief" that, as Junior put it, "nepotism was good for business"— Junior made but little progress in finding himself.

After graduation, Junior "was handed one of the company's prime [sales] territories." Here was the result:

> On the first business day of 1940, I became the company's top salesman when U.S. Steel Products, an account that had been thrown into my territory to make me look good, came across with a huge order. With one day's "work" I filled my quota for the entire year.

The company celebrated Junior's triumph with headlines in its house organ about how he was the first man to make the 100% Club.

"I felt demeaned," said Junior. "Everybody knew that I was the old man's son" and that was the reason for his "success." Within the company, he was also patronized. People threw business his way "to curry favor with Dad." Within the family, things were no better. He lived with his parents in their luxurious town house at 4 East Seventy-fifth Street. This is located a few feet east of Fifth Avenue and is to this day as prestigious as any address in New York City and in the nation. When Junior did score a sales success on his own, Dad "never praised me for my work." Instead, he seemed to pass up no opportunity to attack any self-worth Junior might have been trying to develop:

> We'd be having a casual conversation at home and he'd say, "What do you think of the new sales plan?" or "What do you think of Mr. Jones?" No matter how I responded, he'd listen for a minute and then come back with something ter-

ribly cutting like "You know, you really are not experienced enough to have an opinion of Mr. Jones."

Why would his father torment Watson Jr. this way? We can only guess. One senses the same pleasure that John Patterson experienced by controlling how people felt about themselves. Perhaps Watson felt some resentment at the ease of his son's life. Remember the contrast between how these two men grew up. Father pushed pianos through the wilderness, while sonny was flying airplanes around Paris.

This incident may be another version of a common and age-old conflict. On the one hand, the father wants the son to grow up, to succeed, to have some influence in this world, and to help him in his work. On the other hand, not so fast. This father in particular is far from ready to step down or be edged aside. He wants to hold on to his worldly power and his superior position with regard to his son. So he toys with him in this unworthy fashion.

It takes, we should note, two to toy. Even in this brief episode, we feel that this was a conflict in which both these men wanted to engage. The son chose to live with Daddy and Mommy in their sumptuous town house. He was in his early twenties, he was earning good money thanks to easy arrangements at IBM, and there was no housing shortage in New York City for people of his means during the depression. Even if he had stayed at home, Junior could have handled the exchange recounted above more deftly. When Dad led off with his question about Mr. Jones, surely Junior knew what was coming next. He could, for example, have asked: "Dad, do you think I have the experience to render an opinion on Mr. Jones?" Instead, he led with his chin, which is where his father's metaphorical fist landed.

To assuage his "sickening self-doubt," Junior, unsurprisingly, began to goof off. He charmed the secretaries into covering for him when he would take afternoons off so he could go flying. In the evenings, there were high-class nightclubs where he could drink and dance. This was Manhattan, not Endicott.

One of the most intriguing aspects of the life of Thomas J. Watson Jr. is that he did not degenerate into a playboy. There are many stories of rich sons of famous fathers being overwhelmed by their inability to establish themselves as individuals and solving the problem with alcohol. What came between Junior and that fate was the right woman and World War II.

The woman and the war were intertwined. Junior met Olive Cowley on a blind date early in 1939. She was an "astonishingly lovely girl," a professional model "earning her own way and making her own decisions" who "came from a good family but didn't have much money." Junior's sisters told his parents that he was dating a model. They were not thrilled.

> But I wanted somebody who would give me sweetness, love and support—and somebody who wasn't going to feel upstaged if I actually managed to accomplish something in my life. When I started bringing Olive to family occasions, Mother kept her distance at first but Father unbent and welcomed her. He could be very pragmatic about matters of the heart.

For all the repeated blows to his self-esteem, young Tom never completely lost faith that he would "actually manage to accomplish something." It was that ambition and innate ego strength that saved him from a life of dissipation and early cirrhosis. He wanted a help-meet in the achievement of his goals. If his father had been able to describe the woman he wanted to marry when he was ready to get married, the description would probably not have been all that different from his son's. Jeannette became not only the mother of his children, but the mother of IBM and thus of his ambition.

The reaction of Tom Jr.'s parents to Olive was not surprising. Jeannette must have realized the moment she laid eyes on Olive that she was going to lose her little boy. As for Tom Sr., he was sixty-five or sixty-six years old when he met Olive. This was the year of the world's fair; and as we noted when discussing it, he had no interest in becoming old. Few things can rejuvenate such a man as much as the deferential affection of a lithe, lovely young woman. His son had chosen well.

As far as the war was concerned, Junior could not get into it fast enough. He wanted, of course, to be a flier. By 1940, he had been flying for seven years and had over a thousand hours of experience as a pilot. How many twenty-six-year-old Americans could have said that in 1940? One hundred? Two hundred? Five hundred? Surely not many more. Yet President Roosevelt announced that the United States was going to build fifty thousand planes a year. Who was going to fly them?

There was a threat to Watson's hopes. A problem with his eye muscles meant he would fail the test for the Army Air Corps. As with most bureaucracies, his actual experience was trumped by a "one size fits all" rule. But Watson discovered that he could get around this stupidity by joining the National Guard, which had different rules for pilot qualifications. Soon Watson was a second lieutenant in the 102nd Observation Squadron.

In the fall of 1940, the president mobilized the National Guard; and Watson moved with his squadron for training at Fort McClellan in Anniston, Alabama. "I was free from IBM," said Junior; and he had achieved that freedom in a fashion to which his father took no exception.

Young Tom was falling in love with Olive; and as war approached, things started to happen fast. He began to realize that it was "high time to grow up." Visiting New York in November 1941, he took her dancing at the Starlight Room of the Waldorf and, armed with a diamond ring from famed Fifth Avenue jeweler Harry Winston, popped the question. They were engaged. Almost immediately after Pearl Harbor, they were married at Fort McClellan, where the chapel was "banging out weddings every fifteen minutes." Not the romantic and elaborate ceremony that would otherwise have taken place. But this was wartime.

I asked my father to be best man, which wasn't the conventional thing to do. . . . At that point, Dad was very much on my mind. Underneath all my resentment and underneath all the he-bores-me, he-embarrasses-me-with-his-folderol-about-IBM-Day attitude—underneath all that was a great love and respect. I couldn't have resented him as much as I did unless it was based on some much deeper emotion.

CHAPTER 13

Watson at War

Thomas J. Watson Jr. served in the armed forces of the United States of America from the fall of 1940 to the end of 1945. When he joined the service, he was twenty-six years old, unmarried, depressed, drinking too much, and suffering from low self-esteem. When he was mustered out, he was a few days short of thirty-two years old. He was married and had fathered two children, the first dying in infancy and the second, named Tom, without health problems. He entered the service an unproven individual working—if that is the right word—for his father and living in his parents' home. He left the service full of self-confidence bordering on bravado. What accounted for this transformation?

Watson had found in World War II a wholly legitimate way to escape his family's house and his father's company. He saw his father on a number of occasions each year during the war, but they did not discuss business. Watson did not pilot planes on combat missions, but he did some unquestionably dangerous flying over Africa and all across Asia from Baghdad to Kuybyshev to Moscow to Tashkent to Urumchi to Ch'eng-tu to Chita to bleak Yakutsk on the banks of the Lena River in the desolate wastes of Siberia. He flew the famed route "over the Hump" of the Himalayas between China and India.

He had his share of close calls with regard to life and, literally, limb. (He almost lost a leg trying to fix some landing gear in flight.)

Both father and son were well aware that the son might lose his life in this war. As usual, Senior expressed his feelings nonverbally. He hired an artist from the Kansas City Art Institute to paint his son's portrait.

Watson was dying (at the risk of an inappropriate metaphor) to get into the thick of the war. It is worth asking why. He had spent some time in both Germany and Japan. "The callousness of the Germans" under Hitler toward the Jews, which he witnessed in 1937, "made me very uneasy." Seeing Japanese troops departing for war against China "really opened my eyes to Japan's militarism." On the other hand, he did not seem to have a powerful animus toward either country or its leadership. He did not appear to have any Jewish friends, at least not any close friends. When one thinks of how and where he lived from his birth to the war, it is possible that, unlike his mother, he did not meet a Jew during that period. As far as Japan was concerned, though he witnessed firsthand some of the devastation caused by the Sino-Japanese War of the late 1930s, he did not express particular indignation about it.

Watson did not return from either Germany or Japan with the feeling that the United States had to play a more vigorous role in world affairs to fight fascism. He was apolitical, accepting his father's support of Roosevelt because it was good for business, and seemingly satisfied with his father's belief in "World Peace through World Trade." If Watson was particularly patriotic as a young man, there is no record of it. He was far more concerned with his chaotic and miserable inner state than with the great big world outside. He was in training in Anniston, Alabama, on December 7; and when he and his classmates heard the radio broadcast reporting the attack on Pearl Harbor, they were stunned and silent until someone finally said, "This means major changes in all our lives." He recalls no one declaiming against the attack and those who carried it out.

Why, then, was Watson so anxious not only to serve but to play an active role in the war? I graduated from college in 1969, and only a handful of middle-class boys my age were trying to figure out how they could wangle their way into a combat assignment in Vietnam. Some wanted to go, but they were a small minority. More were like President Bill Clinton, who avoided serving in the military, or Vice President Dan Quayle, who managed to secure a position in the National Guard which guaranteed his remaining in the United States. Or think of the contrast between the forty-first and forty-third presidents of the United States. George Herbert Walker Bush could not wait to join the fray. He enlisted on his eighteenth birthday, June 12, 1942; and when he received his wings the following year, he was the youngest pilot in the navy. In 1944, his plane was shot down and his two crew members were killed. He finished the war a decorated hero.

It is said that one reason then-president Bush could not believe he would lose to Clinton in 1992 was that he did not think it possible that Americans would elect a draft dodger. But times had changed. No better index of this change was the election of George W. Bush, who had pulled strings to get into the Texas Air National Guard, in which his service was undistinguished if not unforgivable, over Al Gore, who had served in Vietnam.

For Watson Jr., serving in World War II—the good war, the just war—was natural. It probably never entered his mind not to serve. It was as natural for him to do as it was for him to have children. Like John F. Kennedy, George H. W. Bush, and thousands of other sons of rich parents, this was the thing to do.

World War II brought a number of other unplanned and unanticipated benefits to Watson Jr. By mere chance, he had taken an interest in flying when he was ten years old in 1924. It was an interest that he cultivated through the years, and it was an interest which his father did not share. So he had something which was all his own. Because of the war, experienced pilots suddenly became a very hot commodity. At last, Terrible Tommy Watson was in the right place at the right time.

The war also enforced a separation between the son and the father and his company. Thus, that interlude away from the family firm which so many young people spend prior to their return to it now took place for Junior. In his case, he was to spend half a decade not at McKinsey or Goldman Sachs, but in the armed forces.

This is not to say that he was completely free from the long arm of IBM. When it appeared that he might get stuck in an insufficiently exciting assignment, he had no trouble asking Dad to use influence to arrange a transfer. Watson's commander, Major Victor E. Nelson, did not like him; and the feeling was mutual. "Whenever I'd make a suggestion to improve our procedures, Nelson would make fun of me. He thought I was a spoiled rich boy; I thought he was about the poorest leader I'd ever met." Watson was stuck flying submarine patrols in boring old planes off the West Coast of the United States. He wanted a chance to replace one of the crews that were being shot down by the Japanese in New Guinea, on the other side of the Pacific.

Dad, who always started at the top, sent for his faithful retainer, Fred W. Nichol. (Nichol had a song dedicated to him at IBM. To the tune of "Tramp, Tramp, Tramp, the Boys Are Marching": "V.P. Nichol is a leader / Working for the I.B.M. / Years ago he started low / Up the ladder he did go / What an inspiration he is to our men!") Nichol was dispatched to meet none other than George C. Marshall, the chief of staff of the United States Army. He later authored the Marshall Plan for the reconstruction of Europe (the European Recovery Program) and was awarded the Nobel Peace Prize in 1953. In 1947, President Truman called him the "greatest living American" and appointed him secretary of state. President Roosevelt declined to give Marshall command of the D Day invasion of Europe in 1944, because, he said, he could not sleep with Marshall out of the country.

So V.P. Nichol was not going to see the sergeant at the local recruiting office.

And V.P. Nichol got results. Watson was transferred to the

Command and General Staff School at Fort Leavenworth, Kansas. Olive moved with him and played a key role in helping him study and helping him act his age. Watson, now twenty-eight years old, still enjoyed practical jokes. My guess is that he needed to do something to relieve his anxiety. Leavenworth was a high-powered place, and Watson had to gather all his concentration to avoid washing out. "This girl," he said of Olive, "I'd married for her beauty and kindness saw how desperately I needed to avoid another failure."

Practical jokes are odious—funny, perhaps, to the people who concoct them—not so funny to their victims. Watson seemed to have no sense of the hostility behind so many practical jokes nor of their potential for giving offense. Olive did. After one such caper, she told him in no uncertain terms to cut it out. "When you graduate," she told him, "your father's going to be here, and you don't want to be the class clown." Watson immediately understood that "when it came to Dad's expectations, she had a better idea than I did about what constituted the straight path. From that night on, she helped keep me on it."

In June 1942, Watson caught the eye of Major General Follett Bradley (not to be confused with Four Star General Omar N. Bradley, who was one of the top commanders of the American forces which invaded Europe in World War II). Follett Bradley, the son of a general, was a career soldier born in 1890. In 1942, he was the inspector general of the U.S. Army Air Corps. Impressed by Watson's use of rudimentary flight simulators to train pilots, he asked him to serve as his aide. Watson had misgivings. He was far more interested in becoming a line officer than in serving on someone's staff. There were also the best interests of Olive to consider because "the wives of generals' aides always end up working as aides to the generals' wives." But Watson decided that this was too good an opportunity to pass up. Bradley was clearly going places, and Watson wanted to go with him. Watson came to believe this was among the most important decisions of his career. "I have worked for two great managers in my life. My father was one and the other was Follett Bradley."

At first Watson thought that his assignment as Bradley's pilot would turn him into merely an "aerial chauffeur." To his credit, however, Watson figured out a way to make himself important to his boss. He lived by the same rule his father had adopted back at the Cash. He glued himself to the man giving the orders. Wherever Bradley went, Watson went, writing reports and recommendations about what Bradley saw. Bradley found these unsolicited reports astute and helpful.

Unlike Dad or any other authority figure whom Watson had encountered, Bradley was unstinting in his appreciation of Watson's work. The more Bradley encouraged him (or, in today's parlance, gave him "positive feedback"), the harder and more effectively Watson worked. Bradley turned into a true mentor. Watson said these early months with Bradley were vital to his maturation "because he showed me that I had an orderly mind and an unusual ability to focus on what was important and put it across to others." We have here a rare moment of modesty. It was Watson who demonstrated these qualities to Bradley. He would never have had the opportunity to do so had he not taken the bit between his teeth by following Bradley around without being asked and writing those reports.

Watson put his ego on the line by showing this initiative. He could have merely done his job and waited at the airfield for Bradley to return from whatever he was inspecting, chewing the fat with the locals, and playing periodical practical jokes. All his life up to this point, he had been patronized by his father's minions, who were desperate to curry favor with the Old Man. Bradley did not patronize him. Nor did he put him down. Gone were the days of "What do you think of Mr. Jones? . . . You do not have the experience to assess Mr. Jones." Now the questions were real, not mind games. The answers were so good and so much appreciated that within months Bradley had Watson promoted to captain and took him on an important mission to Moscow. Whether in Moscow, in Britain, or in the Pentagon, Watson's work with Bradley was essential to his conquest of the demons within him. He was coming to believe in himself.

In 1943, Bradley had a heart attack and was forced to retire from the service. Watson's next boss was a grave disappointment, a "terrible fuddy duddy" named Junius Jones who "got to depend on me, but . . . to dislike me too." The result was that Watson got stuck as a lieutenant colonel because Jones would neither promote him nor let him go. Jones did not matter, however. In his mind, Watson's evaluation of him was more important than his view of Watson. There were plenty of adventures between Bradley's retirement and the end of the war, but the key internal work was complete.

There were important developments on the home front as well. Watson had the opportunity to spend some precious time with Olive. They had their share of arguments. These included arguments about money. Dad did not tell Junior the size of his trust fund, and Junior did not know his assets. Far more important was the fact that their relationship grew stronger.

Olive and Tom's first son, his father's first grandchild, was born in December 1942. Two months later, tragedy. The baby died in his sleep, apparently suffocating in his crib. Watson was able to join Olive immediately after hearing the news. They were bereft. But they were together and able to comfort one another. In March 1944, Olive gave birth to another son, Thomas J. Watson III.

As 1944 progressed, Watson began to give some thought to what he would do at war's end. Dad and his company had not intruded on his career. Yet there was a sense of their omnipresence. IBM was a global company which grew very fast during the war and played a not insignificant role in the military effort. Watson stopped by IBM offices from Washington to Rome to get some military business done when he needed to. Dad was sufficiently well known that more than once at an introduction Watson was asked: "Are you the son of? . . ." It did not bother him. He may not have been a war hero, but he had some remarkable achievements both personally and professionally of which he could genuinely be proud.

August 1944 found Watson in New York. He had at length determined what he wanted to do with his life—"owning and running a small aviation company would be just about right"—and he wanted to let his father know. He had expected a fight, but Dad proved "very shrewd." He seconded Fred Nichol ("V.P. Nichol is a leader. . . .") to scout opportunities. Junior decided that becoming a pilot for United Air Lines was the best move after the service.

The following spring Watson Jr. was back in Washington. Follett Bradley, now a vice president of the Sperry Gyroscope Company, a defense contractor, was visiting on business. Watson picked him up after a day at the Pentagon to take him to his apartment for dinner with Olive and him. The two men had not kept in close touch after Bradley's health had forced him to leave the Air Corps.

On the drive from the Pentagon, Bradley asked Watson about his plans after the war, and Watson told him about becoming a civilian pilot. "Really?" responded Bradley. "I always thought you'd go back and run the IBM company."

Watson was shocked. "I concentrated on driving for a moment or two, and then I asked the question I suppose had been buried in my mind from the time I got up from the curb as a boy and went home crying." Did Bradley really think he had it in him to do it? "Of course," was Bradley's response.

Watson told Olive about Bradley's views and asked for hers. "Tom, you're a fun-loving boy and it's hard to believe you really want to do it. But when you put your mind to something I've never seen you fail." Within a day, Watson called "my old man" and said, "I may be coming back to IBM if you will have me." With "warmth and happiness in his voice," his father replied, "I'd be delighted, son."

Thomas J. Watson Jr. rejoined the International Business Machines Corporation on the first business day of 1946.

CHAPTER 14

Father, Son, and Charley Kirk

Young Tom had not kept close track of IBM during the war, but he did know the firm was growing fast. When Watson joined the service in 1940, sales were $45 million and profits were $9 million. The firm had 12,656 employees. When he again became a civilian at the end of 1945, sales had grown to $130 million. Profits stood at $11 million, and there were 18,257 employees. Profits could have been higher, but Dad "was very sensitive about making money from war production. . . . So he had a rule that IBM could make no more than one percent profit on munitions." If return on sales in 1945 had equaled the performance in 1940, IBM would have made over $27 million. Sales in these five years tripled, with a compound annual growth rate of 25 percent.

Although there would inevitably be problems reconverting IBM to a peacetime basis, there was every reason to believe that the market for data processing was going to grow after the war. With IBM's commanding market share and superb sales force, this was a company that was going places.

Young Tom believed that he would be going places within the

company, and his calculation that he would quickly hold an important position was one of the reasons he returned to the firm. As he
put it, "[T]he prospective competition for the top jobs wasn't great."
The old guard had retired and, despite IBM's rapid growth, had not
been replaced. There was, however, one new man at headquarters
who did give Junior pause. His name was Charles Albert Kirk.

Watson Sr. had brought in Charley Kirk to replace Fred Nichol
as number two man at the company. Nichol had started out as
Senior's secretary. When it came to sycophancy, Nichol, it would
seem, was second to none. "[H]e was the kind of fellow to whom
Dad could say, 'why don't we build a tower to the moon?' and receive
the reply, 'Yes, sir, I'll order the steel this afternoon.'" Charley Kirk
was a very different kind of cat.

Charles A. Kirk is now quite forgotten, but he was once a very
important IBM executive. Nobody ever gave anything to Charley
Kirk. "He came from a rough background," observed Junior, "somewhat like Dad's." Born in Bucyrus, Ohio, on April 12, 1904, Kirk
became a salesman for IBM in Cleveland in 1927. At the time, it
was a pretty small company. But of course it had the man of men
with his sense of mission at its helm. Kirk bought into the Watson
Way wholeheartedly. IBM was going to the top. Charley Kirk
wanted to get to the top of IBM.

Watson Sr. hated formal organization structure and the charts
that go with it, yet Kirk's ascent illustrates that there was a ladder to
the top. From a salesman in Cleveland, he moved up to managing
the Columbus office in 1931, and thence to Pittsburgh, where he
was a special representative for two years; next he went to Chicago
to manage the service bureau from 1935 to 1937, and finally he rose
to running a major regional office, St. Louis, from 1937 to 1940.
This is how Charley Kirk climbed the ladder of success.

It was in 1940 that this "prodigious worker, [who was] aggressive and yet very popular with the men" whom he supervised, and
who had "made a reputation as a supersalesman," was plucked from
the ranks by Senior and brought to Endicott to manage the expan-

sion of IBM's principal manufacturing facility for World War II. Kirk's success combined with the nervous breakdown of poor Fred Nichol prompted Senior to bring Kirk to corporate headquarters in New York City and promote him to executive vice president with a seat on the board of directors.

Young Tom first met Kirk in September 1945, and the fact that this man had his father's confidence and had become the second most important man at IBM came as "a terrible shock." "I never had anything in mind but to aim for the top job," said Tom Jr., and the way seemed clear. With Kirk on the scene, the way seemed suddenly cloudy indeed. "[A]ll I could think of was that if Dad ever got sick or died, Kirk was the logical successor."

When young Tom walked into his father's office to report to work at IBM, Dad told him he was going to be working for Charley Kirk. "I'm sure I shook Kirk's hand and said how glad I was, but I was so surprised that I don't remember doing it." Dad and Kirk had "formed a tight bond."

Kirk must have been feeling pretty good about himself on that January day in 1946 when Senior told him that Junior would be working for him. He had mastered both marketing and manufacturing; he had won the boss's full confidence; and the boss, though in good health, would turn seventy-one the following month. Senior may have wanted to work forever, but nobody lives forever, and Junior recognized that Kirk was Senior's "logical successor" in 1946. Kirk was only forty-one. He knew the business intimately. What Kirk did not know was that when Junior returned to the company, he was destined to play the barley to Junior's millstone.

Kirk threw himself into the role of Junior's instructor with the same vigor and ability with which he approached all his responsibilities. "I have to hand it to Kirk . . . ," Junior reported. "[H]e treated me fairly and went flat out to teach me the business." However, "friendship between Kirk and me didn't seem to be in the cards." Quite an understatement.

"Part of my dislike of Kirk stemmed from competitiveness and jealousy of his relationship with my father. . . . I couldn't understand why they were so close." Some of Junior's dislike was a matter of class prejudice. Kirk "wasn't very polished," while Junior had grown up lavished with every advantage one can imagine. Young Tom thought of his father as having "raise[d] himself up culturally," but Kirk is reported to have "had no impulse" to do likewise. Kirk "was not prepossessing looking—he was of average height, balding, pear shaped, with rumpled clothing and wire-rim glasses, and he was never without a cigarette." Kirk could also take a drink; and young Tom, who had done his share of boozing in college, was temporarily on the wagon.

Kirk was not without charm. He enjoyed playing the piano, and people at the IBM country club at Endicott liked to sing the songs he played. In fact, everyone liked him. Everyone except the one man whose dislike he could not afford.

In April 1947, about a year and a quarter after Junior had started working with Kirk, he told his father that he would have to make a choice. Junior simply could not stand Kirk any longer; nor would he abide the thought that should Kirk succeed his father and work until he was sixty-five, Junior would be fifty-six "before I get a chance at command."

Dad was seventy-three when he got the ultimatum that he would have to choose between his son and Kirk. Kirk had proven an invaluable lieutenant, but Senior had his heart set on both his sons remaining at IBM. He asked Junior to take Kirk on a tour of IBM facilities in Europe. In the meantime, Senior said, he would find a way out of the dilemma.

The following month, Kirk, young Tom, and their wives sailed for Europe. For Kirk, the trip was a dreadful humiliation. Junior was thoroughly familiar with Europe from boyhood. He spoke some French and knew how to handle himself. The first stop was in Zurich, where their host (who spoke English as well as French) gave a speech to IBM executives in French, so Junior could understand it but Kirk, who spoke no French, could not. The host spoke at length about Junior's prospects and the importance of family in business. He concluded by saying that

Junior would be IBM's next leader and that that would be terrific. "There was an absolute ovation." Kirk thought (not without reason) that the applause was for him. He "looked around and just beamed." Whether Kirk found out what was actually said no one will ever know.

If people are not getting along, traveling together is generally not a good idea. This trip went from bad to worse. "Finally," according to young Tom, "Kirk and I almost came to blows" over a matter so inconsequential the details are not worth recounting. Watson, who was to become famous for his anger attacks, was "damn mad," but Kirk "hung right in there." "The vehemence of that silly argument," recalled Junior, "is hard to describe." His wife, Olive, put a stop to it, and "I'm glad it stopped when it did."

The night of the argument, Charles Albert Kirk died of a heart attack.

Kirk was forty-three. He left his wife, Mildred Pearl Steenrod Kirk; two daughters, Shirley Ann and Sally Kay; his mother, Mrs. Albert Kirk of Cleveland; and two brothers, George H. Kirk, also of Cleveland, and H. E. Kirk of Snyder, New York. He also left what could have been a marvelous career.

Young Tom's final comments are so revealing they are worth quoting at some length:

> Dad felt Kirk's death as a personal loss—Kirk was his number-two man and one of IBM's own. Probably he also felt relief that a huge problem had been solved, and I'm sure he felt guilty at that relief. I could see those emotions in the funeral he gave Kirk in Endicott. It was really something. Dad trotted out college presidents, there were a number of eulogies, and the service took over two and a half hours. For the first and last time at a great occasion Dad didn't give a speech. I later heard that during the procession out of the church, Dad was so emotional that he forced his way between two pallbearers and grabbed an edge of the coffin himself.

There was reason for Senior to feel guilty. He had placed his biological son and his surrogate son in a competition that any straight-thinking person should have seen could lead only to disaster. The astonishing thing about the above description is that there is no mention of any guilt that Junior may have felt. Kirk's death solved a very big problem not only for his father but for him as well. His hostile, infantile behavior during the European trip could not have helped Kirk's health. Kirk may have been "of average height, balding, [and] pear shaped," but Junior was not. He was tall, slender, and quite physically imposing. He had just had a shouting match with a man he could have pummeled but who, because Junior was the boss's son, could not have hit him back. Charley Kirk had to keep it all inside. He could only do so for a few hours.

CHAPTER 15

God Damn You, Old Man!

How many people reading these words have passed their seventy-third birthday? How many of those are still running their own company? How many of those have a son whom they plan to be the next CEO? There cannot be too many.

Why ask? Because this was the situation of Tom Watson Sr. after Charley Kirk's death in 1947. No matter how much we try to understand who he was, how he felt, and why he did what he did, our effort will perforce be at least partially thwarted. Very few people have ever been (or will ever be) in Watson's situation. It is difficult to walk a mile in his shoes.

Let us consider for a moment Watson's health. He was a good-looking man, and he was always well turned out. Even at the age of eighty-two, when he at last retired six weeks before his death, though he looked aged his looks were age appropriate. Yet through much of his life, Watson experienced considerable physical pain.

Watson never had surgery. How many people who reach the age of eighty-two can make such a statement? When thinking of Watson we must always keep in mind his origins. He was born in 1874 in Steuben County, New York. As late as 1910, the authoritative Flexner Report on American medicine concluded that an ill person ran a pretty big risk from an encounter with a doctor. This makes his aversion to surgery, even minor surgery, more understandable than it might otherwise be. When Tom and Olive Watson's first son died in infancy in 1942, he was very solicitous but also upset that Olive did not sit with the deceased baby's body for twenty-four hours, which, apparently, was the old-fashioned way.

Watson talked about the future constantly; but, like everyone else, he was a product of his past. Rather than surgery, he elected to live half his life with two painful hernias. More serious were his gastrointestinal difficulties. He had a severe case of gastric reflux (a problem which today can be well managed with a medication called Omeprazole). "For as long as I could remember," his son wrote, "Dad had trouble with his stomach. . . . As a boy I used to listen to him let out tremendous belches behind closed doors and then go about his business." He also had bleeding ulcers. His son reports that these "never [caused] any pain."

His son's assertion that Watson's ulcers were not painful is difficult to credit. Perhaps that is what Dad said. Perhaps he suffered in silence. But ulcers can hurt like hell. Combine them with a gassy gut (which caused the eructation, that is, the belching) and the pain of hernias; and you have the recipe for a good deal of physical discomfort. Consider also that Watson was a man with a stammer who did a great deal of public speaking. Delivering an address before hundreds of employees when you are acutely nauseous and your body is telling you that one more minute on the platform and you are going to vomit or to pass out demands an iron will. This kind of battle with one's body, even if it results in victory, takes a fearful toll. It is a battle in a war that never ends. The next speech in the next town demands the same unforgiving self-control.

Such self-control exacts a price. Watson's anger attacks—hereditary, legendary, self-defeating—were probably caused in part by the fact that he spent a lot of his life in physical pain, which was sometimes chronic and sometimes acute but never wholly absent. To play his chosen role as the man of men required that he conceal his pain. This he did until he could do so no longer. The dam would burst and he would become enraged. His outbursts were often followed by reconciliations which were as shrewd and maudlin as the outbursts were uncontrolled.

Often, Watson would insist on details with regard to, for example, large meetings which would drive his staff crazy. Dozens of people would be working on arrangements for meetings which hundreds would attend; and all of a sudden, the day before the big event, Watson would show up and pull the pin on a grenade. His demands would seem arbitrary and inconsiderate to the point of being cruel.

We must remember, however, that we cannot put ourselves inside his skin. Earlier, we observed that before he was in a position to "dish it out," Watson had to learn how to "take it." In a sense, I believe, he saw himself as taking it his whole life. The proof is in his X rays at the end of his life. "Your father's stomach looks like the battlefield of the Marne," Watson's doctor told his son in the 1950s. The cause of his death in 1956 was the accumulation of scar tissue in his digestive system. The scars caused strictures which blocked digestion. Watson died of starvation.

An order from Watson which might seem frivolous or self-indulgent to others would present itself as perfectly reasonable to him. Those charged with carrying out his commands might think: "How can he throw a monkey wrench into arrangements which have been made for weeks and designed especially to please him?" He would think—or rather, feel—such perceptions did not rise to the conscious level: "I have given up so much for this company and the people in it. Can't I have just one little thing go as I want it?"

As he grew older, Watson's physical condition, not surprisingly, deteriorated. As it did, his rigidity and his insistence on having his own way intensified. The longer he lived and the bigger IBM became, the more the company had to be governed by rules and procedures. The strictures within him seemed to exist outside of him as well. He fought back, indulging himself in the surprising gesture that broke these rules, such as publicly and on the spur of the moment promoting a young person who had caught his eye over a couple of layers of management, shocking everyone else present.

In 1947, Watson was the living embodiment of the violation of a rule he himself had made. He was still running the company at the age of seventy-three. Mandatory retirement was sixty-five. In the world outside IBM, Watson's importance steadily increased. For decades, he had been thinking about the future. Suddenly the future was now.

Here is just one example. From the 1920s Watson cultivated a relationship with Columbia University's formidable and imperious president, Nicholas Murray Butler. Butler served as Columbia's president from 1901 to 1945. He was awarded the Nobel Peace Prize in 1931. In 1933, Butler asked Watson to join Columbia's board of trustees. Watson donated not only money but machinery to the university, where new experiments were developed using it. Butler was forced by age (he was eighty-three) and infirmity (blindness) to give up his position in 1945. By this time Watson had become the most powerful member of the board of trustees. He played a key role in offering Butler's former position to none other than Dwight David Eisenhower, thus providing him with the perfect perch on which to alight in 1948, when he retired from the army. Watson, in numerous realms, had become a power broker of the highest order.

IBM was itself growing fast in size and strategic importance as the computer revolution moved forward. Sales and profits in 1947 were $139 million and $24 million respectively. By 1956, the year the baton was passed from father to son, sales had increased to $892 million and profits to $87 million. Over seventy thousand people worked for IBM that year. It was now genuinely big.

Within IBM, Watson Sr.'s word was law. This was the man, aging and fallible, with whom young Tom was going to work—not necessarily an enviable assignment.

Charley Kirk was now out of the way. Young Tom was about to discover that Kirk had been not only a "barrier" between him and his father. He had been a "buffer." Ever since coming to CTR in 1914,

Dad had enjoyed the services of a right-hand man. How would Tom Jr. take to that role?

IBM's world headquarters in 1947 were located at 590 Madison Avenue in Manhattan. Dad's office was on the seventeenth floor. Junior's was on the sixteenth. Whenever Dad wanted to see his son, he would press a buzzer. Young Tom would climb up the flight of stairs that separated them without knowing why he was being summoned. It could be anything from "Son, I want you to meet Mr. Alfred P. Sloan" to "Tom, I'm really dissatisfied with the way things are going west of the Mississippi." Young Tom now found himself both working for and competing against a man by whom he never felt sufficiently loved.

These two men began to fight. They fought about all aspects of the business. These fights were brutal and awful. The company was changing. The customers were changing. The technology which IBM's products had to embody was changing faster than ever. The threat to the business posed by the antitrust laws was increasing. Everything, in short, was changing; and every change was an opportunity for a fight. "Fight" is the word. Not "disagreement." These two men fought; and, as Watson Jr. put it, their fights were "savage, primal, and unstoppable."

Here is an episode from 1952. A senior executive in the Typewriter Division died that summer. This man's widow was convinced that her husband had suffered heart failure because he had lifted too many heavy typewriters. She was angry and resentful toward IBM for, as she believed, mistreating her husband; and she was talking about suing the company. Tom Jr. thought it important to defuse the situation by attending the funeral, so he decided to fly from New York to San Francisco accompanied by the head of the Typewriter Division. In 1952, the flight from New York to San Francisco took nine hours aboard a four-engine propeller-driven Lockheed Constellation.

Just as young Tom was about to leave for the airport, his father summoned him, and the two "had a terrible argument." At last, Junior told Dad that he had a plane to catch. He walked out.

The man of men had not achieved that lofty position by letting people walk out in the middle of a discussion with him. He hustled down to his limousine and got to La Guardia before his son. He was driven out onto the tarmac and walked toward where his son was about to ascend the stairs to the airplane. Junior described his gait as painful. "I thought," he said, "he was playing his age for all it was worth." When he reached his son, he grasped his arm with his "gnarled" hand. Young Tom "completely lost my temper" and said, "God damn you, old man! Can't you ever leave me alone?"

With that, Tom "ripped my arm away with great vigor, turned my back, and went up into the plane." He said he did not actually strike his father, but he had committed a gesture of some physical violence by ripping his arm away. And the words he spoke were not very nice. What followed was the predictable remorse and reconciliation. But this kind of dreadful encounter is terribly depleting. Even Junior was astonished "that two people could torture each other to the degree that Dad and I did and not call it quits."

What caused these fights? Here are young Tom's views: "Dad was constantly trying to change me, and I was trying to change him. I wanted an easy old-shoe pal and he couldn't be that. He'd have liked me to be more pliant and defy him less. Each of us wanted something the other couldn't give."

There is probably some truth here. There are other reasons as well. We can never know the whole story because this account has been based on Junior's recollections. Senior never set down his version of events. Even if he'd had the opportunity, one doubts he would have been willing or able to do so. All we can do is guess, but these fights were so central to the relationship between the Watsons that speculation is needed. This is, moreover, not only the story of interpersonal conflict. I am convinced the relationship between these two men exercised a significant influence on the development of IBM.

One reason for these fights is not speculation but is a simple fact. Tom Jr. decided to come to work at IBM after World War II.

His expectation was that, fairly quickly, he would become the chief executive officer. Tom had worked for his father in the late 1930s, between his "graduation" from Brown and his enlistment in the National Guard; but there is no record of such fights at that time. That is because young Tom had very little ambition at the company then. He blew it off, flying planes and nightclubbing. After the war, he wanted to run the place. He had, he said in one of those bursts of ignorance about himself which accompany the genuine insight in his autobiography, "no illusions about becoming Dad's equal." His ambition was, in reality, boundless.

Dad did not greet the idea of being superseded by his son with unmixed joy. As the 1940s turned into the 1950s, Junior was taking on more responsibility for the operation of the firm. He was becoming more prominent and receiving more publicity. It was he, not Dad, who adorned the cover of *Time* magazine's March 28, 1955, issue. He was identified as "IBM's Thomas J. Watson, Jr." Dad never made the cover of *Time*. Was he proud of his son? "He didn't talk to me about the article at all," reported Junior. "He never said, 'Great Going!' and I never brought it up." Even at the age of eighty-one, Dad was in no hurry to be known merely as the father of a new man of men.

Father and son were capable of being kind to one another when things were going badly. Dad was quite understanding and accepting of his son's academic problems. Young Tom was equally decent when his father's age got the better of him. It was one another's strengths each man could not abide.

The second reason why they fought was chemistry. These two men tried to love each other. They knew they were supposed to. But the love that was supposed to be there was forced; it was not quite natural. Young Tom once said that he was the "apple" of his father's eye, but he was not and he knew it. His father's favorite was his second child and oldest daughter, Jane. Junior was well aware of this preference. He competed with her for Dad's love. Jane was sharp and knew how to play the game. Not just as a child but all her life, she referred to her father not as "Dad" or "Father" but as "My Joy." Senior must have enjoyed talking to Jane.

Yet another reason for the fighting, perhaps the most important, was that these two men *wanted* to fight. Senior's father had been known for his anger. Temper tantrums ran in the family. Both father and son had their share of the "savage, primal, and unstoppable" locked within them. They let it out because it felt good to let it out. The fights let them give vent to what was primitive within them.

This is speculation, but it is not without evidence. "Our worst fights," according to young Tom, "were not at the office, where outsiders might hear but at my parents' townhouse" on East Seventy-fifth Street, in the heart of Manhattan's "silk stocking" district. (These fights were ideally to be strictly a family affair.) Junior, unseparated as he was, would periodically spend the night there if he had a late event to attend in Manhattan and did not want to commute back to his home in Greenwich. "Looking back now," he wrote in 1990, "I'm not sure why I kept doing that." It was at night at that town house that the two men would have their most "hellacious" fights.

Why did Watson "[keep] doing that"? Perhaps because when he did, he got precisely what he wanted: a "hellacious" fight.

A psychiatrist will tell you that boys around the age of five tend to become competitive with their father and want to take his place. However, they also want their father's love, approval, and support. Ideally, a five-year-old boy will come to understand as he matures that he can achieve rewards through competition with other boys his own age. It was this step that young Tom did not seem quite able completely to take.

To be sure, Tom was competitive with people his own age. He was competitive with everybody. But he remained competitive with his father much longer than was healthy. Not long after his father died in 1956, when at last there was only one Thomas J. Watson at IBM, Watson said of his father, "I still needed him emotionally." At the time, Watson was forty-two years old. Needing his father did not make Watson a problematic figure. It was rather what he needed his father for. There would be plenty of fighting and shouting during Watson's tenure as IBM's CEO from 1956 to 1971. But the feeling of being intensely alive and in touch with something within himself that Watson achieved when he and his father were exchanging primal screams ended when his father died. Something within Watson would never be quite worked through. After 1956, he competed with the memory of his father.

During the nine years that the Watsons were running the company at the same time—it could hardly be said that they were working as a team—the impact of both their strengths and shortcomings was evident in the firm. I have mentioned before that this heritage survives to the present day, and we will encounter a number of instances in which their relationship has been woven into IBM's fabric. Some of these examples are based on inference. In other cases, we will be on stronger evidentiary ground.

Imagine for a moment that you are Wiz Miller in the summer of 1952. Who, you ask, is he? Wiz Miller was the head of IBM's Typewriter Division who accompanied Watson on the flight from New York to San Francisco to attend the funeral of the executive in his division who had suddenly died. What was going through his mind when young Tom lost control of himself and said, "God damn you, old man!"?

A not unreasonable question would have been, "What am I to make of the leadership of this company?" The son was, obviously, the future; but who really was the son, and what kind of future did that airport encounter portend? Miller doubtless sat next to Watson during the nine hours between New York and San Francisco. Here is Watson's description of the trip: "That was the longest nine hours I ever spent in my life. I was beside myself, terrified that he'd be dead before I could talk to him again, and that I was going to have to live the rest of my life with the knowledge that I'd cursed my father." Those nine hours were probably long for Wiz Miller also.

Miller was not the only top executive to have the opportunity to deal with such issues. After an "awful battle" in young Tom's own office, he "ran out of the room" and found himself in the office of a distant cousin of his father's named Charlie Love. He "threw myself on the divan, and sobbed, while Charlie sat there at his desk."

Of one thing we can be certain, father and son could not contain these fights in Dad's town house. They spilled over into the company.

The son, as we just mentioned, was the future. However, the father had gotten into the habit of not dying. As long as he was around, executives found themselves having to make choices between the two. The older group of executives, who had been with IBM for years, clustered around Dad. Junior found these people to be mere courtiers and looked forward to their disappearance. Dad was not necessarily enthusiastic about Junior's favorites either.

What did this split between the two Watsons mean to the people at IBM? Here is an example. Young Tom became executive vice president in 1949. He began a drumbeat of complaints to his father that IBM's engineering research was second-rate. The Engineering Department was "a source of the old man's pride," and attacks on it would not go unanswered. At one point during such a "discussion," Dad summoned the vice president of engineering. This gentleman appeared almost immediately, and he could not have been very happy with what he confronted. Dad and Junior were having another one of their arguments, and somehow he had gotten involved. "My son tells me," said Senior, "that we don't have any kind of research organization. Is that true?"

Imagine yourself in the vice president's position. The odds are that you were promoted to your present position by Watson Sr. It is also likely that prior to Senior's asking the question at that moment, you knew that he and his son had been arguing about you and your department. How would you answer this question?

"The vice president thought a while. He wasn't being glib. He said . . ." (Permit me once again to ask you, the reader, to pause, to ask you not to be "glib," and to think of how you would answer that question at that moment in that circumstance.) Here is what the vice president said, "We have the finest research organization in the world."

Here was young Tom's observation on that statement:

> That was the end of him as far as I was concerned. All businessmen get asked a question like that sometime in their lives. They either answer it with courage and get fired or promoted, or they answer like a patsy. He'd just made a major mistake, because Dad wasn't going to live very long and I was never going to want the vice president around me again.

This incident is an artifact of the family firm. Not the question itself. Difficult questions are asked in every company. This difficult question, however, was asked by the father, who you know felt one way, in front of the son, who you know felt another. The father ran the company now; the son would in the future. So in addition to the legitimate business issues raised there were all the emotional problems of the Watson family with which you had to deal.

Pugnacious young Tom pronounced this executive a "patsy." Not quite a "real man." He suggested an answer which would have gotten this executive off the hook. More likely, the suggested answer would have enraged both father and son. If the vice president had pointed out the problems in his department, thus agreeing with Junior, Dad would have been irate. He would have asked how what he viewed as one of the company's great strengths had degenerated to such a low estate. Dad, said his son, was not going to live very long. But it does not take very long to say, "You're fired." In any case, this encounter took place in 1949. Dad did not retire until 1956.

Junior said that everyone is asked a question like this at some point. But of course no one ever asked *him* such a question. And it is relatively easy for a rich man to talk about the "courage" involved in facing the loss of your job.

This story, and much else of what you have just read, casts the

Watsons in a negative light. Yet we should also be aware that there was another side to these men.

Both Watsons were capable of great and disinterested kindness. Many people—perhaps numbering in the thousands—benefited personally from their generosity over the decades. Not to know this is not to know them. And it is not to know something important about the company they ran.

CHAPTER 16

Siblings: A Brief Introduction

Thomas Watson and Jeannette Kittredge Watson had three other children in addition to Tom Jr. They were Jane, Helen, and Dick. In this Darwinian environment, you needed a niche. Jane and Helen, as readers of this page have doubtless noticed, were girls. That set them apart from the boys and meant they were destined to play no role in IBM other than as owners of stock and as confidantes, to some degree, of the men in the family who ran the company. (Women did play a role in IBM management, but not Watson women.)

Helen apparently figured out that a good strategy was to keep her head down, and this she did. In his 446-page autobiography, Watson mentions her twice. She is also referred to in the acknowledgments to the book; and one infers from reading (hard) between the lines that she got along reasonably well with her older brother.

Jane, Helen's older sister, was a different story. Her niche was to be the favorite of "My Joy." In her words, "I am so thankful that God gave me such a wonderful My Joy and am so glad to know and be sure that you are the very best man and father in the whole wide world."

This did not endear her to young Tom. She was also assertive. According to Tom, "If you had to pick who was the strongest and hardest driving of T. J. Watson's children, it would be a toss up between Jane and me." He did not like her, and the feeling was mutual. In 1958, two years after the death of her father and the assumption of his position by young Tom, Jane sold a million dollars' worth of IBM stock. That constituted a third of her holdings and marked the first time a member of the Watson family sold IBM stock. Her brother did not interpret this as a vote of confidence in his leadership. Needless to say, he let her know it.

With Jane's aggressiveness and competitive spirit, it is noteworthy that she did not consider (and was never considered for) a position within the firm. Female executives were certainly not unknown in post–World War II America.

IBM, in fact, was a leader in this area. In 1935, T.J. Sr. delivered an address to the Institute of Women's Professional Relations. His presentation elicited complaints from the audience about the lack of opportunities for women in business. Watson was something of a romantic in the nineteenth-century sense, by which I mean he tended to "[glorify] the improbable event, and [deny] the predictable pattern." He always enjoyed the dramatic gesture which burst the bonds of bureaucracy.

The complaint from the audience caught Watson by surprise. His response was, "I would be willing to hire twenty women immediately." This offer, coming in the middle of the depression to a group discriminated against by most employers, generated a flood of job applications. The result was a training program specifically designed for women. In 1943, Ruth M. Leach, a graduate of this program, became the company's first female corporate vice president.

The idea that women could work for IBM, therefore, certainly would not have scandalized Watson. Jane, however, never worked for the firm, although she did help her father in his job. It was Jane, for example, who accompanied him to the scene of the train wreck at Port Jervis in 1940. But Watson Sr. apparently figured there was room for only two of his children at the top of IBM. Those two were to be the boys.

Dick Watson, the last of Tom and Jeannette's four children, was not the fire-eater that Jane and Junior were, nor was he as divorced from the action as Helen. Dick was born on April 23, 1919, while the family was still living in Short Hills. He graduated from Hotchkiss, a prestigious prep school, and from Yale (where the Computer Science Department is today housed in Arthur K. Watson Hall) in 1947. (His college education was interrupted by World War II. He was an army officer for almost five years.) Although he did not graduate until 1947, he is officially a member of the Yale Class of 1942.

Dick Watson's life and his career at IBM are the perfect illustration that to survive in the Watson family (and IBM itself was a part of the family—as the *New York Times* put it, Watson Sr. "considered [the corporation] an extension of his blood family and therefore to be treated with the same care and consideration") you needed a niche. Although he never would have said such a thing, because it would have violated his Norman Rockwell image of his family and because he never could have known it consciously, Senior did know it instinctively. He knew it better than anyone else in the family. Dick Watson's career is the proof. His history at IBM is also another illustration of the degree to which family dynamics exercised a direct influence on the business.

Dick Watson actually had two careers at IBM. The first was as chief executive of IBM World Trade. This was a complete success. The second was when he was recalled to the home office in Armonk, New York, to assist with the big push to get the System/360 out the door. This was a complete failure. We will say a word about the first part of his career in this chapter and turn to the second a little later.

IBM had been doing business abroad almost from its inception. Dad, as we know, thought Europe was going to be "a big deal" back in the 1920s, which is why he spent so much time there. In the 1930s, when he was touting "World Peace through World Trade," Dad fully anticipated that IBM would benefit from that trade.

In 1946, Senior began to complain that IBM's "foreign department" was not achieving its potential. He did not push the issue; and the domestic business was growing so quickly that the foreign department wound up on the back burner. Europe was still devastated by the war, and no one saw any reason to exploit opportunities which were invisible. No one, that is, but Dad, who even in his mid-seventies kept thinking about the future. In 1948, he began working on IBM's international business in a concentrated way. His idea was to create a wholly owned subsidiary of IBM which manufactured and marketed IBM products everywhere but in the United States. IBM had operations in numerous countries; and by shipping semifinished machines across borders it could minimize tariffs, thus creating something akin to its own free trade zone. This idea, which is more complicated than the above brief description makes it sound, was visionary. It was a vision which young Tom did not share—mistakenly, as he later graciously acknowledged.

IBM World Trade was organized in 1949 and formally split from the parent in 1950. IBM Domestic would handle finance and research and development for the whole company; but with the exception of those centralized functions, IBM World Trade was on its own.

How was World Trade to be organized? Senior appointed himself chairman, and he made a veteran IBM executive president. The vice president would thus be in a position to run IBM World Trade after what would probably be a brief apprenticeship. Senior appointed Dick to the vice presidency. This was to be Dick's niche.

Tom Jr. had been jealous of Dick through childhood and early adulthood. Dick was more athletic, his grades were better, he had gotten into Yale on his own merits (as far as we know) rather than through Dad's heavy-handed intervention, he was more charming, he was the life of every party. Instead of the younger brother looking up to the older brother, the older brother resented the younger.

This resentment abated during the war, as Junior began to win his battle against low self-esteem. After he returned to IBM in 1946, he did, despite all his conflicts with his father, achieve notable successes he could call his own, and he was beginning to make a reputation for himself. Now, with the creation of IBM World Trade, it suddenly "looked to me as if Dad was about to hand over half of IBM to my brother."

Tom Jr. understood (in the same way his father did—instinctively rather than consciously) that you needed a niche in the Watson family. He also understood that Dick was handicapped in his search for one.

> As the youngest in our family, he was low man on the totem pole. Not only did he have Dad over him, but he had me five years in front. To complicate things still further, there was our sister Jane, who was always Dad's favorite. So Dick grew up in a very, very tough position. Maybe because of this, Dick's relationship with Dad was different from mine. If Dad got mad at me, I'd get mad right back and we'd fight. My brother had just as strong a temper as I did, but he seemed to believe that in order to get ahead, he had to take what T.J. dished out. Knuckling under was traumatic for Dick. He had asthma, and sometimes when my father lit into him he'd get so short of breath he'd need a shot of adrenaline.

Thus, Tom sympathized with Dick's predicament. When it turned out that Dick's niche was to be carved out of Tom's, however, he became a good deal less sympathetic. He advanced numerous business reasons why splitting IBM into two parts was a bad idea. Some of these reasons were genuine. There are always reasons why decentralization is problematic. The opposite is also true. But as Tom, his father, and his brother well knew, business was not the driving force behind young Tom's objections.

The argument about the creation of IBM World Trade was endlessly unproductive. At length, when Junior continued raising ever more objections about the organization to his father, Dad let him have it: "What are you trying to do, prevent your brother from having an opportunity?" "Those words killed me," Junior later wrote. "They set me up against my brother, who was right there. Dad would say that kind of thing without thinking, because he always aimed to win."

Junior's reaction is not easy to understand. The old man was right. It was vital that Dick have a place of his own. Junior was a dangerous man to whom to be too close; and Dick was, after all, his brother. Dad did indeed "say that kind of thing without thinking." Dad was full of disavowal. Like so many people in positions of great power, he had no real idea of his impact upon others. Perhaps that is not quite the best way to put it. He was in a perpetual state of what Sigmund Freud called "knowing-but-not-knowing" with regard to those over whom he had power. He knew that what he said put young Tom in an impossible position. But he did not know how destructive he was being. He did not have to.

Dad "always aimed to win," complained young Tom. That was correct. He did.

IBM World Trade was organized in 1949 and opened its doors officially in headquarters across the street from the United Nations Building in New York City on January 1, 1950. Like the rest of the family, Dick Watson had been to Europe on numerous occasions. In 1948, his father took him on a European trip which served as an apprenticeship. Tall (six feet two), handsome, charming, and sophisticated, Dick was well suited to be the face of IBM World Trade. He was smart and kept himself well briefed. At home in French and competent in Spanish and German, Dick was on the road about half of each year.

It is not easy to transport ourselves back into the world of 1950. From a political point of view, it was the "democracies" (never called "capitalists" in the Western media) versus the "Communists" (also known as "Godless Communists" or simply as "Reds"). It was a "bipolar" world which it seemed would forever remain that way because of something new under the sun, nuclear weapons. From a business point of view, the Communist world did not count, despite the fact that about 40 percent of the world's population lived under its sway. It was difficult to export products to a Communist regime. Communist economies produced almost nothing that was competitive in world markets.

In the "Free World" of capitalism, the United States stood alone, at the head of the class. It accounted for 39.3 percent of gross world product, compared to 11.1 percent for the European Community, 5 percent for the United Kingdom, and a mere 1.5 percent for Japan (at this writing the world's second largest economy). In almost all sectors of economic activity, the United States not only led the way, it was dominant. To take one example, seventeen out of twenty automobiles manufactured in the world were produced in the United States in 1950.

This was to be the "American Century," and it is not surprising how many American companies were managed by men (upper management was almost all male) whose attention was directed predominantly if not exclusively to the home market. IBM really stood out in its global view.

Even at IBM, however, foreign work had usually been relegated to less talented executives (it was known to some as a "dumping ground") and to aristocrats who had well-known names but not much money. Dad believed that the patina of aristocracy brought with it a certain *je ne sais quoi* to the tabulating machine business.

At first, it appeared that IBM World Trade would follow this pattern. But that changed quickly. Working at World Trade turned out to be very appealing for a lot of reasons. One of those was growth. In the year of its founding, World Trade's sales were $51 million and its profits $7 million. In 1963, the year Dick Watson left World Trade to take a position at corporate headquarters, sales and profits had climbed to $788 million and $105 million respectively. If IBM World Trade had been an independent company in 1963, it would have ranked high on *Fortune* magazine's list of the nation's five hundred largest companies.

IBM's consolidated sales and earnings (including World Trade) skyrocketed from $214.9 million and $33.3 million in 1950 to $2.86 billion and $364 million in 1963. The growth rate of World Trade slightly outpaced corporate. World Trade did benefit from the fact that corporate bore the cost of new product development. It is also true, however, that the need to manage around tariffs pushed World Trade's expenses higher than they would otherwise have been.

By the late 1950s, World Trade's growth began to outpace corporate's significantly because of softening U.S. defense expenditures and booming foreign markets. Employment increased along with sales and profits. The need for executives able to take on greater responsibilities increased as well. World Trade started to look like a pretty good place to advance one's career.

Some of these executives were *plus royaliste que le roi*. The head of IBM Deutschland, which did about $80 million in sales in 1960, was Hans Borsdorf. Among his favorite books was Norman Vincent Peale's *The Power of Positive Thinking*, copies of which he cheerfully passed out to visitors.

If, on the other hand, you wanted to be part of IBM without necessarily partaking in full measure of a corporate culture that could be stifling as well as inspiring, World Trade offered opportunities. In different countries you were allowed, to some extent, to adopt local customs even if they departed from standard IBM behavior.

Whatever the method might have been, IBM World Trade worked. It dominated the markets in which it competed, which was everywhere in the "Free World." Those markets were growing, but World Trade was growing even faster, four to five times faster than the gross national product of the European markets in which it participated, for example. In Japan, IBM refused to be forced into the joint-venturing agreements which other companies engaged in. Japan could not do without IBM's technology and had to accept it on IBM's terms.

The brothers Watson had a lot in common. Both presided over businesses that dominated one of the world's most important industries. Neither was at home with the technology that made their companies great. Both were superb representatives of their businesses to the outside world. Both lived in fear and awe of their father and, after his death, his memory. Both had drinking problems. (This was truer of Dick than of Tom.) Both had inherited their father's temper, which aspect of their patrimony served neither well. Both lived in suburban Connecticut. Both had six children.

One, however, was the other's ultimate boss. Tom Jr. was the CEO of all of IBM after his father at long last stepped down. As author Nancy Foy put it, "Dick had separate but almost equal status with his brother in the corporation itself." That word "almost" would come to mean a great deal in 1964.

CHAPTER 17

Awakening the Electronic Brain

Whate is a computer? If you ask people who study these machines for a definition, you are liable to get a different definition from each one. If you had asked for a definition in 1940, you would probably have been told that a computer was an individual who computed. That definition lasted a long time. I remember a textbook I had in seventh grade (1959–60) entitled *Learning to Compute*. This book had nothing to do with computers (there were no such machines in the Dade County, Florida, school system at the time). It was about learning arithmetic. We have already seen that the word "computing" in IBM's original name in 1911 (Computing-Tabulating-Recording) did not refer to the work of modern computers. The computing in its name referred to the Computing Scale Company, which produced scales enabling a clerk in a store to determine simultaneously the weight and the price of an item. During World War II, the need for mathematical calculations increased with a dramatic intensity unprecedented in history. Projects as diverse as determining the trajectories of artillery shells, breaking codes through which messages were sent, building and refining frames for thousands of airplanes, and creating the atomic bomb all demanded speed and accuracy in computation. "This war is changing everything," said Watson Sr. in 1943. He had no intention of "sitting on the curbstone waiting for the parade to come by." He wanted—he demanded—that IBM seize the high ground and lead the changes which were gripping its industry.

Let us ask again the question with which this chapter begins: What is a computer? Ask twenty computer scientists today and you are likely to get twenty-one different answers. We can at least say that each of these answers would be different from any answer you would have received at the beginning of World War II. One expert told me that the most comprehensive definition of "computer" he knew was "a machine that can run algorithms." The definition poses the obvious dilemma of finding an understandable definition of "algorithm." To make the complex simple, let us say that an algorithm is a "recipe." Thus, a computer may be thought of as a machine that is capable of preparing recipes.

This is a good deal less melodramatic than our chapter title, in which we refer to the computer as an "electronic brain." This title is useful, however, for two reasons. First, it captures the magnitude of the onset of the computer age and the awe with which it was greeted. Even today, "electronic brain" sounds big and important. In the 1940s and 1950s, people were dumbstruck by the phrase. Second, the term shows a tendency to anthropomorphize the computer. In other words, people began to speak of it as if it had human characteristics. People have brains, not machines. People have intelligence, not machines. Yet here was a machine which seemed to bridge the gap between science fiction and fact. The distinction between simile and description was so close that to some people it became blurred. If a machine could think, how did it differ from a person? In 1981, a Pulitzer Prize–winning book was published entitled *The Soul of a New Machine*. Did a machine really have a soul?

Many volumes have been written about such issues. More are to come, because as the computer becomes more sophisticated, its capabilities will continue to surprise us. So will its incapabilities. While some of the applications of the computer were unexpected by even the most imaginative scientists and philosophers of a half century ago, the computer has also disappointed us.

On the one hand, no one conceived of the computer in its early years as a device for communication. It was, as its name suggests, a machine that computed, that performed calculations. Although electronic mail had been toyed with as early as 1940, as IBM demonstrated at "IBM Day" during the New York World's Fair, no one then or forty years later thought that E-mail would come to play the role that it has in our society. No one imagined the Internet.

On the other hand, computers have also disappointed. They cannot understand English (or any other human language either). Consumers have been told for decades that voice-recognition is just around the corner. But we seem to be approaching it asymptotically. Engineers keep getting closer to a voice-recognition system that is within the reach of the mass market and that really works, but don't quite reach the goal. The way almost everyone uses a computer is through a mouse plus a nineteenth-century technology, the typewriter keyboard. The Internet brings wonders into our home, but among them are pornography and sadistic violence that were better kept out. Computers may be like people in some positive respects. They also, unhappily, suffer anthropomorphic maladies. They catch "viruses." Some of these are serious enough to make them take the day off from work. Sometimes they take the week off. Some viruses are fatal. On top of all this, computers, which we are informed are created by the application of the most demanding formal logic, are maddeningly counterintuitive. The next time you turn your computer off, take note of where you move the cursor on the screen, or "desktop." You move it to the lower left and click the mouse on "Start." Why does it not say "Stop"?

Despite its shortcomings, the computer has changed the world in which we live. It stands at the center of the most important industries of the early twenty-first century. What is the secret of its impact? The Nobel Prize–winning economist Herbert Simon wrote an essay which draws a distinction between a general-purpose invention and an invention designed to solve a specific problem. The impact of the former is great because there is no telling what its boundaries might be. A good example is the steam engine. It could pump water from a coal mine. It could power a textile mill. It could run a railroad. This same suppleness has made the computer so central to our lives.

The world was on the cusp of the "computer revolution" (not, perhaps, the best of phrases, since this "revolution" arrived in so many increments) during World War II. The same year that Tom Watson Sr. announced that the war was going to change everything, a project was inaugurated at the University of Pennsylvania's Moore School of Engineering, funded by the Army Ballistic Research Laboratory, called the ENIAC, an acronym for Electronic Numerical Integrator and Computer. The project was not completed until after Japan surrendered.

The ENIAC bore but little resemblance to the computer at your home or place of work. It was the size of a large room. It featured forty plugboards and some eighteen thousand vacuum tubes. These tubes generated both light and heat. The heat meant that everyone who worked around the machine sweated constantly. The light attracted moths. Sweeping up dead moths became a normal feature of the ENIAC's operation, and it is this practice that gave the modern term "debugging" its name. Moreover, one of those eighteen thousand vacuum tubes was always blowing out. The blown-out tube had to be located among the forest of them and replaced.

The ENIAC attracted a lot of publicity among people that mattered. These people can be defined as representing institutions in both the government and the private sector who needed machines which could perform a lot of calculations very quickly. The senior member of the ENIAC team and his second in command, John W. Mauchly and J. Presper Eckert Jr., decamped from the Moore School, which had instituted a new patent policy designed to capture all the patents generated by researchers while in the employ of the university. (This is a terrific example of myopia.) They founded their own company in the summer of 1946.

Talented engineers but not great businessmen, Eckert and Mauchly sold their company to Remington Rand early in 1950. By this time, they had developed the UNIVAC (Universal Automatic Computer); and this acquisition meant that Remington Rand was suddenly a factor in the computer market.

IBM had not stood on the sidelines as information technology moved forward. Far from it. The firm experimented during and after World War II with a variety of machines which, while perhaps not pushing the frontiers of science, were exploiting technology as advanced as the market would accept. Governmental agencies in general and the military specifically were ideal customers—demanding excellence but price insensitive. The company's leadership was anxious to exploit this happy situation.

Unlike Remington Rand and new entrants into the industry like General Electric and RCA, however, IBM had a great deal to lose with the waning of old information technologies. It is impossible to do anything more than hint at the technological changes taking place, but one set of them does deserve special mention. That deals with the fate of the beloved punched card. In 1928, IBM developed an eighty-column card with almost twice the storage capacity as the previous forty-five-column card. The card's rectangular rather than round holes were more readily detectable electrically. The new cards were stronger, and sufficiently distinct from their predecessor to be patentable. "Perhaps most important," explains IBM historian Emerson W. Pugh, "the rectangular holes gave punched cards a distinctive appearance that could not be copied by others. Recognizing the marketing value of this patented appearance, Watson began promoting it as the IBM card. It was not *just* a punched card." In the ensuing years, IBM made a fortune from these cards.

However, innovations were coming which were to threaten the value of this franchise. Among the myriad innovations coming to information processing was the migration from electromechanical machines to electronic machines and concomitantly the development of magnetic tape and later magnetic drums for recording the information processed. Electronic machines were far faster than the speediest mechanical ones. As Tom Jr. noted, the quickest punched-card machine could perform four additions per second. The ENIAC could perform five thousand. One did not have to hold a Ph.D. to understand that a difference of over three orders of magnitude in handling just this one arithmetic operation was going to mean a lot.

Then there was the matter of memory. Watson Sr. had the artisan's affection for things that you could touch, feel, kick. How well would this point of view greet the concept of information storage on magnetic tape? "Having built his career on punch cards," wrote Jr.,

> Dad distrusted magnetic tape instinctively. On a punch card, you had a piece of information that was permanent. You could see it and hold it in your hand. Even the enormous files the insurance companies kept could always be sampled and hand-checked by clerks. But with magnetic tape, your data were stored invisibly on a medium *that was designed to be erased and re-used.* Imagining himself in the customer's shoes, Dad said, "Why, you might be going ahead and thinking you are storing information on that magnetic tape and when you try to get it off, you might find you have nothing there!"

With the benefit of hindsight, it seems obvious that electronic, ENIAC-type machines were the future for IBM. It is easy for us to draw a straight line from electric accounting machines, the mainstay of IBM's product line, to electronic data-processing machines. When studying history, however, we must never forget the dictum of the great British historian Frederick W. Maitland that what is now in the past was once in the future. There were many reasons, some of them quite understandable if we put ourselves in the context of the times, which would have caused IBM to hesitate before diving into the deep end of the pool of electronic brains.

One of these has just been mentioned. Watson Sr. was right about the leap required from the world of an IBM card which you could hold to magnetic tape which you could not. How would your customers feel if they recorded over that tape and their vital information disappeared? They would not be very happy about it.

There was the question of speed. Without doubt, electronic machines could process data far more quickly than mechanical machines. But how necessary was that increased speed for IBM's customers? The world seemed to have gotten along just fine in "mechanical time." Why did it now have to switch over to "electronic time"? Would customers pay for higher rentals for features they did not need?

There was the question of size. The ENIAC was gigantic. Have you, the reader of this page, ever seen the giant sequoias in Yosemite National Park in California? They are stupendous. If one has grown up around the pleasant suburban maples of the Northeast, the sight of a sequoia is disorienting. Is this thing, which may have taken root a half a millennium ago, really a tree in the same sense that the sweet little maple is a tree? Or is it something altogether different?

There was reliability. IBM machines were famously dependable. Could the same be said of a behemoth with thousands of vacuum tubes which were constantly blowing out?

Finally, there was the dilemma faced by every organization and especially by winners—institutional rigidity. IBM had a winning formula. The company had for decades been involved in continuous improvement, better to serve the evolving needs of its customers. That meant that everyone was getting better at electric accounting machines. But now, all of a sudden, came electronics and magnetic tape. These were devices of which IBM's engineers knew not of. Did their advent mean that all the accumulated knowledge in the company was rendered obsolete? People are often very frightened when they have to confront their ignorance. Would IBM engineers have to go back to school to master the new devices showing up in universities? Would they be able to master them if they tried? Wallace Eckert (no relation to J. Presper Eckert of the ENIAC) was hired to work in the Watson Laboratory at Columbia University in March 1945. Eckert was a scientist and the first IBM employee with a Ph.D. Would IBM's engineers feel threatened by the new direction toward which the company might be inclining?

Remember the story (in chapter 15) of the vice president who was summoned to settle an argument between the Watsons about the quality of IBM's research. An unenviable assignment indeed. His name was John C. McPherson. He was hired by Senior himself in February 1930. He had graduated from Princeton with a degree in electrical engineering, but his formal education ended there. No Ph.D. His decision to side with Senior—and how could he have decided otherwise?—capped his career. Surely others learned of his predicament and did not want to share his fate.

How much easier it was to say that these new electronic developments did not really have to do with us. Perhaps they were for special military applications, for pure science, or for problems that were of solely "academic" interest. These machines came out of universities. Maybe that is where they belonged. They were "one-off," specialty machines—Bugattis in a world of Chevrolets.

Oddly enough, there were plenty of universities that were less than enthusiastic about the new "electronic brain." At the other end of Pennsylvania from the Moore School in Philadelphia, at Carnegie-Mellon University in Pittsburgh, the first computer was purchased in 1958. It was an IBM 650 (which had originally been marketed in 1953). "When we got it," Herbert Simon recalled, "we didn't have any idea what we were going to do with it. The electrical engineers didn't want to be associated with it because they were afraid they would have to maintain it; the mathematicians didn't want to be associated with it because it seemed beneath their dignity." Institutional rigidities existed among some prospective customers as well as the suppliers.

It was Charley Kirk's idea to visit Eckert and Mauchly at the University of Pennsylvania in the company of young Tom in March 1946. "I remember the ENIAC vividly," Watson recalled decades later. "It was made up of what seemed like acres of vacuum tubes in metal racks. The air was very hot." The ENIAC "didn't move me at all. . . . [F]rankly I couldn't see this gigantic, costly, unreliable device as a piece of business equipment. Kirk felt the same way."

One encounters this kind of reaction often in the history of technology. There is a lot to lose by abandoning the old skills, the old formula, the old profit model. The future promises only uncertainty. In 1948, top IBM executive Louis H. "Red" LaMotte counted nineteen noteworthy computer projects in various stages of development. Not all of these were going to succeed. So where do you put your money? As important, where do you put your management time?

Not all IBM's customers were shy about advances in information technology. It was, in fact, these technologically fashion-forward customers that convinced both Watsons that electronics and magnetic tape were the future.

The insurance companies were among IBM's most important clients. James Madden, president of Metropolitan Life and, needless to say, a friend of Dad's, invited young Tom down to his offices on Madison Avenue and Twenty-third Street to give him a concrete illustration of why IBM had no choice but to embrace the future. He said, "[Y]ou're going to lose your business with us because we already have three floors of this building filled with punch-cards and it's getting worse." He could not afford this kind of storage space, especially if magnetic tape was available.

Two of IBM's ten biggest customers, Prudential (like Metropolitan Life a very large insurance company) and the Bureau of the Census (which had put Herman Hollerith's Tabulating Machine Company in business in the late nineteenth century), placed orders for the UNIVAC in 1947. The heart of IBM's market was doing more than merely speaking. It was acting. We would like to keep doing business with you; but if you do not change your products, we will change our suppliers.

Even at his advanced age and with so many years of success behind him, Watson Sr. did not fall prey to "winner's curse." Times change. Institutions usually resist change. But Watson knew that IBM did not have that option. Customers like Northrop Aviation had engineers who were experimenting with IBM products to speed them up and make them more efficient. Watson Sr. heard the market speak. One can tell a lot of stories about IBM's dawdling in the face of the computer revolution. We have already run across one such story in the response of Watson Jr. and Kirk to the ENIAC. Then there is the fact that the elder Watson was prejudiced against the very word "computer." He thought it was frightening and implied that a machine so named would replace people. (Remember that in his lifetime a computer was a person who computed.) As a result, IBM's early computers were known as "automatic calculators" or "sequence controlled calculators." In 1952, the UNIVAC scored a terrific public relations coup when the "giant electronic brain" was featured on CBS television news to predict the outcome of the 1952 presidential election on the basis of a small sample of votes. The impact was instant and lasting, even on a five-year-old like me.

Despite all this, Emerson W. Pugh, the authority on IBM's early electronic computers, has concluded that "contrary to widely held perceptions, IBM had the fastest start in the market for electronic computing capability. It did not have to catch up as most accounts of this era suggest." His father put young Tom in charge, and he spent a fortune leading IBM into the age of electronics. New engineers and scientists were hired. New facilities were built. New pricing strategies for leasing the new machines were developed.

In addition to the Watsons' own skepticism, there were plenty of senior executives at IBM who felt electronic computing was going to be difficult indeed for the company. Cuthbert C. Hurd, hired by IBM in 1949 and holding a Ph.D., emphasized the leap involved in the move into electronics. General-purpose electronic computers differed from traditional punched-card equipment "in terms of components, methods of control, amount of human intervention involved." Hurd summarized the views of many top people in IBM:

> They told me . . . that general purpose computers would not be used in great numbers by IBM's customers and would not contribute significantly to IBM's profitability. They also told me that . . . general purpose computers had nothing whatsoever to do with IBM or IBM's main line of equipment, IBM's customers or the problems those customers wished to solve. They told me that they could not imagine that enough problems or applications could ever be prepared by IBM's potential customers to keep a computer busy because such machines were to have the capability of performing several thousand operations per second.

W. Wallace McDowell, a top IBM engineer, concurred that there was considerable opposition within the firm to the development of a big, electronic computer. A lot of people believed "we would be foolish to spend the time and money on that kind of effort as compared to . . . the field in which we were primarily competent, the punched card equipment." Stephen W. Dunwell, a leading IBM engineer, also found the prospects of manufacturing and marketing giant computers daunting. There was, he said,

> no evidence that a machine of such complexity could be made to work reliably or could be maintained in working condition. . . . No one had ever programmed a machine of that kind except on paper, and even such questions as how to get the machine started taxed our imagination. Every single instruction used by the machine had to be written by hand

and an error of a single bit in a program was sufficient to make the entire process inoperative.

I am not writing a history of computer technology, so there is room here only to suggest the endless number of technical problems at hand, as I have done above. When facing this kind of inflection point, most companies historically have failed. The past is too comfortable; the future, too unimaginable. It is standard practice to mock the changes coming on. "Who needs such gigantic machines?" "No one will ever make them work." "This is pure science, not accounting, subscription, or actuarial work. The customers are not ours."

In a seminal article entitled "Marketing Myopia" published in 1960, said to be the most reprinted in the history of the *Harvard Business Review,* Theodore Levitt told executives to ask what businesses they were really in. He explained that the answer to that question was defined not by the products they manufactured or the services they promoted but rather by their customers. Customers were in the market for solutions. They were buying not three-inch drill bits but three-inch holes. If the Hollywood motion picture makers had understood that they were in the entertainment business, not in the movie business, they would have viewed television as an opportunity rather than a problem.

It is, however, extraordinarily difficult to embrace change even though history consistently demonstrates the necessity of so doing. The familiar is simply too comfortable and too comforting. One would have thought that carriage makers, for example, would have understood sooner than anyone else the importance of the internal combustion engine. In 1900, horses deposited 2.5 million pounds of manure and sixty thousand gallons of urine on the streets of New York City every single day. Any contrivance that could mitigate that situation would have seemed obviously to be desirable. But carriage makers did not see things that way.

At the convention of the Carriage Builders Association in 1899, one speaker, in response to the assertion that the automobile would replace the horse, declared that "this is a fallacy too absurd to be mentioned by intelligent men. . . . The horse is and to all appearances will continue to be for years to come the cheapest motive power other than mechanically prepared tracks such as the railroad."

How could this speaker have been so wrong? Why did he not understand that he was not in the carriage-building business, he was in the personal transportation business? This speaker looked at the past five years and noted that 350,000 carriages had been sold in New York City alone as opposed to 125 automobiles. Didn't that really say it all?

In fact, these numbers said nothing. This man, like so many of the rest of us, was marching backward into the future. Only one carriage maker, Studebaker, made the transition to the automobile age; and Studebaker was hardly an impact player. Its last car rolled off the assembly line in 1967. Many people reading this book have never heard of it.

IBM, however, was able to cross the technological chasm. How? Why?

The answer emerges out of a constellation of circumstances, some of which were pure chance. For starters, we must pay tribute to Tom Watson Sr. The classic capitalist, he remained future-oriented even though the future in which IBM would have to invest was not one which a man in his eighth decade of life had a right to believe he would live to see bear fruit.

Second, young Tom was coming along. With Charley Kirk having died in 1947, Junior was the presumptive heir to the company. Despite the fact that he was initially unimpressed with the ENIAC, he had some early successes marketing small electronic arithmetic calculators. In October 1949, young Tom became executive vice president. His father remained chairman of the board and CEO, but he was seventy-five that year. The president of IBM at the time was a placeholder.

Tom Jr. has said of his father that "electronics was the only major issue on which we didn't fight." Despite his misgivings, the old man well understood that electronics was IBM's future. He also seemed to know that at his age, he was not the man to lead the company into the promised land. He met with Eckert and Mauchly, but antitrust concerns meant that IBM would never be able to buy their firm and thus buy its way out of punched cards and into electronics.

Leadership into electronics would have to be internally generated. Young Tom grasped the opportunity. In the opinion of Emerson W. Pugh, this was an opportunity that his father had endowed him with. "By not emphasizing his own early role," Pugh has written,

> Watson Sr. provided his son with ownership of the company's thrust into electronics. The master salesman had made one of the most important sales of his life. His son had chosen to be responsible for the company's activities in electronics. The senior Watson could now concentrate on traditional EAM [electric accounting machine] products and a planned expansion of the electric typewriter business....
>
> The record . . . reveals a father who enticed his son into taking responsibility for a new technology. . . . Having done so, the elder Watson had the unenviable task of balancing the company's priorities *and* tempering his son's otherwise unconstrained drive to make the company's drive into electronics a resounding success.

Pugh's analysis contains assertions that are clearly true and others that are questionable. It is a fact that IBM quickly became committed to electronics despite all the obstacles, including prior commitment in terms of facilities, people, and organizational know-how to an altogether different technology, as well as all the unknowns that the new world would bring. They included all the business questions that could not be answered in advance, such as how many customers really existed for this new machine and, critically, how it should be priced.

Another question that had to be answered on the basis of highly imperfect information was how much money IBM was going to have to spend to develop electronic machinery that would work well enough so that it could maintain its reputation. In 1951, young Tom estimated that making a major commitment to electronics would cost $3 million, which was as large as the company's entire research budget in 1949.

What is a little more difficult to accept is the selflessness attributed to the elder Watson in this process. To be sure, Senior was capable of acts of remarkable generosity. He supported people financially whom he knew from the days in Painted Post. It is easy to find letters of gratitude for his beneficence. Yet Watson was also a man who was greedy for credit. It is no accident that his was the largest entry in *Who's Who* or that so many songs were sung at the company in praise of that "man of men." If Senior was this self-sacrificing, it would have been quite out of character. Father was competitive with son as long as he was physically able to be.

The point is that, quite by chance, the information-processing industry had reached a critical inflection point at the same time that IBM's leadership was being passed off from father to son. To grasp the new world, it was not necessary for one individual to change his mind and perhaps to fire people who had been with him for years. Nor was it necessary—as occurred in the early 1990s—for the old leadership to be thrown out because of its resistance to changing times.

By pure luck, IBM was able to make the leap into the electronic world with a certain security because, in one sense, as its products changed, its leadership remained stable. The CEO in 1946, 1956, and 1966 was a man named Thomas J. Watson. After May of 1956, it was simply a different Thomas J. Watson.

Yet another factor opening up the possibility of electronics was the Korean War, which lasted from 1950 to 1953. The cloak of national security has protected high-priced, high-risk technology in the United States since World War II. With Korea, once again decision makers in both the public and private sectors were willing to take chances which might in other times have caused them to balk. The cold war (which occasionally turned hot, as in Korea) led to "technology forcing." It certainly combined with the other reasons just advanced to help IBM avoid the trap of marching backward into the future.

CHAPTER 18

Death of a Salesman

The battles between father and son continued into the 1950s. When the two started to fight, the fight quickly took on a life of its own. This was especially true of young Tom's decision to sign a consent decree with the antitrust division of the Department of Justice, which was entered into in January 1956. Senior had cherished an abiding hatred for antitrust enforcement authorities ever since his conviction for violating the law in 1914. Father and son had a typical "hellacious," "savage," "primal," "unstoppable," etc., battle followed by the standard maudlin reconciliation in the course of this decision.

As the 1940s turned into the 1950s, however, the frequency of the fighting began to diminish. Dad "was deferring to me," commented Junior, "serving more as mentor than as boss. He had pretty much stopped fighting with me, but it took me a while to notice." In January 1952, young Tom became president of IBM. He was beginning to take charge of more matters in the company.

At the same time, as his father's strength waned, young Tom became more protective of the old man. Indeed, "protective" is the very word he used; and the examples are touching.

I remember once, on a [train] trip from Indiana to Washington, I looked in on him and he wasn't there. So I put on my clothes and started searching. I found him walking through the train fully dressed in a business suit and tie. I said, "Are you all right, Dad?"

"Yes. I had a peculiar feeling, so I thought I'd take a walk. But I'm all right."

Young Tom speculated that his father had experienced a premonition of his death.

Dad's public speaking was not what it had once been. Young Tom tried gently to let him know and to shield him at corporate annual meetings. As Tom grew older and his father grew old, the son wanted Dad to hang around indefinitely. "Most of the time my life was enriched by him. . . . Mainly I wanted him there."

We see here a role reversal. During Tom's troubled youth and his academic struggles, his father was for the most part kind and consoling. When he became a competitor, they were vicious toward one another. When Dad's age and infirmities began to catch up to him, Tom became lovingly solicitous. His respect for his father increased as his father declined. Listen to this:

The old man had bursts of amazing vigor right up to the end. I will never forget the last time I saw him before an IBM audience. It was at a sales meeting in Washington that March. There were perhaps five hundred people assembled in a large hotel auditorium. The man running the meeting spotted him in the back of the room and said, "I see that we have the honor of Mr. Watson's presence. Mr. Watson, won't you come up and take the floor?" Dad was a wispy old man of eighty-two and he started carefully down the inclined aisle toward the stage. The men jumped to their feet and were clapping and shouting. The more they clapped and the farther he got down the aisle, the more erect he became. He stood up straighter and straighter and walked faster and faster until he finally got to the steps leading up to the stage. He went up them with such a surge of energy that he seemed to take them two at a time. The thrill of salesmen's accolades was so great that Dad shed about thirty years on the way down that aisle. He grabbed the podium and made a very stirring speech, punching his fist into his hand and telling the men how they must take advantage of the great opportunities before us, and how IBM was going on forever.

A magic moment. After decades of choreographing his public appearances before employees down to the words on the plaque he was presented, his final such appearance was completely spontaneous. Those men who were cheering him—many of them had shaken his hand at previous conventions. Many of them had benefited from the generosity for which he was famous at times of need, when they were facing health problems or when they lost a loved one. Many of them remembered his open-handedness when it came to supplementing their pay during World War II. All of them knew that the money they were making in 1956 was in no small part due to his devotion to his job, which translated to devotion to them.

Now, they all knew an era was drawing to a close. By leaping to their feet, by shouting and clapping, they wanted to infuse the old man with some of the energy and spirit with which he had spent a lifetime inspiring them.

There were five hundred people in the hall at that time. Have you ever addressed such a large group when, physically, you did not feel up to it . . . when you really did not know whether your desperate desire to give a good account of yourself could compensate for your failing flesh and blood? It is hard. No one in that room knew whether Watson would make it to the podium, much less mount the steps, much less give the speech of his life. What if he had tripped and fallen? But he didn't. He went out as he came in, a winner. All those present were able to say thank you in the only way that mattered.

At the end of his life, Thomas J. Watson Sr. presents himself to us as one of nature's noblemen, as the stuff of legends. He had come a long way from the mud of East Campbell, New York (the tiny hamlet near Painted Post where he was born), to international fame and fortune. From a bed of sponges to the lap of luxury. He had had a great teacher in the person of John H. Patterson. At least as important, however, was the fact that Watson could learn. He was coachable. He could grow. After he graduated from National Cash Register, he became capable of teaching himself the lessons he learned from his own experience of life. That is why he was as open as he was to massive change in his business that came late in his own life, even though the change was to a technology he could not possibly have understood.

Watson was very much like Patterson in being sometimes wrong but never in doubt. He epitomized a model of business leadership which is quite out of fashion. He held himself forward as the man with the answers, the man who could boost you to success if you emulated him and followed his dictates.

Another notable difference between Watson's era and today is in corporate governance. He was the leader in fact as well as name. In not one instance after 1915 did the board of directors or the stockholders voice effective opposition to what he wanted. The family never owned more than 5 percent of the stock, but he acted as if IBM were his private property.

Watson was much more than the CEO of a big, important company. He was a citizen of the nation and the world and spoke out when the spirit moved him. Sometimes, especially when assessing leaders abroad and most especially Hitler, his assumption that there could be simple answers to complicated problems ("World Peace through World Trade") made him look like a fool. At other times, however, his refusal to run with the pack served him well. He was a Democrat when most big businessmen could not stand Roosevelt.

Like Robert Wood Johnson (of Johnson & Johnson), in politics as in so many other matters, Watson followed his own dictates.

On May 8, 1956, two months after the sales meeting at which he was so robustly cheered, Watson finally stepped down as CEO and turned the company over formally to young Tom. Within a week, he did the same thing at IBM World Trade.

Permit me to switch gears and take a look at another giant of enterprise. At ten minutes to one o'clock on the afternoon of Monday, March 14, 1932, George Eastman—founder of Kodak and, of course, an acquaintance of Dad's—committed suicide by shooting himself in the heart. He left a note: "To my friends. My work is done—Why wait?" Watson did not commit suicide, but he did decline to have a surgical procedure which stood some chance of prolonging his life. Young Tom believed Dad "willed his death by refusing medical treatment. . . . I suppose he thought, 'It has been a good life. I guess it's about the time.'"

After such a tumultuous life of striving, seeking, finding, and not yielding, Watson drifted through his final days peacefully, surrounded by his wife, his four children, and a great deal of love. He had private conversations with the five members of his immediate family during his last days. All the conflict disappeared. There was nothing but affection and the understanding that all of us have one thing in common. All our lives and the lives of our loved ones end. When a loved one is lost, there is no further communication or communion in this world. He (or she) will reappear, perhaps daily, in our thoughts. We will dream of him; and the dream will be so vivid that upon awakening we will not know whether reality is found asleep or awake. Of his father's dying, Watson said, "It was a joyous and very sad time."

Watson's funeral was appropriate for a man who was also a monument.

"Thomas J. Watson Sr. Is Dead; IBM Board Chairman Was 82" was one of the headlines in the *New York Times* on June 20, 1956. The subheadline read: "'World's Greatest Salesman' Built [$]629

Million Company—THINK Slogan." This two-column article appeared on the front page, quite a rarity for the obituary of a businessman. The funeral took place on June 21, and it was crowded. "Watson Funeral Attended by 1,200," reported the *New York Times.* "Overflow Crowd at Brick Church Hears Tribute to IBM Industrialist." Watson had been an elder of the Brick Presbyterian Church for sixteen years. One of the three other life elders was John Foster Dulles, the secretary of state of the United States. Dag Hammarskjöld, secretary-general of the United Nations, was in attendance. So were David Rockefeller, grandson of John D. Rockefeller; Grayson Kirk, president of Columbia University, on whose board of trustees Watson had served for almost a quarter of a century; Democratic Party stalwart and Franklin D. Roosevelt's postmaster general in the 1930s James A. Farley; Bernard Gimbel, president of Gimbels; Philip D. Reed, chairman of the board of General Electric; Charles F. Kettering, the great inventor; General Lucius D. Clay, commander in chief of U.S. forces in Europe and military governor of the U.S. Zone in Germany from 1947 to 1949, during the Berlin Airlift; Arthur Hays Sulzberger, president and publisher of the *New York Times....* In a word, there were a lot of important people present.

Not all of the forty-two honorary pallbearers were able to attend; but their names adorned accounts of the funeral, and they also were people who mattered. Bernard Baruch, financier and adviser to presidents; Sherman M. Fairchild, CEO of Fairchild Camera and Instrument and the largest individual IBM stockholder; Admiral Richard E. Byrd, naval aviator, explorer of the North and South Poles, best-selling author; corporate executives; university presidents; others. President Dwight D. Eisenhower had already issued a statement lauding Watson, "this truly fine American." . . . "I have lost a good friend, whose counsel was always marked by a deep-seated concern for people." The first lady wrote a separate, unpublished letter to Mrs. Watson on behalf of herself and the president.

New York is a big city, and it did not grind to a halt the day of the funeral. On the other hand, twelve hundred people at the corner of Park Avenue and Ninety-first Street must have caused something of a stir. Doubtless cars were parked for many blocks, including two blocks to the west, at Ninety-first Street and Fifth Avenue, the block occupied by the home Andrew Carnegie purchased soon after his retirement and in which his widow lived until her death, a decade before Watson's.

Watson was buried next to the grave of his infant grandson in the cemetery that is also Andrew Carnegie's last resting place, the Sleepy Hollow Cemetery near Tarrytown, New York, about twenty miles north of New York City. For Watson, the choice of the cemetery was perfect. He was born in upper New York State. His company had extensive facilities up and down the Hudson River valley. Towns such as Poughkeepsie greatly benefited as IBM's growth exploded during the final years of Watson's life and in the three decades following his death. The same was true on the New York side of the border with Pennsylvania. IBM had a very large facility in the town of Endicott. It is not surprising that Charles F. Johnson, president of Endicott-Johnson, came down to the city for the funeral.

At the funeral service, the minister described Watson as "peculiarly loyal to his past. He never separated himself from it or from the small upstate town where he was brought up." Yes and no. He certainly never forgot Painted Post and talked endlessly of his early days on the road. But he was, if anything, more "peculiarly loyal" to the future. For a business to prosper, Watson insisted, it had to "look into the future and study the demands of the future." The creation and development of new products to cover new fields" was always high on his agenda. He never lost this cast of mind, which is why he was able to say yes to electronics at the end of his life.

If the eulogist at Watson's funeral was not quite accurate in emphasizing his respect for the past over his belief in the future, the headline writer for the *Times* could not have been more right.

"'World's Greatest Salesman'" is what the headline read. The phrase is in quotations, indicating it is a claim and a belief rather than a proven fact. Such a description can never be a proven fact. But there can be no question that Watson would be on any short list of the greatest salesmen ever.

Watson's powers of persuasion were awesome. Not only could he persuade customers to buy his products, he could persuade his employees that they were capable of exceeding their own expectations. He could persuade men of great wealth and power to do things they did not want to do.

For an example, let us look at George Eastman again. On February 9, 1931, Eastman was the guest of honor at a banquet at the Hotel Commodore in New York City. The event was the annual celebration of the Society of the Genesee, an organization of leading figures from the Genesee River valley region of upstate New York. (The Genesee River runs through Rochester.) Over a thousand admirers attended.

Eastman's loathing for this kind of event was without bounds. By the time this one took place, he was in ill health and depressed. There is nothing one can think of about a trip to New York City in the depths of winter during the Great Depression which was designed to cheer him up. For a decade, the Society of the Genesee had been asking Eastman to be its guest of honor, and Eastman had been turning the invitation down. "After a decade of saying, No, No, No, he capitulated to . . ." To whom? To Thomas J. Watson. Like so many other great executives of the turn of the century, Eastman had been influenced by Watson's mentor, John Henry Patterson. Patterson had created a program for employees to suggest improvements at National Cash Register; and Eastman imported the practice to Eastman Kodak in 1898. Watson met Eastman sometime between 1899 and 1903, and he earned Eastman's admiration. When Watson asked, and kept asking, Eastman at last "capitulated." Watson was the toastmaster, and his speech was graceful and gracious. He praised Eastman's ability and his philanthropy and described him accurately as having "a devotion to sound business principles seldom met with in the maelstrom of industrial life."

What did the headline in the *Times* announce? It was selling, not technology, which made the papers. This is ironic because IBM was, for many years, at the center of the most technology-intensive of industries. But it is also accurate. Selling and marketing were the heart of IBM's competitive advantage as the industry grew. Watson's death was the death of a salesman. But unlike Willy Loman in the Arthur Miller play of that name, Watson was a dreamer whose dreams came true.

CHAPTER 19

On His Own

There is a picture in young Tom's autobiography of him shaking hands with his father on that day in May of 1956 "when he finally gave me control of IBM." Dad was eighty-two, and he looks his age. His face appears gnarled, bringing to mind the tree trunks back in the Steuben County of his youth in the 1870s and 1880s. When he was forty-two, which was his son's age at the time of this photograph, he stood about six feet two inches and weighed about 175 pounds. His son was also six feet two inches, and he appears a bit taller in this picture than his father, who has given up some height with his years.

Dad is staring intently at his son's face. The moment to step aside in favor of young Tom, longed for yet dreaded, has arrived. What is he communicating to his son? This picture is on the jacket cover of this book, so you can judge for yourself. To me, the look is inquisitive. Still, after all this time, he seems to be trying to find something out which is eluding him.

Tom Jr., erect, handsome, and youthful, is nattily attired in a double-breasted suit. His body language bespeaks rock-solid self-confidence; but his facial expression does not. What is he thinking? Perhaps: "The top of the greasy pole" at last, in Disraeli's famous phrase. Perhaps: Now I can make the changes that this firm has needed for so long. Perhaps: Am I looking at my future?

Neither man is smiling or looking at the camera. We will never know the inner thoughts of either.

What we do know is that when "the shock of Dad's death finally hit" him, it hit young Tom hard. After his father's death and that huge funeral, Watson, Olive, and two of their daughters took a vacation in Bermuda. Suddenly, one night, "I had a horrible allergic reaction. . . . My throat swelled up and I couldn't breathe." This acute episode was followed by rashes. Tom's doctor told him he was taking his grief out on his body.

It was difficult to return to work effectively. Although Tom had been making progressively more operating decisions from 1952, to be the boss in name as well as in fact required a leap. His mother sold the town house immediately after her husband's death. Tom took his oldest child on a trip to Alaska, both to get closer to him and to escape IBM's offices, where everything reminded him of his father. There is a picture of Watson in his autobiography with the caption: "The fall of 1956, after Dad died, was the loneliest time of my life." He looks like a very different man from the one who had shaken his father's hand and taken over the company a few months before. There are bags under his sunken eyes. His clothes are a bit rumpled. Freud said that the death of a man's father was the most important day in his life. That may well have been true for Watson. He was still in deep mourning months afterward. His father, indeed, played a living role for him until he himself passed away. He remained unseparated.

A surprising, and often unpleasant, discovery which you make when someone who has been an important part of your life dies is that the world keeps turning. Things keep happening. There will be a funeral; but after that, everyone else will go home and continue their daily routines. You will go home with a hole in your heart. You will have a feeling that others cannot comprehend. If you are going to lead an organization—if you are going to step into the shoes of the "man of men"—you do not have time to mourn. You have to keep it to yourself.

Watson wanted to move fast to show the world that there was a firm hand at the helm. He gave an interview to *Fortune* which was published in September 1956 and, with the exception of the forlorn photograph which was later published in the autobiography and which perhaps communicated more than was intended, succeeded in that goal. The interview for the article took place a few days after the funeral. The reporter wanted to talk about the "past, present, and future of I.B.M." He began by apologizing "for pressing such questions at this particular time," to which "Watson merely replied, 'Pop would have wanted it that way.'"

"The worst thing that can happen when a leader dies is for his followers to carry on like robots," said Watson. At this crucial juncture, Watson handled himself admirably. Dad was gone; and although "I didn't realize how much I still needed him emotionally," that neediness had to be kept in its place; and where its place was not was the business. "Dad had taught me that a good businessman has to be an actor," and Watson learned that lesson well.

In November 1956, it was an IBM computer, not a Sperry Rand (the Sperry Corporation merged with Remington Rand in 1955—thus the name change) UNIVAC, which the networks used to forecast the presidential election. More important for the company was the momentous Williamsburg, Virginia, meeting of the 110 top executives of the corporation. The meeting's goal was to reorganize the company. But its other purpose was to announce to the world through this, "the first major meeting IBM had ever held without Dad present," that the baton had passed smoothly to the next Thomas J. Watson. "In three days we transformed IBM so completely that almost nobody left that meeting with the same job he had when he arrived." As late as 1947, Dad had "38 or 40" executives reporting directly to him. He wanted to know everything that was going on in the corporation. He always hated formal organization charts.

Tom Jr. became president in 1952 and along with Al Williams was making most of the day-to-day decisions involved in running the company. Williams is quite an interesting character because, despite all the qualifications, he avoided being ground up in the Watson mincing machine. He had attended accounting school and was a numbers man. He had been attracted to IBM because of the high pay and had been hired by Dad in 1940.

Williams fit the formula for destruction quite well. He was young, only three years older than Tom. He was a favorite of Dad's. He was upwardly mobile. Sounds a lot like Charley Kirk. But Williams found out how to help young Tom. He understood accounting and finance, while Watson "never had any pretension about understanding money." A businessman like Watson who literally did not know the difference between debt and equity needed—desperately—a combination partner-assistant whom he never felt embarrassed to ask a question. Williams never competed for Dad's affection. He never aspired to be IBM's chief executive. He shunned the limelight. "The funny thing about Al," Watson observed, "was that he was terribly modest and didn't like to promote himself." There was nothing odd about this at all. Williams knew his boss, a man with an uncertain ego and explosive temper, the "most powerful force" in whose life was the "fear of failure." In a culture which putatively encouraged contention, he understood that the way to deal with Watson was to manage up with great care. Part of this process was Williams's decision, announced well in advance, to take early retirement at the age of fifty-five. Williams's father was a section boss in a coal mine who was fired during the depression and was blacklisted for siding with the workers. Williams never got a college education, but he finished his career serving as president of IBM from May 1961 to March 1966. Watson described these as his "happiest years at IBM," and it would appear that his happiness derived from working with "my friend, Al Williams," a very deft executive indeed.

Williams had been working closely with Watson for years prior to the Williamsburg conference. The first organization chart of the company was put together by Watson, doubtless with the help of Williams, in November 1954. By that time, there were seventeen people reporting to Watson. In the more comprehensive organizational structure created at Williamsburg, two executive vice presidencies were created. They were responsible for all company functions outside World Trade. One of these positions was held by Al Williams, the other by Louis H. "Red" LaMotte, who had the distinction of being one of the few people who talked back to Dad and survived in that company.

At Williamsburg, the goal was a structure that would push decision making down into the organization through the strengthening of the divisions and the establishment of a powerful corporate staff. The staff was created from within IBM rather than by hiring experts from outside. Watson said that he had spent years "weeding out Dad's yes-men." These had been replaced as line executives by "fierce, strong-willed decision makers." Outsiders hired for newly created staff positions "would have been eaten alive . . . , [b]ut by shifting our stars into the staff we enabled it to command the respect of the divisions." One of the many individuals coming out of Williamsburg with a new job was Al Williams, now the executive vice president for corporate staff.

Two other executives also must be mentioned because their fates were soon to become intertwined. Dick Watson was one person whose job did not change. He remained the president of IBM World Trade. His brother did, however, place him on the Corporate Management Committee, "which was IBM's ruling council." This was the first organization chart on which Dick's name ever appeared. It clearly showed that he reported directly to his brother. I believe this was a new development. While Dad was alive, Dick reported to him, not to Tom.

On the same level on the Williamsburg organization chart as Dick Watson was T. Vincent Learson, the newly named vice president and group executive. Learson graduated from Harvard, where he majored in mathematics, in 1935 and remained with IBM his whole career, serving as CEO following Watson from June 1971 to September 1972. (He kept a seat on the board for a decade thereafter.) Learson's first job was as a sales trainee in Boston. He was in charge of the Philadelphia office when young Tom picked him out of the crowd of IBM executives as a man destined for great things.

At six feet six inches in height, Learson stood out in a crowd. He got his big break in the spring of 1954 when IBM and Remington Rand were in the thick of competition for the large computer market. Remington Rand was in the lead with about twenty installed to IBM's fifteen. UNIVACs were delivered to such high-profile customers that year as Du Pont, General Electric, Metropolitan Life, and U.S. Steel (which bought two). According to historians of IBM technology, "As showcase UNIVACs began to replace large card-machine installations, an atmosphere of crisis pervaded IBM branch offices with large accounts."

IBM's answer to the UNIVAC was its 702 Electronic Data Processing Machine. Although some analysts talked the 702 down, the sales force had no trouble booking orders. Unfortunately, the 702 had problems which threatened its quality. Watson told Learson to fix it. Learson was confronting the kind of Gordian knot so often encountered in this industry. It was essential that all the parties involved, from product planning (which had begun back in 1947 for the 702) all the way forward to sales, work together. Instead, each protected itself. In the wings were punched-card old-timers who would not have minded seeing the 702 fail.

Learson, driving the engineers "ferociously," cut the Gordian knot. The 702 turned into a "triumph," as Watson put it. Learson had earned himself a place at the top of IBM's management. He, too, was a member of the Corporate Management Committee.

Organizationally, the stage was now set for System/360.

CHAPTER 20

The New Thomas Watson's New IBM

During the 1950s, IBM's growth was dazzling. Sales in 1950 were $266 million, and profits were $37 million. In 1956, the year of the transit of power from father to son, sales and profits were $892 million and $87 million, respectively. Employment reached seventy-three thousand, an increase of just under two and a half times the thirty thousand of 1950.

Watson wrote that for five years, "I had a ritual I used to follow on the anniversary of my father's death. I would spend a quiet evening taking stock of what IBM had accomplished in his absence, and then say to Olive, 'That's another year I've made it alone.'" The first full year that Watson "made it alone" was 1957, and he could only have been happy with the results. Earnings rose more than 25 percent to $110 million. In its forty-sixth year in existence, IBM's sales topped $1 billion for the first time. They hit $1.2 billion, an increase of almost 35 percent from the previous year. Eighty-four thousand employees, up 15 percent, worked for the company. Sales, profits, and employees continued to climb for the remainder of the decade. Watson's "quiet evenings taking stock" must have ended pleasantly. As the decade drew to a close, things just kept getting better. In 1959, the company employed ninety-five thousand people to generate $1.6 billion in sales and $176 million in profits.

Watson's fifth full year running the company without Dad around was 1961. Sales were just over $2.2 billion. It had taken forty-five years for IBM to become a $1 billion company. It took a mere four years more for it to become a $2 billion company. Profits soared to $254 million, just under two and a third times the 1957 figure. Productivity was increasing as well. Sales per employee were about $14,300 in 1957. That figure rose to almost $19,000 for IBM's 116,000 employees five years later.

With business moving ahead so quickly, one might assume that an atmosphere of happiness, perhaps even playfulness, pervaded IBM from top to bottom. One would be quite wrong. Watson's family life had been full of competition and argument. That spilled over into his professional life when, during the decade after World War II, he and Dad had their "hellacious" fights. Watson had no intention of seeing that gut-clutching way of life disappear merely because his father had passed away.

Around the time of the Williamsburg conference, Watson formalized in his own thinking what had been de facto conduct at IBM since the early 1950s, as his control of operations increased. This was what became well known not only in the industry but in business generally as the system of "contention management." It was a mode of running a company that Watson saw as completely different from his father's. His father attracted sycophants, who disgusted young Tom. The combination of Dad's uncontrollable temper and his unquenchable need for praise had, in his son's view, "silenced too many people."

Under contention management, there would be no silence. To the contrary, there would be as much fighting as in the good old days when Dad and Watson had their "primal" battles. Contention management institutionalized fighting. "Not only did it make staff versus line conflicts acceptable; it actually encouraged them." These conflicts either resulted in eventual consensus or were moved to a higher level. The contending line and staff men would have to "air their differences before the corporate management committee, which did not suffer indecisiveness gladly . . . The best way to motivate people," Watson declared with more self-assurance than the topic permits a prudent man to possess, "is to pit them against one another, and I was constantly looking for ways to stimulate internal competition." What Watson had with Dad from 1945 to 1956 he wanted to metastasize throughout the whole company.

There are a couple of observations which call out to be made about all this. First, although internal competition did work in Watson's IBM and has worked elsewhere, internal cooperation can also work. There is such a thing as team play not only in sports but in business and indeed in life. True teamwork can mobilize the power of the spirit of self-sacrifice. When one person says to another— "Life is not a seesaw where I'm down if you're up; it is the opposite: Your success is my success"—the enormous power of generosity is unleashed. Great things have been done with this approach to challenges. To state as an immutable principle of human nature that the "best way to motivate people is to pit them against one another" is highly questionable. It is true if that is the business culture you foster. But it is very far indeed from some eternal verity.

Another aspect of human relations at IBM under Watson is noteworthy. The company moved people around a lot—both geographically (IBM came to be known by insiders as "I've Been Moved") and with regard to their assignments. If a man was promoted to a job that was over his head, he would be reassigned "to a level where he could perform well." In this process, according to Watson, "we would sometimes strip a man of a fair amount of his dignity, but we would then make a great effort to rebuild his self-respect."

This "recycling" of executives can be done successfully and is a practice some well-run companies use today. Intel is an example. But it is a process which must be managed with exquisite tact, a trait for which IBM was not famous.

There is no doubt that IBM could rob a man of his dignity. It certainly succeeded with Charley Kirk. The rebuilding part is a little more questionable. A lot of things have to be true for the rebuilding to work. The man who has found himself "parked" or placed in the "penalty box" has got to have a combination of pride which can withstand such humiliation and self-control so that the pride does not result in either depression or rage rendering him beyond rehabilitation. Moreover, the company's culture has to reward people who help retrain this individual and guide him back to the promotion track. These people must be deft and skilled at managing delicate situations. Since we know that people with this kind of talent are going to be busy, they may find themselves questioning this investment of their time.

It is interesting that this is similar to the way John Patterson managed the National Cash Register Company when Dad started out there at the turn of the century. Dad got a sales job at the Cash he could not handle. His manager, John Range, berated him for his shortcomings. Having broken him down, Range then built him up. It worked. Dad regained his self-respect and became one of the greatest salesmen ever. But that was a world away from IBM in the era of the "organization man."

Many things could be said of the executive corps Watson put together, but apparently "nice" was not a word one would use to describe them as a group. The enemy of effective business management, in Watson's view, was "the nice guy you like to go on fishing trips with."

> Instead I was always looking for sharp, scratchy, harsh, almost unpleasant guys who could see and tell me about things as they really were. If you can get enough of those around you, and have patience enough to hear them out, there is no limit to where you can go.

Watson declared that his "most important contribution" to IBM was "my ability to pick strong and intelligent men . . . and then hold them together by persuasion, by apologies, by speeches, by discipline, by thoughtfulness . . . , and by using every tool at my command to make each man think I was a decent guy." When he looked in the mirror, Watson saw a "pretty harsh and scratchy guy myself."

Watson wanted every executive at IBM to feel the urgency he felt—"whatever they did, it was never enough." He knew that he was hiring men who were intellectually his superior; but he felt he could make a vital contribution by driving them as hard as he could.

Is this the best way to run a company? Had Watson been asked, he could have said what Dad said when people complained about his leadership: "Look at the record." Indeed, Watson took more than one leaf from Dad's playbook. When Dad unloaded on Red LaMotte in the late 1940s for failing to make a sale, LaMotte—who had become something of a legend in the company for landing the Social Security account—resigned. Dad hustled over to LaMotte's home on posh Gramercy Park and, with him in the room, addressed himself to his wife. "Lois, I've made a great mistake and I need your help. Red is one of the people I count on to move IBM ahead. He has resigned, and I'm here to apologize and make sure I'll have him back with me."

The business world is full of tension, and there are many companies populated by shouters and screamers. "Acting out," as a psychiatrist would call this sort of thing, can serve to relieve stress. On the other hand, there are plenty of companies which have done very well without manufacturing melodrama. Sam Walton did not scream at people and then beg their wives to coax them back to the company.

Watson in the late 1950s was, however, in a different position in his company from Walton's when he founded Wal-Mart in 1962. Watson inherited IBM. Walton was the entrepreneur who founded Wal-Mart. More important—much more important—Walton was a man of such innate self-confidence that he did not have to tell the world what a great man he was. He was a natural leader, a man who chose to lead by inspiration rather than intimidation. He could be hard. There are hard moments in business as in life; and if they are not faced, the business might fail. It certainly will not achieve its potential. But there seems to have been a bright line in Walton's life which separated "hard" from "harsh." I have never seen Walton referred to as harsh, except, perhaps, by the competition.

Another big difference between Watson and Walton pertains to their knowledge of what it was that their respective companies actually did. It could be argued that Sam Walton was the greatest retailer who ever lived. He knew more about how to get the right product to the right place at the right time for the right price than anyone else. He loved retailing with a passion difficult to communicate. He believed you could learn from anybody. His hunger for knowledge from his employees and from other retailers was legendary.

Walton's expertise in retailing was responsible for the success of Wal-Mart in numerous ways. Unlike the marketing of computers, retailing is a business in which contact with the customer takes place with the lowest-paid employee. The clerk at the counter and the person stocking shelves receive the minimum wage (if that) and are often part-timers. Walton viewed his ability to motivate as perhaps his greatest asset. If you can motivate your workers, they will figure out new ways to make customers happy. If you listen to what they have learned, you can spread that knowledge throughout the company. Before you know it, each customer is a little bit happier with each encounter with a Wal-Mart employee than when he or she shops at a Kmart, Woolco, or Target. You have created a competitive advantage which is real, palpable, and bankable even though it is difficult to quantify.

Walton's genius extended far beyond the point of sale. He had his own searing insight into the nature of his business—small towns could support big stores if those stores provided staple goods at prices sufficiently attractive to draw customers from wide trading areas. Wal-Mart grew by building the most efficient distribution system possible in a forgotten part of the country dotted by dozens of towns nobody on Wall Street had ever heard of.

Such knowledge of what his company actually did was denied to Watson. Dad knew a lot about cash registers back at NCR, and he knew enough about the electromechanical accounting machines which IBM produced to make fairly detailed suggestions about their improvement. Knowledge of even these machines was tough for young Tom. Remember he needed a tutor in Endicott. As the world of processing data moved toward the computer, the intellectual requirements for an in-depth understanding of what IBM was providing its customers with increased enormously. If Watson could not "plug up a board" at the Endicott training school in the 1930s, what chance did he have of understanding the problems of compatibility within IBM's product line? Obviously, not much.

How important is it to have a technologist running a technology-intensive company? A difficult question. History is replete with examples of CEOs rich with technological expertise who chose the wrong path and ruined promising companies. On the other hand, if you do not have an in-depth knowledge of your product, you run the risk of making demands that cannot be satisfied because they are technologically impossible.

Managerial ability and technological expertise are two distinctly different talents. Rare indeed is the individual who possesses them both. Andy Grove is one of the few examples that come to mind. Others include Alfred P. Sloan Jr. in the great days of General Motors, and Pierre S. du Pont a hundred years ago.

The usual practice is to hire the half that is missing. That was Watson's path in the computer era. IBM's staff grew ever larger and more powerful because the staffers were engineers and scientists who actually knew what went on inside those big, handsome cabinets which housed the computers the company sold or, more often, leased. The staff's power derived from its knowledge. Wal-Mart did not have any comparable institution because it was not needed. Sam Walton knew more about his business than anyone else.

At times, Watson described the relation between line and staff at IBM as a system of checks and balances. Nevertheless, he also often said that a business must be a dictatorship if it is to move forward. There was no question who the dictator was at IBM.

On the domestic front, Watson and his family were beginning to attract attention from general-circulation magazines. Both *Life* and *Sports Illustrated* ran fawning stories about them. Rich and good-looking, the family owned a house in the palatial Connecticut suburb of Greenwich, a ski lodge, a yacht, and sundry other trappings of a superabundance of cash. They boasted glamorous friends. Reality, however, was not as rosy as reportage.

Watson did not check his attitude in the foyer when he left the office and came home to his wife and family in Greenwich at the end of the day. He had six children who were born between 1944 and 1956. A certain amount of disorder is to be expected in such a ménage, but Watson could neither expect nor accept it. The instances of disarray that greeted him upon coming home

> would strike me as crises that needed to be resolved right away, and yet [after a hard day at the office] I had no energy to bring to bear. I'd feel a desperate wish for somebody else to step in and make the decisions so I didn't have to. That's when I'd blow up. The kids would scatter like quail and Olive would catch the brunt of my frustration.

These episodes would balloon within Watson, making him feel "totally thwarted and boxed in. Those were the blackest moments of my adult life." He would become "so morose that the only thing I could do was hole up." Acting out precisely the "boxed in" feeling of which he was complaining, Watson would lock himself in his dressing room, leaving poor Olive on the other side of the door trying to coax him out. When she gave up, she would call her brother-in-law, Dick, who lived in the equally ritzy nearby town of New Canaan. Dick, Watson recalled, "always knew how to make my responsibilities seem lighter and draw me back into the world."

Watson's behavior was quite similar to his father's. In Dad's case, it was bringing a half dozen executives home for dinner and expecting Jeannette to entertain them on the spur of the moment. For Watson, the problem seems to have been more one of bringing IBM home in spirit. Everything was an extension of the company. When something or someone did not behave accordingly, Watson lost control of himself.

Before too long, Watson's demons would put his marriage at risk; and they would cost him his relationship with his brother.

CHAPTER 21

Threats from Without and from Within

Not only was IBM growing quickly in the late 1950s, so was the whole industry. According to a study prepared by a well-known consulting firm in 1957, the increasing number of clerical workers, almost doubling in the years from 1940 (4.5 million) to 1956 (8 million), made it obvious that "there is a growing market for any device which will simplify or cut back on the load of accounting, record keeping, cost analysis and all the other paper work that must inevitably accompany big business." The report asserted that there were about 250 electronic digital computers already installed and that letters of intent showed there were more on the way. In 1951, it had been estimated that there were only four computers in the whole world.

This report, prepared by Arthur D. Little, Inc., discerned three distinct but interrelated markets: business, science and engineering, and government. It named twelve "major producers of digital computers." Although it described the number of companies in the market as "comparatively few," the report also asserted that "competition in the field was becoming more severe." Included among these dozen competitors in addition to IBM were Bendix, Burroughs,

Honeywell, NCR, RCA, Raytheon, and Sperry Rand. These were big companies, experienced in technical products and business-to-business marketing. Some, like Sperry Rand and NCR, had been competing against IBM for years. Others, like Raytheon and RCA, were new to IBM's competitive set.

Traditional or new, they were certainly not welcome. Sales of Sperry Rand were higher than IBM's in 1956, and RCA was larger than Sperry Rand. RCA is today merely a brand name and not terribly well known even as that. In the 1950s, it was at the apex of corporate America. It had pioneered radio in the 1920s and was leading the pack in television in the 1950s. Its research and development capability in electronics was unquestioned. In David Sarnoff, it boasted not a standard CEO but another "man of men" type much like Dad. (Coincidentally, the "General," as Sarnoff was always known, arranged to have his son Robert succeed him as CEO in 1956. The result was disastrous.)

Al Williams thought that RCA was one of the two companies that could cause IBM a lot of trouble in the future. The other had not yet entered the industry, but it posed a potential threat of major proportions. That was General Electric.

More than four times the size of IBM in 1956, General Electric was still a consumer rather than a producer of "giant brains" in the mid-1950s. However, it had all the tools to enter the industry if it wanted to do so, including cash, engineering expertise, and research capability. General Electric dwelled in the land of the giants. In terms of sales, it ranked fifth on the Fortune 500 list in 1956. Its 280,000 employees put it second behind only General Motors. This was a company founded by Thomas Edison and financed by J. P. Morgan. Its scientists and engineers were second to none.

Although IBM always exuded a sense of confidence and command, the thought of the menace posed by RCA and potentially by GE made top executives realize that "Ever Onward" was not merely a song title, it was a necessity. As Watson said, if either of these companies "had decided to hire away some of our best people and commit large amounts of money to this [market], they would have wiped us off the map." IBM was being driven forward not merely by habit or inertia but by what top executives perceived correctly as competitive necessity.

It is notable that Watson focused on the potential loss of "our best people" to larger competitors with deeper pockets who could pay them more. This was smart. People do not show up on a balance sheet along with property, plant, and equipment; but talented engineers and scientists were the most precious asset any competitor in this industry could possess. If GE and RCA hired away IBM's technical people, the game was over.

Let us ask as we have previously: What holds a company together? Money would certainly rank high on any list, and Watson and Williams saw to it that through salary and stock options the people IBM counted on most did not go hungry. But money was not all there was to it. People at all levels want to feel they are doing something important. They want to feel valued. They want to feel like winners playing on a winning team. In short, "psychic reward" is real and counts for a lot. To many of IBM's key people, Watson seemed like a prince. Dad devoted his whole career to telling his troops that the grass was not only green at IBM, it would grow a lot greener with time. Watson understood the value of that attitude, and he built on Dad's heritage.

IBM was well positioned in the computer business in the late 1950s. It was, however, far from safe. The 1956 consulting report inadvertently captures the confusion which abounded in the marketplace:

> The first thing to point out is that the whole field is enormously active. Almost every company in the business is doing what it can to improve its present equipment—to make it more flexible, more reliable, faster, better suited to a great number of applications.
>
> In one sense, electronic computers are more or less in their infancy; but in another, it is unlikely that we shall see any radical change for perhaps ten years or more.

One of the miracles of the consulting business is that clients actually pay for reports that say this sort of thing. The guidance provided above is about as useful as a weather forecaster telling you there is a 50 percent chance of rain. All that can possibly mean is it either will or won't rain, which one knew prior to the forecast. In fact, the prediction that there would be no "radical change" in this industry for a decade or more proved quite wrong.

There were a number of characteristics of the computer market in the late 1950s that bore directly on IBM's position in the industry. The first and perhaps most important was insatiable demand. Even though the barriers to entry in this industry are very high because of the capital required, the essential engineering expertise, and the marketing ability to manage customers successfully, industry incumbents are going to find themselves facing new entrants if demand is sufficiently great. IBM's top management was shrewd to worry about General Electric. Their worries were borne out when GE did, in fact, enter the market.

The second characteristic of the market was that no matter how great the demand, it seemed infinitely segmented. Each company, each university, each arm of the government seemed to want the one "giant brain" which it leased out of the 250 installed in 1956 to do something a little different from the other 249. Communicating with the computers of the 1950s was a task of considerable difficulty. Computers at the time were all about analyzing and processing data. They were not about communication. When Tom Watson Jr. took over IBM, no one had the slightest inkling of something like the Internet. It has been estimated that in 1960, there were "twenty commercial whole systems [architectures] in production or under design . . . in addition to ten whole systems [architectures] in research institutions and universities." Not one of these "commercial whole systems" could interface with another. In other words, there was no compatibility.

In the 1950s, virtually all computers had instruction sets that were literally hardwired into their control logic and arithmetic units. This high degree of interdependence also characterized input/output design, the processor-memory linkages, and all hardware and software interactions. Because the design parameters were so interdependent, each new system had to be designed from scratch; hence every market niche had a different whole system matched to it.

This paragraph captures the heart of the dilemma faced by IBM in the late 1950s; but for those of us not familiar with how computers actually work, the problem is not easy to grasp fully. There is no product quite like a computer, so it is difficult to come up with a commonplace analogy. But let us look at a product which may shed more light on the situation.

Suppose it is the late 1950s, and you are in the market for an automobile. You buy a Chevrolet. Suppose further that you live in Miami, but you decide to move to Boston. You would like to hitch a U-Haul trailer to the rear of your car to bring your belongings up north. Unfortunately, you can't. U-Haul and Chevrolet have not created a coupling device. You will have to ship your belongings to Boston.

You arrive in Boston in July. By December, you have discovered that it snows in Boston as it did not in Miami. You are advised to buy snow tires. There are plenty of tires on the market, dozens of different brands and sizes, but not one of them fits the wheels of your Chevrolet. You are not going to buy new wheels, so you are going to have to chance making it through the New England winter on tires designed for Miami, a city where, if you believe the chamber of commerce, it has never snowed.

The reason it snows in Boston is because it gets a lot colder there than it does in Miami. You are advised to put antifreeze in your engine so the engine block does not freeze and crack. You cannot do so, however, because you discover that Chevrolet has designed the automobiles it has sold in Florida in such a way that they cannot use antifreeze. You now have a real problem.

Let us further suppose that the reason you have moved to Boston is because you have found a job which pays you more money than you made previously. As a symbol of your advancement, you decide to trade in your old Chevrolet, the utility of which you are beginning to doubt anyway, in favor of a Pontiac. You want to stick with General Motors automobiles because of the company's reputation.

The expectation of this kind of migration is, indeed, why General Motors designed its product line as it did. The corporation wanted to create a "car for every purse and purpose"; so if you wanted to move up in class, you would still be a General Motors customer. *Fortune* magazine described GM's product policy as "Chevrolet for the *hoi polloi* . . . , Pontiac for the poor but proud, Oldsmobile for the comfortable but discreet, Buick for the striving, Cadillac for the rich."

You go shopping for a Pontiac but discover to your shock that the differences from the Chevrolet are far greater than the styling of the chassis. Our imaginary Pontiac has only three wheels! Driving it demands considerable retraining. Merely starting the vehicle poses a dilemma. The Chevrolet had a key you turned to ignite the engine. Our Pontiac has a bunch of toggle levers, which you must set in a precise configuration. The configuration varies depending on weather conditions, the number of passengers, the amount of luggage, and the nature of the errands you plan to run.

This three-wheel-drive automobile is ideally suited for the small, snow-clogged streets of Boston. However, when you want to drive back to Miami to visit some friends, you discover that it is not nearly the comfy road cruiser your Chevy was. It is unsteady at high speeds and subject to wind drift when a big truck drives by in the opposite direction.

A consumer facing a set of such dilemmas might well find himself starting to look at other upscale cars. Perhaps he would take a Dodge, DeSoto, or Mercury out for a test drive and find that they are not only more prestigious than his Chevrolet but also easier to drive. Four wheels not three. Keys not toggle levers. Perhaps one of them even has an attachment on the rear for a U-Haul trailer.

Let's add one more ingredient to the mix. Let's say that our motorist never owned that Chevrolet but has leased it. He can return it to Chevrolet in Boston and be done with it. The result is that Chevrolet loses and General Motors loses.

The situation IBM faced with its customers bears some similarities to this automobile story, which is why its executives had plenty to worry about. In the decade from 1952 to 1962, IBM alone produced seven "families of systems—the 1400, 1620, 7030, 7040, 7070, 7080, and 7090." The incompatibility of these systems posed severe problems to customers.

The heart of the difficulty lay in the fact that the computing needs of customers rarely remained static. They grew and changed. If you leased one of the smaller systems for the purpose of, for example, processing your payroll, IBM would provide you with support in programming, training of your data-processing staff, and field service. You would manage your own applications engineering.

If your company grew and your need to process payroll increased, becoming more complex perhaps because of multiple locations of employees, you might need to move to a larger system. Or perhaps you might launch a new product for which not merely payroll but market research data might need analysis. In either case, you would need a bigger machine. But in order to upgrade, you would be responsible for the laborious task of entering all your old customer and accounting information from scratch. None of the applications your staff had programmed for, say, the 1401 or 1410 would be portable to the 7030. Not only did this cost you time and money, you ran the risk of losing precious data or having it corrupted in some way. In the words of Bob O. Evans, who rose from being an engineering manager in the General Products Division in Endicott to become vice president of the Data Systems Division in Poughkeepsie and eventually to become the product champion of the System/360, "User migration from one architecture to another was usually difficult—if possible at all."

This was the key point. IBM did have a product line which

encompassed a wide range of applications; but each time a customer needed something more or something different, there was no way seamlessly to obtain it. There was no "migration." Rather, each upgrade to a new machine family was a leap into the unknown of a machine which was dreadfully complicated and difficult to get information into and out of.

From a marketing standpoint, this leap posed an intolerable problem. The customer now was at a fundamental decision point. He owed it to himself to review all possible options from all possible suppliers. IBM was unable to "lock in" its customers. To the contrary, it had institutionalized a system in which its customers periodically surveyed the market to see if there was a machine out there with a superior price/performance ratio. Why take a chance on what might turn out to be a three-wheeled Pontiac if the dealer down the road had a Dodge on the lot with four wheels on sale and ready to go?

Whoever invented the six-pack carton for Coca-Cola was a genius. Buy a six-pack, and that is five fewer times to make a decision about whether Coke or Pepsi was the order of the day than if that consumer had bought just one bottle.

In addition to encouraging customers to look around, product proliferation was causing serious operational difficulties for IBM. For each discrete processor architecture, the company had to train all the support personnel its customers required. From a manufacturing point of view, product proliferation meant parts proliferation, which posed the danger that manufacturing economies of scale would be sacrificed. Then there was the issue of peripheral equipment. Quoting Evans, "Usually the small volume of sales for any single system or family could not justify a disk or tape drive optimized to that particular architecture. Thus new peripheral devices were suboptimized across differing architectures, and throughput potential was not being realized."

There was simply no question about it. A compatible product line was essential if IBM was both to protect its market against current competitors, to prepare itself for the onslaught of new entrants waiting in the wings, and to maximize the return on its assets. The industry had to be organized, or IBM might get picked apart. Top management understood this by the end of the decade. So did the company's best customers, who "were telling IBM's sales force and top managers in no uncertain terms just how unhappy they were with the growing cost of incompatibility and the expanding complexity of the product line."

The problem was not figuring out that a compatible product line was valuable. The problem was: Was it technically and organizationally possible to create one?

CHAPTER 22

The System/360

"Set your goals high, but not beyond your reach." Those of us who have sat through enough high school graduations have heard that phrase. Now and again—very rarely—a corporation will act on the first clause in that quotation and ignore the second. The corporation will set its sights as high as possible and commit to achieving its goals no matter what. Decision makers will take a deep dive into the unknown for no other reason than that they cannot know all they need to. They may not even be able to know what they do not know. Such executives make the proverbial "bet the company" decision. Lose and you lose everything. Win and you define your industry's future.

The System/360 was one of the two greatest new product introductions in twentieth-century American business history. The other was the Model T Ford. First marketed in 1908, the Model T organized and defined the automobile industry for two decades. It put America on wheels and changed the way the nation lived and worked. The manufacturing method developed for the Model T ("Fordist mass production") is still studied and, in part and under certain circumstances, emulated today.

The Model T's creation was the product of truly extraordinary effort by the most talented mechanics in the industry at the time. It has been said that "work was play" for these men. Had it not been, according to "Cast Iron Charlie" Sorensen, who was there, "it would have killed them. They were as men possessed. They often forgot to eat." To create the System/360, many men also had to work as if possessed. But this launch skirted the edge of catastrophe. In Watson's words, "Building this new line meant putting IBM through tremendous upheavals. Careers were made and broken, and the mistakes we made along the way changed a lot of lives, including Dick's and my own." Watson described the cost of the 360 as "staggering." It was estimated to be more expensive than any other privately financed commercial venture in history.

A *Fortune* magazine article on the System/360 was entitled "I.B.M.'s $5,000,000,000 Gamble." It asserted that the decision to launch the new product line, which was publicly announced on April 7, 1964, "committed I.B.M. to laying out money in sums that read like the federal budget—some $5 billion over a period of four years." Five billion dollars is about 1.6 times greater than IBM's *sales* the year of the 360 announcement.

A word is now in order about Dick's career. IBM World Trade had been flourishing under his leadership in the late 1950s and early 1960s. In 1960, it posted sales of $350 million, greater than the total sales of all of IBM (including World Trade) just nine years earlier. It was growing very fast, at double the domestic rate. In his autobiography, Watson described Dick as a "merry fellow." This phrase jumps out because no man of business whom Watson respected is ever so characterized. T. Vincent Learson's own mother would probably not have described him as a "merry fellow." Remember that Watson thought "nice guys" were dangerous in business. "Harsh, scratchy" types were more to his liking.

When his mother stepped down from the IBM board on the occasion of her seventy-fifth birthday in 1959—and her presence on the board at that age says a lot about corporate governance at IBM—Watson asked Dick to join. He declined Dick's offer to join the board of World Trade, but nevertheless he was drawing Dick into his orbit. "[T]he organizational split between our two companies, which had been quite useful at first, now [i.e., after Dad's death] seemed more like a formality."

Within the family, "Dick and I had never been closer." The two spent a lot of time with their mother. She was fond of Watson, but Dick was her favorite. He built her a summerhouse on his land in New Canaan, and the three of them lived there while the Watson wives and children summered in Maine. (This is not, it is fair to assert, a typical domestic arrangement for men in their forties, both of whom were married and had six children.) IBM moved its top executives from 590 Madison Avenue to a site in northern Westchester County in 1961. Two years later, new headquarters were established on 443 acres in Armonk, also in Westchester and about an hour's drive north of New York. Armonk was not far from the Connecticut homes of the Watsons, and in the early 1960s the two brothers often commuted to work together.

While this coziness was developing, Al Williams and Watson started thinking about succession planning at the top. Williams never wavered in his determination to retire at fifty-five, which meant 1966. IBM would then need a new president. "The most obvious candidate," said Watson, "was my brother." Eventually the company would also need a new CEO. Dad, who remained a living presence for Watson, "had never said so explicitly"; but Watson "had always understood it was [Dad's] wish" that Dick succeed him at the top. Dick was five years younger than Watson, so if he succeeded Williams and then Watson retired "at a reasonable age," Dick would be able to run the company for as much as a decade.

There were a number of good reasons for Dick Watson to figure in IBM succession planning. Foremost among these was the fact that IBM World Trade had done very well under his leadership. Dick had IBM in his veins and was steeped in its culture. He had never worked for another company. It would have been odd if he were not considered.

Dick also had some liabilities as a candidate, however. He had no technical knowledge. Neither, of course, did his brother. But times were changing, and the industry was becoming ever more complex. Tom had to learn how to manage research and development. This was not required of Dick, because World Trade manufactured and marketed products that were created by IBM domestically. Dick's talents were ideally suited to World Trade. He made friends easily, and he had a natural talent for languages, mastering French, Italian, Spanish, and German.

Dick's greatest liability as a potential CEO for all of IBM was his personality. He lacked the innate forcefulness that was simply essential for survival at the top of IBM, never more so than during the protracted crisis which the 360 became. This recessiveness was clear from childhood. When Dad exploded at young Tom, he often (though not always) found a way to fight back. Dick became traumatized.

Alcohol had been an issue for the Watsons ever since Dad's days selling sewing machines for Wheeler and Wilcox from a horse-drawn buckboard in upper New York State. Lessons from those early, youthful days impressed themselves deeply upon Dad's consciousness and, as a result, upon IBM. He never forgot the other salesmen he encountered.

> Cast free from family ties, these men were rootless, hard-eyed wanderers, always on the lookout for the unfamiliar. . . . Travel offered anonymity along with loneliness; and with no accounting to do except to the head office, they elected to do most of their business where they took their pleasure—in saloons.

The Beldens said that Dad "was to do more than any other businessman in America to divorce drinking from business." He was unapologetic about his adamant attitude. When an executive drank, "it is because he is establishing that as part of his policy." At

IBM, as young Tom explained, "[t]he official policy was that employees did not drink during the workday and that no liquor was allowed at IBM gatherings or on IBM property. The unofficial policy was that excessive drinking, even when done on your own time, could ruin your chances of promotion." Employees were known to have been fired for being drunk in public on their own time and off IBM property.

As we have seen, Tom Jr. was on and off the wagon at various times in his life. He was known as a drinker in his collegiate years at Brown; but when Charley Kirk offered him a drink, he turned it down.

Dick had real trouble with alcohol. Whether or not he was an alcoholic, he apparently was a heavy drinker. Perhaps the bottle was an escape for Dick, who, according to Kevin Maney, a recent biographer of Tom Sr., could stand up to neither his father nor his brother. In Maney's view, Dick "never grew up." His success was "manufactured" by his father. Writes Maney, "Dick proved time and again in his IBM career that he had difficulty managing and motivating people. His temper alienated employees, and he would blame others instead of taking charge." Maney quotes Peter Drucker, who knew the Watson brothers, to the effect that "[i]f Dick hadn't been the son of the boss, he would've been a division manager, at best." (We are not told where Tom Jr. would have wound up if he had not been the boss's son.)

These are tough words about a man who had a lot of success running World Trade. Let us assume for the sake of discussion that they are true. If they are, the dilemmas Dick Watson posed to the family and the firm are unsolvable. His revered father had, apparently, wanted him to succeed his brother as CEO of IBM. But what if he was not the best candidate? How would anyone find out? Once this fact (if true) was discovered, how could anyone act on it? Precisely how was Dick Watson going to be denied the leadership of the company his father created and his brother ran? The answer was, as we shall see, by destroying him.

To keep our story as clear as possible, we have to review some IBM chronology. Young Tom took over in 1956, succeeding his father, who in 1914 had assumed control of a three-year-old company which appeared to be a step away from collapse and positioned it at the center of a booming industry. Dad fit well the definition of an entrepreneur as an executive who seizes opportunities without being constrained by resources currently controlled. First in importance in Dad's world was selling; and, along with his teacher, John Patterson at National Cash Register, he transformed the sales function into a vital tool of corporate success. Salesmen have to have something to sell, and Dad developed a fully articulated marketing function around selling. By "marketing," I am referring not only to selling but also to product policy (i.e., what are we going to sell?), pricing, distribution, after-sales service, brand building through advertising and publicity (the 1939 New York World's Fair being a good example), and other activities.

Dad understood the products. Indeed, records of his meetings, as Maney shows, are full of specific questions about the mechanics of the devices IBM leased and sold to customers. He understood the importance of research and development. It was often said at IBM that Dad was the company's chief engineer.

In addition, Dad was a man who believed in thinking big. Time and again, he made "bet the company" decisions. These date back to his earliest days, when he borrowed money for an already deeply indebted CTR. They included his unwarranted optimism after World War I and his production for inventory in the early years of the Great Depression. In both instances, had the market for its products not grown, IBM would have faced a cash-flow crisis and potential bankruptcy. During World War II, IBM increased its factory space by a factor of two and a half. If demand had not exploded after the war, IBM would have been in deep trouble. But demand did grow, and the company had the capacity to satisfy it. In 1947, IBM's sales hit $139 million, two and a half times the 1940 mark and thus nicely matching the increase in factory space.

Young Tom's tenure as CEO, beginning in 1956, had proven as successful as anyone could have hoped. The industry, however, was on the move. Competition was unquestionably going to intensify. The pace of technological change was accelerating at such a rate that Watson did not have the luxury his father did concerning the company's product line. With no formal training, his father could know all he needed to know about the products his company manufactured and marketed. Such knowledge was denied Watson.

Watson could not know the answer to the most important issue facing IBM in 1960, which was the creation of a compatible product line. No one else could either. However, Watson also could not know the answers to the numerous questions which cascaded from this central issue. He could not even know what questions to ask. No one could begin to come to terms with this project, except in the most general way, without advanced technical training. Indeed, you needed more than that. You needed a philosophy about what computers could do. There had to be a touch of the liberal arts leavening the engineering and the science.

Frederick P. Brooks Jr. provides a good example of the rare mix of qualities that were demanded of the creators of the 360. Born in North Carolina in 1931, he did his undergraduate work at Duke, class of 1953, and earned an M.S. and a Ph.D. from the computational laboratory at Harvard in 1956. He started out in IBM that fateful year—the year of Dad's death and the son's assumption of full power—as an engineer in the Poughkeepsie, New York, laboratory. He moved to IBM research at Yorktown Heights, New York, but returned to Poughkeepsie in 1960.

By 1960, Brooks became an outspoken proponent of a new line of computers IBM was developing, the 8000 series. This was at the same time that ideas were coming together for the System/360, with its own champion, Bob Evans.

After tough corporate infighting, the System/360, as we know, won out in May 1961. In a brilliant stroke of what can only be called corporate statesmanship, Evans, the winner, asked Brooks, the loser, to lead the planning the 360 demanded. Brooks was "dumbstruck at being asked to take charge of the juiciest part of his [Evans's] work, namely the new product line." Brooks had early established himself as a man of "candor, prophecy, wit, fervor, and careful preparation." He was a superb technologist, who was to found the computer science department at the University of North Carolina and write a book on software project management for the layperson, *The Mythical Man-Month*, which is a classic and is presently in its nineteenth printing.

In *The Mythical Man-Month*, Brooks explains why the process of software engineering can actually take more time rather than less to complete if more people are assigned to the project. This is a counterintuitive notion. One would assume that if a task takes one competent person a month, two competent people ought to be able to complete it in half the time. However, "oversimplifying outrageously," as he admits, Brooks's law declares that "[a]dding manpower to a late software project makes it later." Why? Because software engineering demands a lot of time-consuming communication among the team members and also because of the sequential nature of debugging. "Men and months are interchangeable commodities only when a task can be partitioned among many workers with no communication among them." Some tasks simply demand "clock time." In an observation that has become famous, Brooks writes, "The bearing of a child takes nine months, no matter how many women are assigned." (Brooks's ability to distinguish between problems that could be solved by massive resource commitment and those that could not was the result of his experience with the 360. I cite Brooks's law to illustrate the kind of intellectual agility needed to navigate the challenges of the 360.)

Brooks was a charismatic man. Evans's decision to transform him from a competitor to a collaborator on the 360 reverberated among IBM's engineers. Many others in the company who were opposed to or at least skeptical about the 360, followed Brooks's lead. During the development of the 360, Brooks had more of an opportunity than anyone in history of discovering the problems of software engineering. The 360 posed problems of a nature and magnitude which at times did indeed appear insuperable. By 1965, Brooks managed two thousand programmers and a $60 million budget in search of solutions to these problems. In short, the complexity of the issues faced in transforming one simple word, "compatibility," into reality were as great as those faced by any business up to that time.

Organizational changes at the highest levels of the corporation were under way by the end of the 1950s, and these changes would help make the big push to the realization of the 360 possible. In May 1959, the development and manufacturing of computers were removed from the Data Processing Division. These critical responsibilities were given to Vice President and Group Executive T. Vincent Learson. His responsibilities were divided into two subgroups, the Data Systems Division (large computers) and the General Products Division (small computers). Marketing remained with the Data Systems Division. For any new product to succeed, it was critical that manufacturing and marketing coordinate their activities harmoniously. They had to be managed with an intimate understanding of the problems each faced. The series of handoffs—from development to manufacturing to marketing to customer service—had to be balletic . . . seamless. No fumbles allowed.

In 1961, Watson moved Al Williams up to the presidency of IBM; and he appointed himself chairman of the board. Watson remained very much the boss. It fell to Learson "to spur IBM's growth rate." To Learson, it was obvious that a compatible product line was essential. He tried to move his organization in that direction, but the engineers who actually had to do the work were not very interested. Each group liked its own product.

When Learson gave orders, he expected results. If he could not get results through sweet reason, then it was time to apply what he called "abrasive interaction." This meant forcing people to take the side of the person against whom they had been fighting. Out of this process eventually evolved the SPREAD Committee. (SPREAD was a code word. It was an acronym for "Systems Programming, Research, Engineering, and Development.") The chairman of the committee was John Haanstra. Haanstra was president of IBM's General Products Division, which produced the 1401 computer, a very successful model. As work on the 360 progressed, he became less enthusiastic about it and "fought a dogged rear guard action, [continuing] to fund new 1400-compatible products through 1963." The company could not "abandon a winner," which is how he felt about the 1401, in favor of a gamble as risky as the 360. This was especially true in light of Honeywell's unexpected announcement on December 3, 1963, of the introduction of its H-200, which targeted the 1401 directly.

Honeywell almost immediately reported more than two hundred orders for its H-200. John Gibson, Product Division head, was getting a lot of pressure from the sales force to respond to the Honeywell attack. With Haanstra's blessing, he scheduled an announcement of the 1401-S in mid-February. Bob Evans, champion of the 360, immediately responded that this would not only divert resources but sabotage the introduction of the new product line, and indeed was contrary to the whole 360 concept.

At a meeting in Poughkeepsie in early February 1964, the 1401-S was scrapped. Evans had won; Haanstra had lost. When these moves were taking place, the 1401 was the largest-selling computer in the world, and "Haanstra was IBM's most rapidly advancing engineer. His self-assurance, exceptional drive, and success in setting and achieving barely reachable goals made him invaluable in the eyes of top management."

Nevertheless, he lost his job as president of the General Products Division early in March 1964. In the words of Professor Carliss Y. Baldwin and Dean Kim B. Clark of the Harvard Business School, he was "banished from the high councils of the corporation." Haanstra remained at IBM for three and a half more years. At the height of the 360 crisis, he was asked to help get the project on track. In August 1967, he became information systems consultant with General Electric, which was now very much in the computer business. Eight months later, he rose to the position of general manager of GE's Information Systems Division. Two years later, he died in the crash of a small airplane he was piloting.

We have been forced to anticipate our story to illustrate just how high this high-stakes game was. Evans had his way because Learson backed him. Learson had his way because Watson backed him. There were, in fact, a host of good reasons for Haanstra's position. But "bet the company" means just that. There could be no sideshows, however appealing. The 360 would demand all IBM's resources. Even then, its success was doubtful for years. To abandon the 1401-S was to sacrifice a certainty for a vision. To use a baseball analogy, it was preferable to swing for the fences than to settle for an intentional walk. Haanstra and the 1401-S were among the many eggs broken to make the 360 omelet.

Let us return now to the SPREAD Committee. The vice chairman and eventual big winner was a man we have already encountered, Bob O. Evans. Also serving on the committee were Fred Brooks and ten other top IBM computer engineers.

During 1961, Learson felt the SPREAD Committee was dawdling. He got impatient, which was not a good sign if you reported to him. The committee began to meet daily. In December Learson told them all to decamp to the Sheraton New Englander Motel in Cos Cob, Connecticut (a little town off the Connecticut Turnpike between Stamford and Greenwich), and not to leave it until they had a plan for a compatible product line. They emerged on December 28, 1961, having produced one of the key documents in the history of computing: "Processor Products—Final Report of SPREAD Task Group."

Things started going wrong immediately. Issues of design for the hardware and software proved more intractable than predicted. The software, considered by itself, was a gigantic knot in a fishing line, with no way to unravel it in sight. The stock market took a nosedive in May, dragging IBM's stock along with it.

The original idea was that there was to be a phased rollout of the 360 over a year and a half, during which IBM's current product line would be retired. Unfortunately, the competition was not cooperating with IBM's plans. IBM's competitors are often mocked in accounts of the industry's history in the 1960s and 1970s. They are ridiculed as the Seven Dwarfs to IBM's Snow White. They did not look that way to IBM in 1963. Its older computers, on which development was being discontinued, were falling technically behind the competition. "By the middle of 1963," reported Watson, "sales offices were sending in panicky reports that they could no longer hold the line against the competition." IBM salesmen in 1963 "panicky" about the competition? Yes, and not without reason. They had to sell inferior products. IBM's growth was 7 percent in 1963 compared to a 15 percent growth in demand for computers.

Seven percent growth is, of course, a lot better than a decline. But, relatively, these results were obviously not very happy. "The only solution," said Watson, "was to get System/360 out the door fast." He was right. That was the solution. But how was it to be accomplished? By throwing more resources at it? That violated Brooks's law.

It was in the midst of this maelstrom—with agitation at every level of the organization, from the laboratories to the factories to the engineers to the sales force to middle management to top management—that Watson and Williams decided it was time to bring Dick from World Trade to corporate. "Our plan," Watson explained, speaking for Williams as well as himself, "was to groom my brother just as Dad had groomed me, and we figured he would need a couple of years in a big job on the domestic side to establish his authority. Then he'd be ready to take Al's place, and eventually mine."

So in 1963, Watson had a heart-to-heart with Dick. Dick was a star at World Trade, he said. But he was also number one in line to succeed Watson. The question was: Did Dick want to stay at World Trade as the "great internationalist," or throw his hat into the ring as possible choice to be CEO? Dick asked for an evening to consider the proposition. The next day he told Tom that he wanted a chance to be chief. "I thought I was being scrupulously fair," wrote Watson. To his credit, he went on to say that "in hindsight it was the worst business and family mistake I ever made. I should never have forced my brother into a horse race with other executives for the top job."

Watson was right. He should have either bestowed the top job upon him, as their father had bestowed it upon young Tom, or decided that Dick did not have it in him to run IBM, and told him so. Did one really want a "merry fellow" running this business?

CHAPTER 23

The Destruction of Dick Watson

IBM announced the 360 on April 7, 1964—"almost exactly fifty years," as Watson, ever mindful of Dad, observed, "after my father came to work at IBM." The announcement was made with all the noise the company could muster. Press conferences in sixty-three cities in fourteen countries, customer briefings for thousands, a chartered train to take reporters from New York City to Poughkeepsie ... the works. Dad would have approved. We do not know when the 360 was given its name, but we do know what the name was supposed to signify:

> One system number, embracing processors with five distinctive engineering designs, would symbolize the singleness of architecture. The integer 360, betokening all points of the compass, would suggest the universal applicability of the new machines, the broad range of price and performance, and the company-wide scope of the undertaking.

Watson, Evans, and Brooks took questions at the Poughkeepsie press conference. To judge from their presentation, things looked pretty good. They announced some high-profile initial customers, including the Bank of America and the NASA Institute of Space Study. Fred Brooks demonstrated one of the models (although at least one component was cannibalized from existing equipment). So 1964 "had its moments of euphoria." It also, however, had its share of crises in terms of competitive counterthrusts and, most important, problems in getting the 360 up and running.

Despite unmistakable indications of very high hurdles to be cleared before the 360 could serve its potential market, Watson's optimism was greater than his misgivings. Now was the time he chose "to bring Dick into the IBM mainstream." Until 1963, Learson had done the whipping and driving needed to make the 360 a reality. Now, Dick was going to be his partner in this effort. Dick was going to manage production; Learson would be in charge of marketing.

How do you think Learson felt about this? Here is what Watson said many years later: "In hindsight I think Vin deeply resented this change, and with reason—the 360 was his product line, and here we [Watson uses the plural because Al Williams concurred in these assignments] were telling him to go out and sell it while we brought my brother in to finish Vin's job." Learson has left us no record of his feelings, but Watson's after-the-fact supposition seems reasonable. It seems so obvious that the question is: Why was hindsight required?

We must also keep in mind, although apparently Watson did not, that not only Dick but also Learson was suddenly "forced . . . into a horse race . . . for the top job." Once again, the problems of the family firm rear their ugly head. Did Learson feel that the horse race was fair, given that the other jockey's last name was Watson and that his father's ghost still stalked IBM's battlements? The last man who rode in such a race wound up dead. His name was Charley Kirk. Learson probably knew this story. He may even have been at the funeral. He had the opportunity to read about Kirk's death because he was an IBM sales executive in 1947, when it took place;

and the funeral was widely covered in IBM publications and noted in the general-circulation press.

Watson himself knew that "Dick had never launched a major product." But now he was parachuting into the middle of the biggest product launch in the company's history, and one of the biggest launches by any company in the twentieth century. Watson rationalized that Dick "had presided over World Trade's complicated factory system in Europe." So what? In the words of a disinterested account of the 360, Dick had "little relevant experience." Learson must have known that. He must have known that if Dick's last name had been Smith or Jones or, for that matter, Learson, he never would have gotten this position, given the poverty of his previous experience in this area.

"I honestly thought I had given Vin the tougher job," said Watson about assigning Learson to marketing and Dick to manufacturing. Here was his thinking:

> The engineering and manufacturing side of the company had tremendous momentum by then [presumably "then" refers to the public launch of the 360 on April 7, 1964], while the sales force was starting from scratch. Not only did they have to turn the tide against our competition, but there was the danger that the 360 would alienate a lot of customers. Those used to their current machines were almost sure to balk at the idea of rewriting their software to work with the new line. Vin's people [i.e., the sales force] had to convince customers to make those conversions, while competitors' salesmen flocked around, saying "Don't convert. Come to us. Convert to us."

Watson summoned Learson and his brother and "lectured them sternly." To Learson he said that IBM would produce whatever the sales force needed to move the merchandise. He told Dick to respond to what the sales force needed.

Watson's misunderstanding of the challenges the company faced was complete. If we assume that he is telling the truth about his perceptions, we see at this point a vivid illustration of the price a high-technology company can pay for having a technological illiterate serving as CEO. The problems with the 360 were only just beginning with the launch announcement. Producing what IBM promised on April 7, 1964, in the volumes required and to customer specifications was a task of horrifying complexity. Selling what IBM had promised was, on the other hand, with a few exceptions, easy.

The company was inundated with orders for the new product. Over 1,100 came in during the first month. Another 1,100 came in the next four months. Thus, in less than half a year, IBM had orders for the 360 equaling a fifth of its computers installed in the United States.

Watson's misjudgment of the market's response to the 360 was as notable as his inability to comprehend how difficult it was going to be for IBM to deliver product in this quantity. Dick Watson had a far more difficult job than Vin Learson. Dick, who probably would have succeeded at selling the 360 (I probably would have as well), was woefully unprepared to solve his engineering and manufacturing dilemmas. In this regard, he had the same professional profile as his brother Tom. Tom Watson could have sold the 360; but it is indeed difficult to believe that the man who needed a tutor at IBM's Endicott training program to help him deal with machines which, compared to the 360, were mere toys—child's play—would have done any better with the problems he dumped in Dick's lap than did Dick.

Did Watson really "honestly" think he had "given Vin the tougher job"? Let us ask another question: Was the job Learson got tougher for him than the job Dick got was for him? That is the important question; and it strains credulity that Watson, had he posed this question to himself, would have said yes. Learson was thoroughly familiar with the 360 from the beginning. He had worked in manufacturing as well as marketing for years at IBM, while brother Dick was out being a "merry fellow" as the "great internationalist." Learson was, moreover, as tough a man as was to be found in corporate America in 1964. No one would have said anything like that about Dick.

By bringing Dick into IBM Domestic at this time and with the responsibility he was given, Watson set his brother up for failure. He later admitted as much. Did he do so knowingly? He says he did not. Is it not true, however, that Watson *should* have known that Dick had very little chance in this horse race with Learson? That is up to you, the reader, to decide.

As the orders for the 360 began to inundate the company, it soon became apparent that delivering on the promise of April 7 was a critical issue. A half a year after the 360 announcement, Watson created a Management Review Committee composed of Al Williams, Richard H. Bullen (the vice president and group executive to whom the corporate staff reported), Learson, and both Watson brothers. Watson had said he favored "contention management." There was plenty of contention in that group. Dick and Learson were not getting along. Neither were Dick and big brother.

For the first time, Dick was reporting directly to Tom on a regular basis. The Management Review Committee met every Monday, and every Monday the five men who comprised it faced problems which seemed beyond solution. These meetings soon got far beyond tense. To use Watson's words, they became "fierce." In those meetings and in other settings, "I went after my brother in the same way I'd have gone after anybody else in that position."

This was precisely the situation which Dad had gone to great lengths to avoid. The reason for Dad's creation of IBM World Trade in 1949–50 had been to protect Dick from the maw of Tom. It was his niche, and the royal road to his success in it was carefully paved. Now he had been removed from that niche. He was a turtle without a shell.

As 1964 moved toward 1965, production shortages continued to worsen. Watson's worries included the impending retirement of Al

Williams. It was one thing for Watson to get rid of you, quite another to walk out on him. Watson offered to make Williams IBM's CEO if he stayed on past his fifty-fifth birthday in 1966. But Williams refused. The fact that Watson's offer meant not that he (Watson) would resign but that he would become Williams's subordinate may have influenced Williams's thinking. "I would be proud to serve under him for the rest of my career," said Watson. "Al knew I really meant it." What Al knew was that this was an exceptionally crazy idea. He would have none of it.

"By some miracle," reports Watson, hundreds of 360s met their delivery dates in 1965. Nevertheless, pressure for production continued, and shortcomings in software made it look as if it would take years to fill some orders. The bottleneck was always some aspect of production. The 360 was bedeviled by shortages. As 1965 progressed, some units were being shipped not fully finished, and stopgap measures meant they could not perform optimally on the customers' premises.

"Vin did a superb job at rallying the sales force and convincing the customers to make the transition to the 360," said Watson. But Vin and his people constantly badgered Dick for various special functions and features. "Dick, for his part, had a go-for-broke attitude. He said yes too many times." Watson said Dick should have told Learson that he was freezing specifications, and Learson was simply going to have to sell what the factory made instead of accepting custom orders for various industries. But what would Watson's reaction to that have been at one of those "fierce" Monday Management Review Committee meetings when Learson told him why they were losing sales? Doubtless the fights would have become "savage, primal, and unstoppable." Just like the good old days with Dad.

Watson had crafted a calamitous managerial situation. We will never know what Learson was actually thinking. What we do know is that every time one of his people sold a computer, he put Dick Watson, his rival for the top job, deeper in a hole. Every time he honored IBM's most hallowed tradition—giving the customer more than he bargained for—that hole got deeper still. The better he did, the worse Dick did. These two men should have been working together. Perhaps Watson should have told them that if the 360 succeeded they would run the company together. If it failed, they would both be through.

Instead, Watson put Learson and Dick on a seesaw. When one was up, the other was down. Learson was always the one who was up. They were getting along so well that, in Watson's words, "the friction [between them] got completely out of hand."

Unsurprisingly, "Dick was not doing well under such tremendous pressure." His staff support was equally frail, responding to the production issues with a flat affect that enraged Watson. Watson sometimes attacked Dick's staff directly. Dick would try to defend them in the same way he was doing everything else—ineffectively.

In the autumn of 1965, everything, reported Watson, "looked black, black, black." In mid-October, Dick informed senior management that a problem at the factory producing integrated circuits (IBM needed so many such components that it had to manufacture them in-house) would delay deliveries by three months.

"I panicked," said Watson; and in yet another passage of admirable candor, he explained, "[M]y thinking became very self-protective. I was fifty-one years old, I had nine years of fantastic success behind me, and I didn't want my career to be wrecked. . . . Under these circumstances, sparing my brother's feelings was the last thing on my mind." That is a clear description of how he acted—as a panicky man who had no interest in his brother's feelings.

The production delays were trouble enough. The more that was learned about what was now frankly being labeled a crisis, the worse things looked. The usually calm numbers man, Al Williams, was becoming "frantic" about IBM's cash position. IBM—which had made its name leading the market for the mechanization of accounting at companies all over the world—had been unable to keep track of the value of its own work-in-process inventory.

Williams "guessed" that this balance sheet item should be valued at $150 million. The information at his disposal was too uncertain for him to be sure. He assigned the task of finding a number everyone could rely on to John Opel, a young executive with the Data Systems Division and a future IBM CEO.

Opel could not figure out what the work-in-process inventory was either. He asked the factory managers, but they did not know. At length, he insisted that managers at each factory take a physical inventory of what was on hand. The air must have been thick with irony. It was as if Tom Watson Sr. had never lived. It was he who understood that business in the twentieth century was to be all about information. That is why he focused on tabulating machines rather than butcher scales or time clocks when he took over CTR back in 1914. Those tabulating machines played a key role in making business more efficient. Yet now, in 1965, just short of a decade after his death, the very company he had created was, in Watson Jr.'s words, cavorting with "clerks with clipboards walking through the factories counting things." Those factories were Dick Watson's responsibility. The need for this procedure could not have made him look worse.

What Opel discovered, after pulling the teeth of a lot of factory managers, was that Williams's estimate was a bit low. In fact, it was low by a factor of four. IBM had about $600 million in factory inventory. The company was running out of cash and was forced to issue $370 million in stock in the spring of 1966.

By the end of 1965, Watson reports, he and Dick were barely on speaking terms. "The more problems we turned up, the quieter he became, just as he had in the old days when Dad and I argued." Watson later graciously conceded that he would have experienced many of the problems Dick did had he had Dick's responsibilities. The difference, he wrote, was that he always had competent staff at the ready. Dick did not.

"Everybody was scared" late in 1965, reported Watson. As we know, Watson believed that "a business is a dictatorship, and that is what really makes it move." Time for a dictator. Learson was the only candidate.

If you have been wondering how you fire your brother from the family business, this is how it is done:

> I called Dick into my office on a gray December afternoon. "I've got to tell you some things that are not very pleasant," I said. "The future of the business depends on the 360. It looks pretty bad now, and I'm going to have to take the whole project and put it under the person I believe is the most competent to bring it out of the woods."

That, of course, was Learson. Dick would become chief of the corporate staff with no line responsibility.

Dick wasn't happy about this arrangement. Watson describes him as "absolutely furious." Apparently the dam of the quietness with which he customarily managed family crises burst on this occasion. Dick said, "In other words, control of this entire business goes to him, and I'm left with some crumbs." From the company's point of view, this was the right decision. Learson sorted things out; and the IBM System/360—his product—was saved.

On January 26, 1966, the board of directors formally appointed T. Vincent Learson president of the International Business Machines Corporation. Al Williams, moving toward his retirement, became chairman of the board's executive committee. (There always seemed to be titles available at the top of IBM for those in need of one.) Watson, of course, remained chairman of the board and boss. Poor Dick became vice chairman of the board and remained chairman of World Trade. This might have looked good to the uninformed, but anyone close to the situation knew he had been humiliated. He stayed away from the office when he could.

Here is Watson's epitaph for the great 360 drama:

> I felt nothing but shame and frustration at the way I'd treated [Dick]. There were so many other ways to have managed things. . . . [W]e remade the computer industry,

and objectively it was the greatest triumph of my business career. But whenever I look back on it [from 1990], I think about the brother I injured, and the dream of my father's [there's Dad again—never far from Watson's thoughts] that I could never make come right.

CHAPTER 24

Denouement for Dick and for Jane

Dick was never again a factor at IBM. His depression was worsened by the death of his mother in the winter of 1966, not long after he had been marginalized at the firm. Dick had been close to her. So another prop was knocked from under the structure of his life.

Dick hung around the company until his resignation in March 1970. Like his brother, Dick had been a Democrat. In 1968, however, he changed sides. He contributed an estimated $44,000 to the Nixon-Agnew campaign, $5,000 to the Republican Party that year, and another $21,000 to the Republican Party in 1970. These were large political contributions in the context of the times, and Dick was referred to as a "major contributor" in the press. His reward was appointment as ambassador to France, a position he assumed on April 16, 1970.

As Dick was leaving IBM, Jane was in the process of dying of cancer. Watson had been estranged from Jane for over a decade, since 1958, when she sold some of her IBM stock two years after he assumed the reins from Dad—"My Joy" as she always called him.

Jane's "illness made hurt pride irrelevant." Watson visited her several times a week during the final stage of the disease. He found her "a solid, thoughtful, tough gal, and she really fought the cancer."

Jane had married John N. Irwin II in 1949. If ever there was an all-American boy, it was Jack Irwin. As Watson described him, "he was tall, attractive, and probably the best dancer I ever saw." Jack neither smoked nor drank (abstention from these two habits was far less common among people of his class a half a century ago than now). He had graduated from Lawrenceville, not far from, but much more prestigious than, the nearby Hun School, Tom's alma mater. Tom, as we recall, was rejected by Princeton. Irwin was not only accepted, he was president of his class (of 1937) for four years in a row and captain of the track team. He then received a B.A. in jurisprudence from Balliol College, Oxford, and a law degree from Fordham. During World War II, Irwin served on General Douglas MacArthur's staff and rose to the rank of colonel.

Needless to say, Watson felt competitive with Jack and envied him. Jane did what she could to provoke and intensify these feelings. When Watson first visited their home, Jane showed him all Jack's trophies. There was "Jack as oarsman, Jack as track star, Jack as this, Jack as that." Jane rubbed Watson's nose in Jack's accomplishments whenever the opportunity presented itself. "Tom," she asked, "did you know that Jack was a *full* colonel?" Jane had to know that there was absolutely no chance on earth that Tom, who had become a lieutenant colonel (which is one grade lower), was not aware of Jack's rank. Tom replied to Jane's question with a small tantrum: "Yeah, of course I know he was a full colonel. But I was the one flying airplanes all over the world."

Watson says that he actually got along fine with Irwin. The problem was not so much Irwin as Irwinism. Dad also used Irwin to provoke his son. "I don't know why you object to your brother-in-law," he would say with an enraging mock innocence. "He is a very thoughtful fellow. He thinks very carefully before he speaks." The obvious but easily disavowed suggestion that young Watson did not conduct himself in such a fashion did not make Tom Jr. very happy.

When it came to acting like infants, the Watson family was second to none.

In 1970, when Jane was dying, President Nixon offered Jack Irwin the position of undersecretary of state. Despite her illness, Jane urged him to take the position. Her health did not permit her to leave their home in New Canaan and join him in Washington, D.C. (The fact that Irwin would leave his wife to take this job tells us all about him that we need to know.) Watson visited Jane often in her last weeks. He may have seen more of her than her ambitious husband did.

This is yet another example of a pattern of behavior which kept repeating itself in the Watson family. When a family member was strong, he or she was the object of envy and discord. When he or she was injured, those emotions were replaced by kindness and gentleness. The Watsons could deal with weakness, not strength.

If humiliation is a worse fate than death, Dick's remaining years were worse than Jane's. Dick's drinking problem apparently began in the wake of the 360 battle. According to one account, Dick at that time "took to brooding. Although he was always in control while at work, he began to drink heavily."

On March 16, 1972, about two years into Dick's tenure in Paris, the political gossip columnist Jack Anderson published an article about Dick's conduct that must have been devastating to him. Entitled "Ambassador Watson's Playboy Ways," the article asserted that Dick was drunk when he boarded a morning flight from Paris to Washington, D.C. He also "appeared to be foaming at the mouth from white tablets he had been chewing. . . . Before the airliner left the runway," wrote Anderson, Dick

> ignored the "No Smoking" sign, propped his feet up on a lounge chair and yelled at the stewardess: "Hey, you! I want a Bloody Mary!"
>
> When she politely declined until the plane was aloft, he shouted at her: "Who do you think you are?" Thereafter, he

called her a "bitch" and "stupid" and threatened to get her fired.

He kept up a holler for Scotch and grabbed at passing stewardesses. Then he tried to stuff $40 down the fronts of their blouses. Finally, he passed out and slept for about three hours.

After the presidency of Bill Clinton, this indiscretion must seem like pretty weak tea. We must remember, however, that this incident took place in the pre-Clinton era. It also happened before the Watergate revelations. However mistaken they undoubtedly were, average Americans were under the impression that high officials of their government comported themselves with at least minimal decorum. The incident was rendered more ironic by Dick's father's world-famous war on alcohol. Now, in a column with a readership of over 70 million and carried by more than three hundred newspapers, this story was published.

There was talk of an investigation by the Senate Foreign Relations Committee and a subcommittee of the House Foreign Affairs Committee. Dick wrote a letter to a member of that subcommittee in which he acknowledged that he took two sleeping pills and ordered several drinks on the flight. "The most one could say," according to his dignified reply to the story, "is that I was exceedingly, and, I think, uncharacteristically, rude."

Congress dropped the matter. Presumably unbeknownst to him, Dick's conduct was brought to President Nixon's attention on March 14, 1972. Nixon wasn't interested. "Look," he said to his chief of staff, H. R. Haldeman, "people get drunk. People chase girls. And the point is, it's a hell of a lot better for them to get drunk than to take drugs. It's better to chase girls than boys. Now that's my position and let's stop this crap. Understand?" Yet, forgiven though he was, this publicity could not have done much for Dick's state of mind.

Shortly after Labor Day in 1972, Dick resigned his position. The article in the *New York Times* reporting the resignation dealt predominantly with the drunken groping incident. The article also mentioned that a successor had not been selected. (Coincidentally, his successor proved to be none other than John N. Irwin II.)

In 1972, Dick rejoined the IBM board, where "he had no real power or authority." He also had seats on a number of other boards. Essentially, however, he was retired.

In 1973, Dick had a heart attack. On July 18, 1974, he took a fall down the marble staircase in his New Canaan home. He was severely injured and lapsed into a coma. His brother at the time was sailing his brand-new "sturdy blue sixty-eight-foot ketch, not huge as yachts go, but the biggest boat I'd ever owned" north of the Arctic Circle off the coast of Greenland.

On July 18, Watson was readying his yacht to leave Egedesminde, a tiny port in northern Greenland, almost literally at the end of the world. Olive was with him (as was a crew). But "the sun never sets on IBM." Even though he had retired as CEO, he still had an office at the company, and his secretary managed to get a telegram delivered to him in that place on that day. The telegram informed him that Dick had fallen in his home. It provided no information about his condition, concluding with the straightforward line "YOU MUST COME HOME." Watson and Olive did so.

They arrived at the Norwalk, Connecticut, hospital "to stand by helplessly" as Dick remained unconscious. He remained in a coma until his death on July 24, 1974. He was fifty-five years of age.

After the funeral, Olive stayed with Dick's wife, Nancy; but Watson returned to his yacht.

> I was in no state to be of help to anybody, and I was afraid to sit idle because I knew my brother's death was going to haunt me. We had never fully healed our relationship after the System/360 crisis. I'd taken actions that had derailed Dick's IBM career, and I blamed myself. . . . My brother had died, and my feelings were so tangled that I didn't know how to mourn him.

Dad had died eighteen years and one month earlier. As always, however, he was a living presence. Speaking of his brother, Tom wrote: "Hard feelings had darkened our relationship for nine years, even though we were the sons of a man who taught his children never to let the sun set on a family argument. Now I saw the terrible wisdom of Dad's belief."

CHAPTER 25

Denouement for Tom

Late on an afternoon in mid-November 1970, Jane Cahill walked into Tom Watson's office at IBM's Armonk headquarters. Watson did not seem terribly happy, which was doubtless not unusual. This particular afternoon, however, he did not seem well. He was resting his head on his desk. Ms. Cahill, his executive assistant, blurted out, "Are you all right?"

Watson said he was fine, merely fatigued. He was tired mentally and emotionally. His sister's medical condition was worsening. He had just learned of the death of a longtime friend, a "merry guy who loved to play practical jokes and always got me to laugh." His friend's funeral was the next morning.

That night, Watson was awakened by chest pain. It was not severe, but it was persistent. His wife, Olive, was away with friends, so he drove himself to Greenwich Hospital, where he spent the night being monitored. The next morning he felt ready to leave. The attending physician told him he would be staying. He was having a heart attack.

"Impossible" was his first thought. "Dad never had a heart attack." His second thought might have been, "I'm not Dad." It wasn't. His father had become woven into his own life to such an extent that when their paths diverged unexpectedly, the divergence caught him by surprise. He did not spend his days figuring that since his father had never had a heart attack, neither would he. His assumption that his life would mirror Dad's was part of who he was.

The years from the announcement of the System/360 in 1964 to Watson's heart attack in 1970 were not without their ups and downs for IBM. Overall, however, one could not have asked for more. Sales and profits were $3.239 billion and $431 million in 1964. In 1970 they were $7.504 billion and $1.018 billion respectively. In 1964, IBM placed ninth on the Fortune 500 (up from eighteenth the previous year). In 1970, IBM ranked fifth, behind only General Motors, Esso (what is today ExxonMobil), Ford, and General Electric. IBM's market capitalization as of January 2, 1970, was $41.5 billion. This staggeringly high number can be compared to $27.1 billion for AT&T, $20.4 billion for General Motors, $13.3 billion for Esso, and $7 billion for General Electric.

Under fifty-four years of Watson management, IBM had become the most valuable business on earth. The System/360 had swept the field:

> In the late 1960s, in the wake of the introduction and rollout of System/360, IBM appeared close to invincible. Its historic competitors were losing money, or at best limping along. Some, like RCA and GE, left the industry entirely; others refocused their businesses and sought to exploit various niches.

The System/360 had proven to be a "compellingly superior product." Its success was so great that it created new problems. Most important among these was the antitrust suit which the U.S. Department of Justice filed on Friday, January 17, 1969, the last business day of the Johnson administration.

United States v. IBM became something of an industry all by itself. It spawned and was supported by various private antitrust actions against IBM. The suit lasted until January 8, 1982, almost thirteen years to the day from its filing. On that date, the government issued a "Stipulation of Dismissal" in which it declared:

> WHEREAS, plaintiff [i.e., the government] has concluded that the case [against IBM] is without merit and should be dismissed . . .
>
> IT IS HEREBY STIPULATED AND AGREED that this case is dismissed without costs to either side.

That phrase "without costs" is easy to include in a legal document. It was accurate insofar as it meant that no fine would be levied as a result of a legal judgment. However, the costs in every other way were very high indeed for IBM. In terms of dollars, IBM's annual legal fees ran into the tens of millions each year of the suit. (In one instance, an attorney billed IBM twenty-seven hours for one day's work. He worked on the case around the clock and picked up an extra three hours on a coast-to-coast flight. This may be unique in the annals of the law.) Those were merely cash costs. The case absorbed thousands of hours of management time. The suit lasted thirteen years. The trial itself lasted six years, beginning in May 1975. Testimony was taken from 974 witnesses. The trial generated some 104,400 pages of transcript. This was only part of the total number of pieces of paper generated by the lawsuit. Here is just one illustration. "IBM's Proposed Finding of Fact, January 1982" was 5,979 pages long. It is said that the government assembled "more than 760 million documents from the company." If IBM's executives billed their hours in the same way their outside counsel (Cravath, Swaine, and Moore) did, the suit's out-of-pocket costs would have been tens of millions of dollars greater.

The trial itself was quite odd. The judge was David N. Edelstein, who had presided over the proceedings that led to the consent decree of 1956, which Watson negotiated. In this trial, for some odd reason, Judge Edelstein had many pages from depositions read aloud in court. Presumably this was because he wanted to hear them. Why he presumably wanted to hear them is one of life's mysteries. I keep using the word "presumably" because the judge left the courtroom during many of these readings. The exercise seems to have been a pure waste of time.

The court costs and the bizarre courtroom conduct were problematic, but they were not the biggest price IBM paid for this legal action. That price can best be thought of as spiritual. Watson was an aggressive, combative man, and he wanted his company to reflect those traits. Thus, "[I]t depressed me to see IBM back in the lawyers' hands. The antitrust case began to color everything we did. For years every executive decision, even ones that were fairly routine, had to be made with one eye on how it might affect the lawsuit."

The suit affected the vocabulary executives could use. Military metaphors were out. "Market share" was out; "market leadership" was okay. IBM developed "sorts of code words and strange uses of language," which to Watson was "mealymouthing. I wanted IBM to be the best in everything and recognized as such, which meant capturing more market share than anybody else. Instead, we were slowly tying ourselves in knots."

The antitrust suit traumatized IBM for more than a decade. The special "code" being developed to deal with normal business situations introduced an element of unreality into the company. IBM seemed to be living in a dense fog on a rocky coast where the noise of the surf and the density of the dismal clouds everywhere made straight talk and frank honesty difficult. Like the seaside fog, the suit was omnipresent, obscuring reality. The thirteen years that suit lasted did a great deal to change IBM's culture.

By 1970, something began happening to Watson that never would have happened to Dad. He was getting bored with business, with the "constant punch, punch, punch of making decisions and pushing IBM ahead—running from crisis to crisis, going to company dinners, visiting plants." He was beginning to daydream about escaping. The 360 was a success beyond all expectations. IBM was a $7 billion company. What more mountains were left to climb?

Watson spent thirty days in the hospital recuperating from his heart attack (quite a contrast from today's medical practice in which physicians are constantly barraged with memoranda from administrators exhorting them to minimize "LOS," "length of stay"). During this period, he had long discussions with his doctor about his condition and his future (another notable contrast with today). In the course of one of these chats, Watson told his doctor that he was planning to go back to IBM and retire in a few years. He did not sound terribly enthusiastic about the prospect.

Watson's doctor asked him bluntly, "Why don't you get out right now?"

This was an interesting moment because it was so similar to that instant back in the spring of 1945 when Watson was discussing his future after the army with his mentor, General Follett Bradley. When Bradley said to him that he always thought Watson would run IBM, Watson reports "I was stunned." When his doctor asked him why he should not get out from under IBM, Watson said, "I was so stunned." Watson needed permission from an authority figure to do what he wanted to do. Without that permission, he seemed incapable of taking his fate into his own hands.

Watson had kept a "secret list of adventures . . . in my desk drawer for years," and he had the list delivered to the hospital. He wanted to have a big yacht designed for him and go sailing. He kept thinking about Captain James Cook. His oppressed brother Dick sent him a large oil painting of a ship entering an English harbor in the nineteenth century. Dick's note read: "I hope this is the biggest get-well card you'll receive." After the history of these two men during the 360, Dick's gift was a remarkable gesture. I think we should take it at face value, rather than interpret it as a subliminal invitation for his brother just to sail away, to get out of town. Watson was on that boat—that was first conceived while he was still in the hospital—when Dick fell down the stairs of his home.

After further recuperation at his home in Greenwich, Watson returned to work; but there was no fire in the belly for it. Soon, he decided to retire. He and Al Williams had formed a plan for Frank Cary to be his successor. But if Watson retired in 1971, Cary, he and Williams felt, would not be quite ready. Thus in June, when Watson decided to resign, he turned IBM over to Thomas Vincent Learson. Learson ran the company for a year and a half, at which time he reached the age of sixty and stepped aside in favor of Cary. Watson himself experienced Learson's tenure as an extension of his own. Although the two did not particularly like each other, their attitudes toward IBM were sufficiently similar and business was so good that "I hardly felt as if I'd given up my power over the company."

Frank T. Cary was a different story. He held an MBA from Stanford and joined IBM in 1948. He came up through sales and marketing. Cary was the consensus choice to lead the company. His style was cool and analytical, far removed from the gut-clutching Watson approach of management by shrieking from crisis to crisis. Watson described Cary's style as "muted." "He didn't make heroic moves and didn't make glaring mistakes; when he ran into a problem he simply figured out how to fix it." With Cary, Watson "had to contend with the fact that the Watson dynasty, after almost six decades, was over." Why none of Watson's children or nieces and nephews ever played a role in IBM remains a puzzle. Just as it went without question that Tom Jr. would follow in Dad's footsteps, it seems to have gone equally without question that no member of the next generation of Watsons would ever run IBM.

In March 1973, two months after Cary took over, Watson invited him to spend a few days at his ski lodge in Vermont and talk about the company. Cary was in no great hurry to make this trip. "I'm sure he expected a bunch of homilies," Watson commented. If so, his expectation was met. "Act like a beggar, feel like a king," Watson told him.

Cary listened and proceeded to run the company with no particular regard to what he heard.

CHAPTER 26

Denouement for IBM

IBM's dominance in the business world grew during the Cary regime (1973–81) and under his successor, John R. Opel (1981–85), who was also strictly an IBM insider. Another lifetime IBM executive, John F. Akers, succeeded Opel and served as CEO from 1985 to 1993. IBM entered the personal computer business in 1981. By 1984, IBM PC sales were about $5 billion. If its PC unit had been an independent company, IBM PC would have ranked seventy-fifth on the Fortune 500.

IBM's sales peaked in 1986 at $68.9 billion. Profits reached an all-time high in 1984 at $6.582 billion. This was more money than any other company had ever made. Employment at IBM hit its record high in 1985, at 405,535. Yet another record was reached on August 20, 1987, when IBM's market capitalization hit $106 billion.

It is difficult to recapture what IBM meant in the quarter century from the introduction of the 360 to the early 1990s. General Motors has been described in the 1940s as "the company of companies in the industry of industries." That phrase fits IBM during its golden quarter century even better. To be sure, there were danger signs. IBM's share of the value being created by the computer industry was declining

in the 1970s and 1980s. But this was easy to ignore amidst the wel-
ter of happy numbers for the company.

Everyone did business with IBM, and IBM was everywhere. In
the late 1970s, more than half the chief information officers at Fortune
500 companies had worked at IBM. More than sixty of those companies had someone from IBM on their board. In Stanley Kubrick's 1968
motion picture *2001: A Space Odyssey,* the computer which controls
everything is named HAL. (Kubrick directed. He coauthored the
screenplay with Arthur C. Clarke.) HAL, of course, is IBM. Each letter of HAL's name is one closer to the beginning of the alphabet than
I, B, and M.

IBM was a clean company that made clean machines which
operated in clean rooms. They were quiet, nonpolluting, mysterious,
and magical. The company was full of smart people, including
Nobel laureates. General Motors was populated by executives who
were right-wingers. Tom Watson was a staunch Democrat, who
became Jimmy Carter's ambassador to the Soviet Union in 1979.
General Motors had to endure strikes. IBM was not even union-
ized. *Fortune* magazine became positively breathless in its praise of
Watson. In 1976, it inducted him into the "Hall of Fame for Business Leadership," labeling him "the most successful capitalist who
ever lived." In 1987, *Fortune* invited Watson to tell its readers of the
"controlled explosion that was IBM under his leadership." The
magazine entitled the article "The Greatest Capitalist in History."

But then, with shocking suddenness, the great edifice collapsed.
Sales held up, but profits wobbled around between 1986 and 1990.
In 1991, the unthinkable: IBM lost money. And not just a little. It
lost $2.9 billion. That was a good performance compared to 1992,
when it lost $5 billion. And that was a good performance compared
to 1993, when it lost $8.1 billion. This was more than any other
company had ever lost. The conventional wisdom in the early 1990s
was that the company was finished.

IBM had prided itself on its no-layoff, lifetime employment policy
for as long as anyone could remember. With collapsing earnings, that

policy was jettisoned. Through layoffs and early-retirement programs, head count was reduced to 256,207 by 1993. This was about 150,000 fewer people than had worked for the company in 1986. Between 1986 and 1993, IBM let go more employees than the total number who had worked for it in 1964, the year the System/360 was announced.

Amid this collapse, IBM's stock, unsurprisingly, was hammered. It hit its nadir on August 16, 1993, when the company's market capitalization was $23 billion. In the six years since August 20, 1987, about $83 billion in wealth (not adjusting for inflation) had simply disappeared.

During the course of 1992, it became apparent to everyone that John F. Akers, the fourth in a line of handpicked successors as CEO, was not capable of turning IBM around. For years, Akers had been practicing what might be called "management by incantation." He declared, for example, that 1987 should be the "Year of the Customer." But this and similar pronouncements were not followed by clear changes in incentives and corporate structure. They were mere words, followed by nothing to transform them into reality.

From the great days of that man of men, Thomas J. Watson Sr., IBM had been known as a song-singing company. The practice was purposely allowed to lapse under the regime of Tom Jr. There were songs once again in 1992, but they were different from "Ever Onward." Here is one about Akers, sung to the tune of a very bad popular song called "Big John":

> *Every morning at Armonk you could see him arrive*
> *In a big fancy car that a chauffeur would drive.*
> *Kind of big in the wallet and narrow in the mind,*
> *And every VP knew how to kiss the behind of Big John.*
>
> *Big John, Big John, Big bad John.*
>
> *Nobody seems to know why John was the boss.*
> *He just never cared about the profit or loss.*

He didn't do much except raise his own pay.
Many earn in a year what he makes in a day, Big John.

Big John, Big John, Big bad John.

Funny? Yes. Cruel? Yes. Productive of anything useful? No.

What went wrong? The answers are so numerous and all-encompassing that when one is finished with them one finds oneself asking if anything went right.

In any industry, value is determined by what the customer wants. So to get a seat at the table of the musical chairs of business, you have to satisfy the customer. That is not easy. Since about 1880, the history of business has been the story of the development of new products and services. We have already alluded to the story of George Eastman. When he became involved in the world of photography in 1877, it was presided over by a priesthood which had mastered this arcane craft. If Eastman had taken a poll in 1877 to find out how many people might want to buy a camera, he would have learned nothing.

Photography became an obsession for Eastman. Over the course of years, working twenty-four-hour days, he came to believe that if you could create a camera that was easy to use, a lot of people would want it. This became his life's work, and he succeeded. In 1900, his company, Eastman Kodak, brought out the Brownie. The price: $1. The advertising slogan explained it all: "You press the button. We do the rest."

It is probably as useful to tell this brief story to explain the collapse of IBM as it is to recount in detail, as has already been done in numerous books, how the computer became faster, smaller, and less expensive. How a new set of entrepreneurs not bound by the traditions and preconceptions of the past worked twenty-four-hour days to create the personal computer. How they outsmarted the priests of the old religion and beat them not at their own game but by changing the rules of the game.

To the old-timers, the conservators who presided over IBM after Watson and Learson retired, to Ken Olsen at the Digital Equipment Corporation, to the gigantic Japanese companies which seemed the only real threat to the hegemony of IBM, the idea that a bunch of children like Bill Gates, Steve Ballmer, Steve Jobs, and Michael Dell might make it possible for everyone to own a computer was simply not one they could understand. Neither Cary, Opel, nor Akers could imagine why anyone would want a computer on his or her desk. No wonder IBM gave DOS away to Microsoft and sold its investment in Intel. IBM bought 20 percent of Intel's stock in 1983 and 1984 with an option to buy another 10 percent. The investment cost almost $400 million. IBM never exercised its option to buy that remaining 10 percent. It sold its Intel stock in 1986 and 1987 for $625 million. If it had held on to that stock and if it had made a similar investment in Microsoft, *Fortune* would have been running articles on John Akers with titles like "The Greatest Capitalist in History." But in the eyes of the decision makers at IBM, Intel and Microsoft were not the vanguard of a revolution. They were suppliers, just like the companies that supplied their carpet cleaners. Bill Gates received letters addressed to "Dear Vendor." Everyone at IBM felt great to get out of Intel with a 50 percent return on its investment. But what if?

If . . . if . . . if . . .

Dozens of books and articles have been published about how smart (and tricky) everyone at Microsoft was and how slow and dumb everyone was at IBM. I have a lot of sympathy for IBM's executives. I well remember the first personal computer I ever owned. The Harvard Business School bought one for everyone on the faculty in the early 1980s. I could make my PC perform two tasks. I could make it sing a song about how great IBM was, and I could make it produce the following message on its tiny screen (which you elevated by putting a block of wood under it): "Error loading driver." I did not know what the error was. I did not know what the driver was. I did not know how to fix the error I had committed loading the driver. I consulted the manual. It contained no information about what to do if there was an error loading the driver.

In a word, the personal computer in its early days was not a machine designed to make its user feel at ease. What the children of the PC era understood that the mainframe gerontocracy did not was that the personal computer could move in that direction. They understood that consumers (even techno-idiots like me) would find value in a PC. They also understood that to capture the value they could create as profit, they had to maneuver themselves and their industry to a point at which they were strong and their competitors were weak.

Three questions must be answered when you look at a business:

1. What does the customer want?
2. Where am I strongest?
3. Where is my competition weakest?

The answer to the first question defines value in the business world. The answers to the second and third questions determine a corporation's ability to extract that value as profit. Microsoft and Intel answered these questions correctly. IBM did not. As a result, "Wintel" is where the profit dollars flowed. Will those dollars flow there forever? Nothing is forever in business.

At any rate, by late 1992, there was widespread talk of breaking IBM up into seven separate companies. What the government had failed to do after a thirteen-year legal action a decade earlier, the company seemed willing to do voluntarily.

There was also a widely publicized search for a new CEO for IBM. For the first time since Watson Sr. came to Computing-Tabulating-Recording from National Cash in 1914, this CEO would come from outside. On January 26, 1993, it was announced that John Akers had decided to retire. A search committee had been formed to look for a successor. Although insiders would be considered, few believed that was anything more than a formality.

The search committee of the board of directors engaged two executive search firms in the hunt for a successor to Akers. Moreover, committee members, including James E. Burke, former CEO of Johnson & Johnson, and Thomas S. Murphy, CEO of Capital Cities/ABC (which is now owned by Disney), had plenty of personal connections of their own in the business world. Dozens of people were approached. It appeared that no remotely plausible candidate wanted the job.

Jim Burke was the chairman of the committee. He was at the time (and remains to this day) one of the most admired business executives in recent American history. Johnson & Johnson grew smartly during his tenure from 1976 through 1989. He will forever be numbered among the greatest crisis managers in business history. As noted earlier, he was running Johnson & Johnson when Tylenol was poisoned in Chicago in September 1982. People were saying the product was finished. He and his team saved it. Tylenol was poisoned again, this time in Yonkers, New York, in February 1986. Burke and his team saved the product again. The search process and the eventual selection of Louis V. Gerstner Jr. to succeed Akers were surrounded by press reports ranging from derision to mockery.

I have seen not one contemporary report that suggested that this man Burke might actually have known what he was doing.

Epilogue

Lou Gestner was born on Long Island on March 1, 1942. He graduated from Dartmouth, where he majored in engineering, and from the Harvard Business School with the class of 1965. He began his business career at the well-known consulting firm McKinsey. He was a senior partner by the age of thirty-two. The next step was to American Express, which he joined in 1977. From there, he became CEO of RJR Nabisco on April 1, 1989. Four years later to the day—April Fool's Day once again—he became CEO of IBM. You could buy a share of IBM that day for $12.93. Its peak in 1987 had been $43.

When Gerstner took the helm, IBM was in free fall. "Only a handful of people," he has written, "understand how precariously close IBM came to running out of cash in 1993." There was a great deal of attention in the press to the fact that in one of the world's most technology-intensive businesses, Gerstner had neither previous experience running a computer company nor any technical expertise. Indeed, referring to Gerstner's previous job running RJR Nabisco, an IBM employee sent him an E-mail warning him of the danger of confusing "microchips with chocolate chips."

Gerstner was also sharply criticized in 1993 for being without a vision for IBM's future. He had no such vision, and he made no secret of the fact. At his first public press conference as CEO, on July 27, 1993, he said, "There's been a lot of speculation as to when I'm going to deliver a vision of IBM, and what I'd like to say to all of you is the last thing IBM needs right now is a vision." This was the most widely quoted remark he ever made. Usually it was quoted, much to his annoyance, without the words "right now."

What we know today is that Gerstner was right. When you are face-to-face with bankruptcy, you do not need a vision "right now." You need cash. And when your business is in that kind of dilemma, a Harvard Business School education and a decade at McKinsey are arguably a more useful background than an intricate knowledge of, say, the physics and technology of semiconductor devices. IBM as a business was face down in the soup when Gerstner took it over. What it needed to be fixed was a businessman's business knowledge. We are talking about a company that in Europe alone had 142 different financial systems, a company that had hired more than seventy advertising agencies. A great deal of the work of saving IBM was going to be "difficult, boring, and painful." "Fixing IBM," Gerstner has written, "was all about execution." Without execution, the greatest vision in the world will lead to nothing more than management by incantation. Akers tried that. It didn't work.

It is beyond the scope of this book to examine IBM's turnaround in detail. Suffice it to say that it was a success as great as the introduction of the 360. Revenue rose from $62.7 billion in 1993, the year Gerstner took the job as CEO, to $85.9 billion in 2001, his last full year on the job (he stepped down as president and CEO on March 1, 2002). This represented an increase of 37 percent. The price of a share of stock rose from $12.72 the day Gerstner took the helm to $120.96 the last day of 2001. This increase of 850 percent far outperformed the averages. IBM seemed well positioned for future growth. It had moved aggressively into services, which accounted for 23 percent of its income in 1992 and 41 percent in 2001.

The question with which I would like to conclude is: To what extent did the heritage of the Watson era cause IBM's decline? Did exorcising the ghosts of the Watsons, father and son, make it possible for the rebirth of the 1990s to take place? The answer to the first question is: To a small extent. The answer to the second question is: No.

To a small extent, the heritage of the Watsons made the job of
their successors (prior, that is, to Gerstner) more difficult. The Watsons were icons. Frank Cary, John Opel, and John Akers (I am
excluding Learson, who served only briefly and as a matter of con-
venience between Watson and Cary) were not. They simply did not
have the stature of their predecessors in the company or the country.
When *Fortune* was celebrating Tom Watson as the greatest capitalist
since the earth was warm, who was writing anything like that about
his successors?

And Watson did not go away. He was on and off the board at
various times. He lived until the end of 1993, and his seaside Greenwich home was not far from Armonk. These men could never
emerge from the shadow of the Watsons. Junior's presence was never
better illustrated than by his showing up in Gerstner's automobile in
April 1993.

That said, the Watsons handed their successors the dominant
firm in the most important industry of its time. The future was
theirs to lose. I do not feel one can blame the Watson heritage for
the fact that their successors did in fact lose it.

As to the second question, concerning the Watson heritage and
the Gerstner turnaround of IBM, that heritage did not hurt him. It
helped him. The best evidence comes from Gerstner himself.

Gerstner speaks of the Watsons with reverence. Early in his
tenure, he made a set of decisions concerning how IBM could be
saved. Discussing these decisions, he observes,

> You could argue that a lot of [them] represented a return to
> IBM's Watson roots. However, to have announced in July
> 1993 a strategy built around past experience would have
> subjected us to gales of laughter that would have blown
> around the world.

Gerstner's insight was fundamental. It is one from which every
great company that finds itself in deep trouble can benefit today and

tomorrow. He implicitly asked himself: How does IBM have to change in order to survive and prosper? But he also asked himself a second, more profound question: What does IBM have to keep in order to survive and prosper? Gerstner's searing insight was that there was rock-solid muscle under the fat at the company. That muscle had been developed during decades of Watson management. The muscle had to be further strengthened while the fat was worked off. To get rid of everything in a company that had dominated its world, which was what the pundits were urging, would have killed IBM.

The problem with IBM was not Watson principles and practices. It was that those principles and practices had ossified. Rather than being living, breathing, flexible guidelines within which creative people could work and be playful at their work, they had degenerated into mere words which had lost their meaning. They were only limiting, never liberating. The shadow remained; the substance had disappeared.

Thus it was that IBM—the company with a history of making big bets, the company that had successfully crossed that chasm from gears to chips and led the world into the electronic age, the company that had launched the industry-transforming System/360—became known by the early 1990s as a firm from which products were not launched. They escaped.

Let me cite one well-known example of the management of the company's Watson heritage out of dozens that could be discussed. This was the fate of IBM's famous dress code. Here is what Gerstner said:

> It was well known throughout business circles that IBM salespeople—or, for that matter, any IBM employee—wore very formal business attire. Tom Watson [Sr.] established this rule when IBM was calling on executives who—guess what—wore dark suits and white shirts! In other words, Watson's eminently sensible direction was: Respect your customer and dress accordingly.

[As times changed], customers changed how they dressed at work, and few of the technical buyers in corporations showed up in white and blue. However, Watson's sensible connection to the customer was forgotten, and the dress code marched on.

When Gerstner got rid of the dress code in 1995, the move received a lot of publicity. Some observers found it deeply meaningful. But for Gerstner, "It was one of the easiest decisions I made—or rather didn't make; it wasn't really a 'decision.'" All he did was recapture "the wisdom of Mr. Watson" by permitting people to "dress according to the circumstances of your day and recognize [whom] you will be with."

Gerstner wanted to throw out the bathwater, not the baby. This is a cliché, but that does not make it something to be ignored.

On December 31, 1993, Thomas J. Watson Jr. died. He was two weeks short of his eightieth birthday. "As I sat in my pew in his memorial service," reflected Gerstner, "I felt strongly that like most other great people who built great things, Tom Watson was at heart an agent of change." Lou Gerstner thus became the first successor to Tom Watson who would do his job without Tom Watson looking over his shoulder.

Gerstner was succeeded as president and chief executive officer of IBM on March 1, 2002, by Samuel J. Palmisano. On January 1, 2003, Palmisano also succeeded Gerstner as chairman of the board. Palmisano had spent his entire career at IBM. Gerstner has said that the single accomplishment he was proudest of was that his successor as boss and all the heads of IBM's major business units are longtime veterans of the company.

IBM survived a near-death experience. It took an outsider to save it by, in part, returning it to its roots.

Notes

Prologue

xi   "animated," "agitated," "angry," save "my company": Gerstner, 37.

Chapter 1: *Defining Moments*

1   The Fair Grounds covered 1,216.5 acres: Applebaum, xiii.

1   "stupendous, gigantic, super-magnificent": *Official Guide* Book, 79.

1   "biggest, costliest, most ambitious undertaking": *Time* quoted in Gelernter, 13–14.

1   "Chamber of Horrors," "dirty Talmud Jew": Gelernter, 291–293.

1   "showroom for the display of goods," "*World Stage*": Marchand, 292.

2   "Futurama," "share our world": Marchand, 301–311.

2   "The IBM is not merely an organization": Watson, *Men*, 82.

2   "are so much broader than anything": *New York Times*, May 2, 1939, 15.

3   "As a demonstration of the latest device": *New York Times*, May 2, 1939, 20.

3   "somewhat programmatic in nature": "International Business Machines," *Fortune* (January 1940), 43.

3   "a bold and potentially constructive step": *New York Times*, May 28, 1939, 7.

3   "Our endeavor has been to increase the interest": *New York Times*, May 28, 1939, 7.

4   "representation by one painter alone," "well enough upon the whole": *New York Times*, May 28, 1939, 7.

4   The IBM contingent headed back to Manhattan: *New York Times,* May 5, 1939, 20.

4   "Home was no longer on the map": Gelernter, 43.

5   "Nobody had seen anything like it": Watson and Petre, 83.

5   "250 Hurt in Crash": *New York Times,* May 13, 1940, 1.

6   "It felt like," "It felt as if": *New York Times,* May 13, 1940, 10.

6   This 66-year-old man: "Thomas J. Watson," "World Readjustments Which Must Be Made," *Think* (June 1940), 14, 48; Fiorello H. La Guardia, "Unless We Have Peace," *Think* (June 1940), 18, 48.

6   Lily Pons and Lawrence Tibbett: *New York Times,* May 14, 1940, 20.

7   "a story on so small a frog": Drucker, 135–136.

7   "Nobody ever forgot": Watson and Petre, 84.

7   "There's a thrill in store for all," "With Mr. Watson leading": Rodgers, 114–115.

Chapter 2: *The Early Years of the "Man of Men"*

9   "engage in the linen business": "The Man: His Ideas and Ideals," *Think* (July, August, September 1956), 4.

10 "with a wider range of interest," "worked and wandered": Rodgers, 17.

11 "Burned Over District": Cross.

11 the lumber business in Steuben County: Dimitroff and Janes, 58.

11 The company was lured to the town of Corning: Dimitroff and Janes, 59–66; Thrall, 259–261.

11 "gentlemen engaged in the building": Neu, 116.

12 A cluster of glass companies: Martin and Martin, 105–108.

12 Amory Houghton's descendants: Dimitroff and Janes, 60–66.

12 he changed his name back: Rodgers, 18.

12 there is more than one account: George Rogers, "Town of Hornby, Steuben County, New York: Genealogies," Town of Hornby personal Web page, December 30, 2001, http://homepages.rootsweb.com/~hornby/W.html (June 26, 2002); Helena Howard, "Chrisjohn Cemetery," Schuyler County, New York, Genweb page, 1999, http://www.rootsweb.com/~nyschuyl/crisjohn.htm (June 26, 2002); and Sackett.

13 Was the family Presbyterian or Methodist?: Belden and Belden, 4; Rodgers, 20.

13 a church-going family: Rodgers, 20.

14   The word travel: Howard, 172.

14   "ego shattering": Rodgers, 30.

14   "The father's lumber business": Rodgers, 19.

15   "a lively, assertive boy," "a suggestion of restraint": Belden and Belden, 8.

15   "He did not go swimming": Rodgers, 20.

15   "brawny," "black beard and dark, angry eyes": Belden and Belden, 7–8.

15   "brusque, stern, domineering, and fiercely attractive": Rodgers, 20.

16   "loved to write his name": Rodgers, 20.

16   he had spent a year studying business: Rodgers, 21.

16   he topped trees: Belden and Belden, 4–5.

17   "you couldn't even raise a disturbance": Belden and Belden, 5.

17   average value of dwellings: Dimitroff and Janes, 92.

18   more than 1,100 canal boats: Martin and Martin, 93–94.

19   "I was absolutely sure," "I was positive": Belden and Belden, 5.

19   some very good advice: Belden and Belden, 11.

19   "I guess my father": Belden and Belden, 6–11.

20   "His fellow villagers would be surprised": Belden and Belden, 12.

20   "a worldly fellow": Belden and Belden, 13.

20   "They say money isn't everything": Belden and Belden, 13–17.

Chapter 3: Watson and National Cash

23   over 110,000 workers: Chandler (1977), 204–205.

24   "managerial revolution in American business": Chandler (1977).

24   Watson betook himself to the Buffalo agency: Rodgers, 29.

25   "I haven't got any orders," "How far away is it?": Belden and Belden, 19.

25   "Any general advice I consider useless": Quoted in Spears, 109.

26   "I know what you're up against": Belden and Belden, 20.

27   "capable of extraordinary, even complete, subordination": Rodgers, 30.

27   Range took Watson out on the road: Belden and Belden, 20–21.

28   "I know you don't [want to make a purchase]": Belden and Belden, 20.

29   "No relatives employed in the business": Tedlow (2001), 208–209.

29   "strong-willed, competent women": Belden and Belden, 24.

30   They came with him to Rochester: Belden and Belden, 24.

31   "What I learned mostly was what not to do," "small words and big ideas": Tedlow (2001), 194.

32 would have nothing in his store not referred to in the bible: Tedlow (2001), 206–207.

32 "incorruptible cashier": Crandall and Robins.

33 Reciting the Lord's Prayer: Crowther, 166–167.

33 "How I Sell National Cash Registers": Friedman (1998).

33 "Don't answer a question": Tedlow (2001), 205–206.

34 "The best way to kill a dog": Belden and Belden, 30.

34 Once he overheard a Hallwood salesman: Tedlow (2001), 191–192.

34 covert operation: Belden and Belden, 30.

35 He opened a store of his own on Fourteenth Street: Tedlow (2001), 192–193.

36 Watson dressed in silk top hat and tails: Belden and Belden, 31.

36 "You have bought this stock": Crowther, 81.

37 "When you go to a town," "You are representing a first-class concern": Crowther, 111.

37 "Don't do all the talking," "Don't remain idle": Tedlow (2001), 205–206.

37 Role-playing occupied an important place: Tedlow (2001), 208.

37 Patterson turned everything he had learned: Tedlow (2001), 208.

38 "Why, that's just the very reason": Crowther, 124.

38 "Standing before an easel," "Kill them...crush them!": Rodgers, 48.

39 Hugh Chalmers: May, 76–79.

39 "He who overcomes others": Crowther, 230.

40 charismatic leadership: For an excellent discussion of charisma in business, see Khurana.

41 set them on fire: Tedlow (2001), 207.

42 Watson's perseverance paid off: Rodgers, 50–54.

Chapter 4: Crime and Punishment

44 "things are not running very well," "I don't like the idea": Tedlow (1996), 435.

45 "Do you really expect?": Kirkland, 323.

45 "His death coincided": Sklar, 16.

45 "American business must henceforth": Chandler, McCraw, and Tedlow, 2-67.

45 "There will be no other king": Sklar, 16.

46 "As the barons of nineteenth century business": Wiebe, 17–18.

46 "Once great men created fortunes": Hofstadter, 236.

46 "from ingenuity to training": Wiebe, 17–18.

46 "untrammeled and untaxed": Josephson, v.

48 "flagrant commercial piracy": *United States v. Patterson et al.* (District Court, S.D. Ohio, W.D., June 26, 1912), 201 *Federal Reporter,* 714.

48 "We are receiving overtures, " "We are determined to absolutely control," "securing a monopoly," "We are going to absolutely control": *United States v. Patterson et al.* (District Court, S.D. Ohio, W.D., March 13, 1915), 222 *Federal Reporter,* 632–634.

49 The bill of particulars included: *United States v. Patterson et al.* (District Court, S.D. Ohio, W.D., June 26, 1912), 201 *Federal Reporter,* 701–704.

50 "Of course, acts of violence": *United States v. Patterson et al.* (District Court, S.D. Ohio, W.D., February 3, 1913), 205 *Federal Reporter,* 301.

51 "You men belong to the walk of life": Belden and Belden, 72–73; Rodgers, 68.

51 Patterson, Watson, Range, and the others were sentenced: *United States v. Patterson, et al,* 201 Fed., 697; 205 Fed., 292; 222 Fed., 299; 238 U.S. 635. District Court of the United States, Southern District of Ohio, Western Division. No. 862. *Decrees and Judgments in Federal Anti-Trust Cases,* 795–797.

51 "I will not be even with the old man": Belden and Belden, 69.

51 His two children cried: Belden and Belden, 72.

52 "only another illustration": Belden and Belden, 74.

52 "I do not consider myself a criminal," "I want to assure you": Belden and Belden, 74.

52 "We, the jury": Rodgers, 59.

53 "tough on competition": Belden and Belden, 63–72.

53 a womb of top executives: Brevoort and Marvel, 4.

54 the only executive in the company making money: Belden and Belden, 41–42.

54 sales manager: Belden and Belden, 50–51.

54 Charles Kettering: Leslie.

55 "immoderate even when right": Belden and Belden, 40.

55 "insisted that his men go": Belden and Belden, 49.

55 "lightning intuition and spontaneity": Belden and Belden, 47.

56 "Do Right": Belden and Belden, photograph following p. 144.

56   fairness with which the law was being enforced: Belden and Belden, 66.
57   "Look, kiddie, I built this business": Tedlow (2001), 203.
58   twice before been engaged: Belden and Belden, 61.
58   "a beautiful young woman": Belden and Belden, 62.
58   "I was hoping you would marry": Belden and Belden, 63.

Chapter 5: *High Water and Hell*

59   "great cyclonic storms," "glowing wire fences": Sealander, 43.
59   Patterson got up on the roof: Sealander, 21.
60   "roaring rivers over fourteen feet deep": Sealander, 45.
60   Three hundred sixty-one people died: Sealander, 45.
60   NCR started building boats: Sealander, 48.
60   "man of the hour": Sealander, 58.
60   "It is a noble work": Belden and Belden, 81.
60   "without my knowledge or consent," "guilty of no crime": Belden and
     Belden, 81.
60   He organized three railroad trains: Belden and Belden, 80.
61   were married on April 17: Rodgers, 64.
61   The home office set strict quotas: Johnson and Lynch, 252–262.
61   most famous of his innovations: Crowther, 261.
61   "stammering a bit": Rodgers, 64.
62   "resignation" of the two: Belden and Belden, 86.
62   "After being systematically humiliated": Rodgers, 64–65.
62   "stunned": Belden and Belden, 86.
62   "could not seem to relate": Rodgers, 66.
62   "In addition to the speculations": Tolstoy, 37.
63   "a source of great satisfaction," "my earnest desire": Watson to Grant,
     November 29, 1913, photocopied in Grant and Denlinger, 25.
63   bizarre superstitions: Friedman (1998), 565–567.
64   "I am proud of you": Johnson and Lynch, facing p. 288.
64   The similarities could be pushed further: Rodgers, 102.
65   "seemed often not to hear praise": Rodgers, 194.
66   "vowed to build a larger and more successful company": Pugh (1995),
     250–251.
66   Sixth Circuit Court of Appeals: *Patterson et al. v. United States* (Circuit
     Court of Appeals, Sixth Circuit. March 13, 1915). [222 *Fed. Rep.* 599]
67   indictment was dismissed: District Court of the United States,

Southern District of Ohio, Western Division. No. 862. *The United States of America, Plaintiff, v. John H. Patterson et al., Defendants* in *Decrees and Judgments in Federal Anti-Trust Cases*, 798.

67   consent decree: *United States vs. National Cash Register Co.* in the District Court of the United States, Southern District of Ohio, Western Division. In Equity No. 6802 in *Decrees and Judgments in Federal Anti-Trust Cases*, 315–320.

67   Justice Department won a suit against IBM: *United States v. IBM Corporation* (13 Fed. Supp. 11; 298 U.S. 131). See also Appeal from the District Court of the United States for the Southern District of New York to the Supreme Court of the United States, October Term, 1935. No. 758. *Opinion* (December 2, 1935). *Decision* (entered April 27, 1936).

Chapter 6: Down and Out

69   "revered Mr. Patterson": Watson and Petre, 14.

69   "whispering" to Patterson: Watson and Petre, 14. For Deeds, see Marcosson (1947).

70    $50,000 cash severance: Rodgers, 66.

70   Frigidaire, Montgomery Ward: Watson and Petre, 15.

71   "always been impressed," "explained this by saying": Watson and Petre, 14–15.

71   approached him with offers: Belden and Belden, 89.

71   early in 1914: Belden and Belden (p. 89) state that Watson met Flint "late in the winter of 1913," but the following year seems more likely.

72   first great merger movement: McCraw, 327.

72   "organizer or industrial expert": Flint, 309.

73   "haphazard organization": Belden and Belden, 92.

73   Tabulating Machine Company was established: Tedlow (2001), 220; Belden and Belden, 92; Engelbourg, 20–27. For Hollerith, see Austrian; Cortada (1993), 44–63; and Pugh (1995), 1–28.

74   "What are you trying to do?" "Ruin this business?" Belden and Belden, 93.

74   "Why did you leave?" "Because Mr. Patterson": Belden and Belden, 93.

74   "Watson was spared having to face": Belden and Belden, 103–104.

75   president and general manager: Computing-Tabulating-Reporting Company, Annual Reports, 1914–1915.

75 "cigar-chomping guys": Watson and Petre, 28.

76 "was most intense," "could press the button": Watson and Petre, 20.

76 "The chances he took with money": Watson and Petre, 16.

76 Senior managed CTR's finances: Watson and Petre, 14–15.

76 "Balance sheets equal the past": Watson and Petre, 14–15.

77 "worry about money": Watson and Petre, 16–17.

77 refused to hedge his bets: Watson and Petre, 16.

77 "strong on prairie virtues," "torture," "I remember incessant arguments," "The door to their bedroom": Watson and Petre, 18–20.

Chapter 7: *Terrible Tommy Watson*

80 "the biggest presence": Watson and Petre, 20.

80 "Terrible Tommy Watson," "Whenever there was trouble": Watson and Petre, 2.

80 "were always a jumble," "Words on a page": Watson and Petre, 6.

80 "Unless you've had such a depression": Watson and Petre, 30–31.

80 "feel protected and loved": Watson and Petre, 20.

81 "All sons at some point": Watson and Petre, 28.

81 "The very idea made me miserable": Watson and Petre, 26.

81 "on a curb thinking," "I can't do it," "Yeah, but I know": Watson and Petre, 26.

81 his sister Jane: Watson and Petre, 4.

82 "Father would be rude": Watson and Petre, 20–21.

82 "Jeannette Kittredge was a full and true partner": Rodgers, 61–62.

82 picture of the two: Rodgers, following p. 192.

83 "I thought she'd stopped," "so shocked," "conscious decision": Watson and Petre, 21.

83 "knew how to loosen up," "Dad loved to ham it up": Watson and Petre, 4.

84 "clean as a whistle," "the next fellow has the same chance," "I do this for two reasons": Watson and Petre, 29–30.

85 "It's fascinating to make fires": Watson and Petre, 5.

85 "warmth and gentleness," "I wish you were better": Watson and Petre, 34.

85 "I figured I was as good as in," "Hun was filled with playboys": Watson and Petre, 35.

85 smoked marijuana once: Watson and Petre, 35.

85 "Academically I was still a zero": Watson and Petre, 36.
86 "I am looking at your son's record": Watson and Petre, 37.
87 "The campus looked run down": Watson and Petre, 41.
87 "I'm Thomas Watson, I run the IBM company," "He's not very good": Watson and Petre, 38.

Chapter 8: Thomas J. Watson Sr. in 1893 and Thomas J. Watson Jr. in 1933

90 "organ wagon": Belden and Belden, 3–4.
90 "I had the sense to know": Belden and Belden, 3.
91 "a really hot-looking black and red Chrysler": Watson and Petre, 35.
91 "before I was even old enough": Watson and Petre, 22.
91 "He had such astonishing brass": Watson and Petre, 28.
92 "who had the money," "Dad never asked," "When we saw each other": Watson and Petre, 41–42.
92 "Oddly, I never knew if I was really rich": Watson and Petre, 42.

Chapter 9: The Searing Insight

94 "Cut the prices; scoop the market": Livesay, 101.
95 "phrases that paid": Donald Sull, "A Strategy to Meet the Challenges of Entrepreneurship," *Financial Times*, August 12, 2002.
97 Hollerith's machines were so successful: Belden and Belden, 109.
99 stand up and cheer: Belden and Belden, 114.
100 "no shadow of a claim": Livesay, 112–113.
100 "a learned German," "they could not afford": Livesay, 114.
101 "We have realized from experience": Pugh (1995), 55.
102 "top for ordinary businessmen": *Time*, April 17, 1939.

Chapter 10: The Watson Way

103 "This business of ours has a future," "It has a past": Watson (1934), 82.
104 "We are not in business for our health": Quoted in Kaplan, 379.
105 "The trouble with everyone": Belden and Belden, 157–158.
106 THINK, OBSERVE, DISCUSS, LISTEN, READ: Watson and Petre, photograph following p. 114; "International Business Machines," *Fortune* (January 1940), 130.
106 "I mean take everything into consideration": Belden and Belden, 158.

106 "died down abruptly": Belden and Belden, 158–159.

107 "My, but those men look nice": Rodgers, 92–93.

107 sent a note congratulating President Roosevelt: Belden and Belden, 128–129.

108 Watson was "vitally interested": Rodgers, 113.

108 "T. J. Watson—you're a leader fine, the greatest in the land," "He's a real father and a friend so true": International Business Machines, *Songs of the I.B.M.* (IBM, 1931).

109 "sustained outbreak of applause": Belden and Belden, 127.

110 Tears would come to his eyes: Rodgers, 119.

111 "stopped speaking," "Now, you men there": Rodgers, 119–120.

Chapter 11: The Big Payoff

113 A look at some numbers: Tedlow (2001), 234, 472.

114 "Working for such a man": Belden and Belden, 147–148.

115 "the most heartbreaking": Belden and Belden, 106.

116 "where engineers explain": Breckenridge (May 31, 1941), 38.

116 "by talking to friendly minor employees": Breckenridge (May 31, 1941), 38.

117 "many hours at Endicott": Breckenridge (May 31, 1941), 38.

117 treated as an "honored guest": Breckenridge (May 31, 1941), 38.

118 "takes the IBM salesman out": Breckenridge (May 31, 1941), 38.

118 "The great argument": Breckenridge (May 31, 1941), 41.

118 "Mine is the one on the left": Mayer, 53.

118 "Already the battle was more than half won": Breckenridge (May 31, 1941), 41.

119 "Why do we have to sign," "We'll send our customer service men around": Breckenridge (May 31, 1941), 41.

120 "This was in the very depths," "Rand must have thought": Watson and Petre, 33.

122 "I could have survived without it": Pugh (1995), 107.

122 He broke ground for a large new research facility: Pugh (1995), 55.

123 "We want you to make money": Crowther, 116–117.

124 the sale of cards was equal to one-fifth: "International Business Machines," *Fortune* (January 1940), 126.

124 the card business was said to account: Belden and Belden, 301.

124 The net result of all this maneuvering: Belden and Belden, 301; Engelbourg, 272–276.

125 "historic function, like that of the most memorable inventions": "International Business Machines," *Fortune* (January 1940), 126.

125 "should find a market for antifriction bearings": Sloan (1941), 24–25.

Chapter 12: *High Time to Grow Up*

127 soloed following a mere five and a half hours: Watson and Petre, 42.

128 "exercised a profound influence on me": Watson and Petre, 49.

128 "their lives became a regular round-robin": Watson and Petre, 43.

128 "Dad's optimism blinded him": Watson and Petre, 55–56.

128 Watson's and IBM's dealings with the Nazis: Black.

129 "I told the president this didn't make sense": Watson and Petre, 433.

130 "I was delighted by this offer," "hard travel and hard work": Watson and Petre, 51.

130 "I love to buy things": Watson and Petre, 63.

130 "make work," "This was a terrible blow": Watson and Petre, 59.

131 "fooling around on Dad's money": Watson and Petre, 59.

131 That evening his mother talked: Watson and Petre, 26.

132 "We must never feel satisfied," "The IBM is not merely an organization": Watson (1934), 97, 83.

134 one of his final stops was at a local saloon: Watson and Petre, 65.

135 "I had to be assigned a tutor," "I spent many nights," "I lacked the force of character": Watson and Petre, 71.

135 "two miserable winters," "perpetually cold and damp": Watson and Petre, 65–66.

136 "nepotism was good for business": Watson and Petre, 75.

136 "handed one of the company's prime," "On the first business day": Watson and Petre, 85.

136 "I felt demeaned," "Everybody knew": Watson and Petre, 85.

136 "curry favor with Dad": Watson and Petre, 76.

136 "never praised me for my work," "We'd be having a casual conversation": Watson and Petre, 79.

137 "sickening self-doubt": Watson and Petre, 76.

138 "astonishingly lovely girl," "earning her own way," "came from a good family," "But I wanted somebody": Watson and Petre, 82.

138 "actually manage to accomplish something": Watson and Petre, 82.

139 "I was free from IBM": Watson and Petre, 87.

139 "high time to grow up," "banging out weddings every fifteen minutes," "I asked my father to be best man": Watson and Petre, 88–89.

Chapter 13: *Watson at War*

141 He saw his father on a number of occasions: Watson and Petre, 112.

142 "The callousness of the Germans": Watson and Petre, 54.

142 "really opened my eyes to Japan's militarism": Watson and Petre, 61.

142 "This means major changes in all our lives": Watson and Petre, 88.

144 "Whenever I'd make a suggestion": Watson and Petre, 92.

145 "This girl I'd married for her beauty and kindness," "your father's going to be here," "when it came to Dad's expectations": Watson and Petre, 94–95.

145 "the wives of generals' aides": Watson and Petre, 97.

145 "I have worked for two great managers," "aerial chauffeur": Watson and Petre, 97–98.

146 "he showed me that I had an orderly mind": Watson and Petre, 98.

147 "terrible fuddy duddy," "got to depend on me": Watson and Petre, 119–120.

147 Dad did not tell Junior: Watson and Petre, 116.

147 "owning and running a small aviation company," "very shrewd," "I always thought you'd go back": Watson and Petre, 126–127.

148 "I concentrated on driving": Watson and Petre, 127.

148 "Tom, you're a fun-loving boy," "I may be coming back," "I'd be delighted": Watson and Petre, 128–129.

Chapter 14: *Father, Son, and Charley Kirk*

149 "was very sensitive about making money": Watson and Petre, 113.

150 "prospective competition for the top jobs": Watson and Petre, 128.

150 "He was the kind of fellow": Watson and Petre, 130.

150 "He came from a rough background": Watson and Petre, 130.

150 Kirk's ascent illustrates that there was a ladder: *Who Was Who in America*, vol. 2 (1950), 301.

150 "prodigious worker," "made a reputation": Watson and Petre, 130.

151 "terrible shock," "I never had anything in mind": Watson and Petre, 130.

151 "All I could think of": Watson and Petre, 131.

151 "I'm sure I shook Kirk's hand," "formed a tight bond": Watson and Petre, 131.

151 "I have to hand it to Kirk," "He treated me fairly," "friendship between Kirk and me": Watson and Petre, 132.

151   "Part of my dislike of Kirk," "wasn't very polished," "raised himself up culturally," "had no impulse": Watson and Petre, 139.

152   Kirk "was not prepossessing looking": Watson and Petre, 137.

152   "before I get a chance at command": Watson and Petre, 143.

152   Senior said he would find a way out: Watson and Petre, 143–144.

153   "There was an absolute ovation," "looked around and just beamed": Watson and Petre, 145.

153   "Kirk and I almost came to blows," "damn mad," "hung right in there," "vehemence of that silly argument," "I'm glad it stopped": Watson and Petre, 145–146.

153   He left his wife: "Charles A. Kirk, 43, IBM Vice President," *New York Times,* June 18, 1947, 25.

153   "Dad felt Kirk's death": Watson and Petre, 146.

Chapter 15: *God Damn You, Old Man!*

156   When Tom and Olive Watson's first son died: Watson and Petre, 110.

156   "For as long as I could remember," "never caused any pain": Watson and Petre, 277.

157   "Your father's stomach looks": Watson and Petre, 272.

158   Nicholas Murray Butler, Dwight David Eisenhower: Rodgers, 201–210.

158   He had been a "buffer": Watson and Petre, 147.

159   "I want you to meet Mr. Alfred P. Sloan," "I'm really dissatisfied": Watson and Petre, 153.

159   "savage, primal, and unstoppable": Watson and Petre, 213.

159   "had a terrible argument," "completely lost my temper," "God damn you, old man!" "ripped my arm away": Watson and Petre, 223–224.

160   "two people could torture each other," "Dad was constantly trying to change me": Watson and Petre, 212.

161   "no illusions about becoming Dad's equal": Watson and Petre, 162.

161   He didn't talk to me about the article," "He never said, 'Great Going!'": Watson and Petre, 239–241.

161   Junior was well aware of this preference: Watson and Petre, 4.

162   "Our worst fights were not at the office," "I'm not sure why I kept doing that," "hellacious": Watson and Petre, 210–212.

162   "I still needed him emotionally": Watson and Petre, 284.

163   "That was the longest nine hours": Watson and Petre, 224.
163   "awful battle," "threw myself on the divan": Watson and Petre, 212.
164   "a source of the old man's pride," "My son tells me," "The vice president thought a while," "We have the finest research organization," "That was the end of him": Watson and Petre, 200.

Chapter 16: Siblings: A Brief Introduction
167   "I am so thankful that God gave me": Rodgers, 102.
167   "If you had to pick who was the strongest": Watson and Petre, 112.
168   Jane sold a million dollars' worth of IBM stock: Watson and Petre, 298–299.
168   "glorify the improbable event": Wall, 397, 687.
168   "I would be willing to hire twenty women": Pugh, (1995), 58–59; Amonette.
169   "considered the corporation an extension of his blood family": *New York Times,* July 27, 1974, 32.
170   Dick was more athletic: Watson and Petre, 173.
171   "looked to me as if Dad": Watson and Petre, 172.
171   "As the youngest in our family": Watson and Petre, 177.
172   "What are you trying to do," "Those words killed me," "They set me up": Watson and Petre, 178–179.
173   Communist economies produced almost nothing: Foreman-Peck, 248–250.
174   *The Power of Positive Thinking:* Robert Sheehan, "What Grows Faster than IBM: IBM Abroad," *Fortune* (November 1960), 170.
175   "Dick had separate but almost equal status": Foy, 41.

Chapter 17: Awakening the Electronic Brain
178   "This war is changing everything": Pugh (1995), 118.
181   "Perhaps most important, the rectangular holes": Pugh (1995), 49–50.
182   The ENIAC could perform five thousand: Watson and Petre, 189.
182   "Having built his career on punch cards, Dad distrusted magnetic tape": Watson and Petre, 194.
184   "we didn't have any idea what we were going to do": Simon.
185   "I remember the ENIAC," "It was made up," "didn't move me at all": Watson and Petre, 136.

185 nineteen noteworthy computer projects: Watson and Petre, 194–195.

185 "You're going to lose your business": Watson and Petre, 192–195.

186 "automatic calculators," "sequence controlled calculators": Pugh (1995), 142.

186 "contrary to widely held perceptions": Pugh (1995), 155.

187 "in terms of components," "They told me that general purpose computers": Hurd quoted in Fisher, McKie, and Mancke, 14. See also Akera.

187 "we would be foolish to spend the time": Fisher, McKie, and Mancke, 13.

187 "no evidence that a machine": Fisher, McKie, and Mancke, 14.

189 "this is a fallacy too absurd": Critchlow, 45.

189 "electronics was the only major issue": Watson and Petre, 205.

190 "By not emphasizing his own early role, Watson, Sr., provided": Pugh (1995), 150.

191 "electronics would cost $3 million": Watson and Petre, 205.

Chapter 18: *Death of a Salesman*

193 "was deferring to me," "serving more as mentor": Watson and Petre, 267.

193 "Protective," "I remember once, on a train": Watson and Petre, 208–209.

194 "Most of the time my life was enriched": Watson and Petre, 208–209.

194 "The old man had bursts of amazing vigor": Watson and Petre, 272–273.

197 "To my friends. My work is done": Brayer, 523.

197 "willed his death by refusing medical treatment": Watson and Petre, 273.

197 "It was a joyous and very sad time": Watson and Petre, 275.

197 headlines in the *New York Times: New York Times,* June 20, 1956, 1, 31.

198 "Overflow Crowd at Brick Church": *New York Times,* June 22, 1956.

198 Sherman M. Fairchild: "Multifarious Sherman Fairchild," *Fortune* (May 1960), 170.

198 "this truly fine American," "I have lost a good friend": *New York Times,* June 20 and 22, 1956.

199 "peculiarly loyal to his past": *New York Times,* June 22, 1956.

199 "look into the future": Pugh (1995), 110–116.
200 "After a decade of saying, No": Brayer, 513–514, 581.
201 "a devotion to sound business principles": Watson (1934), 474–478.

Chapter 19: On His Own

204 "the shock of Dad's death," "I had a horrible allergic reaction": Watson and Petre, 277.
205 "past, present, and future of I.B.M.," "Pop would have wanted it that way": Robert Sheehan, "Tom Jr.'s I.B.M.," *Fortune* (September 1956), 113 ff.
205 "The worst thing that can happen": Watson and Petre, 285.
205 "I didn't realize how much I still needed him": Watson and Petre, 284.
205 "Dad had taught me that a good businessman": Watson and Petre, 300.
205 "the first major meeting IBM": Watson and Petre, 285.
205 "In three days we transformed IBM": Watson and Petre, 285.
206 "never had any pretension about understanding money": Watson and Petre, 159.
206 "The funny thing about Al": Watson and Petre, 250.
206 "most powerful force," "fear of failure": Watson and Petre, 284.
206 "happiest years at IBM": Watson and Petre, caption to photograph following p. 308.
206 Williamsburg conference: Pugh, Johnson, and Palmer, 652–653.
207 "weeding out Dad's yes-men," "fierce, strong-willed decision makers," "would have been eaten alive": Watson and Petre, 286–287.
208 "As showcase UNIVACs began to replace": Pugh, Johnson, and Palmer, 26–27.
208 Learson cut the Gordian Knot: Bashe, et al., 173–178, 342–347; Pugh, Johnson, and Palmer, 23–29; Watson and Petre, 242–243.

Chapter 20: The New Thomas Watson's New IBM

209 "I had a ritual I used to follow": Watson and Petre, 342.
210 "contention management": Watson and Petre, 288.
210 "silenced too many people": Watson and Petre, 152.
210 "Not only did it make staff versus line": Watson and Petre, 288.
211 "air their differences": Watson and Petre, 288–291.

211 "to a level where he could perform well," "we would sometimes strip a man": Watson and Petre, 289.

211 "recycling" of executives: Grove (1988), 172–173.

212 "nice guy you like to go on fishing trips with," "Instead I was always looking": Watson and Petre, 290.

212 "most important contribution," "ability to pick strong," "pretty harsh and scratchy guy," "whatever they did": Watson and Petre, 290.

213 "Lois, I've made a great mistake": Watson and Petre, 158.

216 *Life*: "Busy Days for IBM's Tom Watson," September 30, 1957.

216 *Sports Illustrated*: "Wintertime and the Watsons," December 14, 1959.

216 "would strike me as crises," "totally thwarted and boxed in," "so morose that," "always knew how to make": Watson and Petre, 315.

Chapter 21: *Threats from Without and from Within*

219 "there is a growing market for any device": Little, 33.

219 there were only four computers: Baldwin and Clark, 159.

220 "had decided to hire away": Watson and Petre, 293.

221 Watson and Williams saw to it: Watson and Petre, 289.

221 "The first thing to point out": Little, 55.

222 "twenty commercial whole systems": Baldwin and Clark, 171.

222 "In the 1950s, virtually all computers": Baldwin and Clark, 171.

224 "Chevrolet for the *hoi polloi*": Quoted in Alfred D. Chandler, Jr., and Richard S. Tedlow, *The Coming of Managerial Capitalism: A Casebook on the History of American Economic Institutions* (Homewood, IL: Irwin, 1985), 519.

225 "families of systems": Evans, 4.

225 "User migration from one architecture": Evans, 4; Cortada (1987), 89–91.

226 "Usually the small volume of sales": Evans, 4.

227 "were telling IBM's sales force": Baldwin and Clark, 170.

Chapter 22: *The System/360*

230 "it would have killed them": Hounshell, 23; Sorensen, 45–55.

230 "Building this new line," "staggering": Watson and Petre, 346.

230 "committed I.B.M. to laying out money": Wise (September 1966), 118.

230 Dick as a "merry fellow": Watson and Petre, 344.

231 "The organizational split between our two companies," "Dick and I had never been closer": Watson and Petre, 345.

231 "The most obvious candidate," "had always understood," "at a reasonable age": Watson and Petre, 343–344.

232 "Cast free from family ties": Belden and Belden, 13.

232 "was to do more than any other businessman," "it is because he is establishing": Belden and Belden, 13.

233 "the official policy was that employees": Watson and Petre, 48.

233 "never grew up," "Dick proved time and again," "If Dick hadn't been the son": Maney, 375–379.

234 had the markets for its products not grown: Maney, 293–325.

236 "dumbstruck at being asked to take charge": Pugh, Johnson, and Palmer, 122.

236 "candor, prophecy, wit": Pugh, Johnson, and Palmer, 119–120.

236 "Adding manpower to a late software project," "Men and months are interchangeable," "The bearing of a child": Brooks, 12–26.

237 Brooks managed two thousand programmers: Cortada (1987), 42.

237 "spur IBM's growth rate": Watson and Petre, 348.

237 "abrasive interaction": Watson and Petre, 348.

238 "fought a dogged rear guard action": Baldwin and Clark, 177.

238 "Haanstra was IBM's most rapidly advancing engineer": Pugh, Johnson, and Palmer, 164.

238 "banished from the high councils": Baldwin and Clark, 177.

238 Haanstra remained at IBM: Pugh, Johnson, and Palmer, 432–433.

239 "Processor Products–Final Report": *Annals of the History of Computing,* vol. 5, no. 1 (January 1983), 6–26.

240 "sales offices were sending in panicky reports," "The only solution": Watson and Petre, 350–351.

240 "Our plan was to groom my brother": Watson and Petre, 346.

241 "I thought I was being scrupulously fair," "in hindsight it was the worst": Watson and Petre, 346.

Chapter 23: The Destruction of Dick Watson

243 "almost exactly fifty years": Watson and Petre, 351.

243 "One system number": Pugh, Johnson, and Palmer, 167.

244 "had its moments of euphoria": Pugh, Johnson, and Palmer, 167–171.

244 "bring Dick into the IBM mainstream," "In hindsight I think Vin deeply resented": Watson and Petre, 352.

245 "Dick had never launched a major product," "had presided over World Trade's": Watson and Petre, 352.

245 Dick had "little relevant experience": Pugh, Johnson, and Palmer, 173.

245 "I honestly thought I had given Vin," "The engineering and manufacturing side," "lectured them sternly": Watson and Petre, 352.

246 The company was inundated with orders: Pugh, Johnson, and Palmer, 169.

247 "I went after my brother": Watson and Petre, 354.

248 "I would be proud to serve": Watson and Petre, 355.

248 "Vin did a superb job," "Dick, for his part": Watson and Petre, 356.

249 "the friction between them," "Dick was not doing well": Watson and Petre, 355–356.

249 "looked black, black," "I panicked," "My thinking became": Watson and Petre, 356–357.

250 "clerks with clipboards," "The more problems we turned up": Watson and Petre, 358.

250 "Everybody was scared": Watson and Petre, 359.

250 "a business is a dictatorship": Watson and Petre, 140.

251 "I called Dick into my office," "absolutely furious," "In other words, control": Watson and Petre, 359.

251 "I felt nothing but shame": Watson and Petre, 359–360.

Chapter 24: *Denouement for Dick and for Jane*

253 "illness made hurt pride irrelevant," "a solid, thoughtful, tough gal": Watson and Petre, 391.

254 "he was tall, attractive," "Jack as oarsman," "did you know that Jack," "Yeah, of course I know": Watson and Petre, 184.

254 "I don't know why you object," "He is a very thoughtful fellow": Watson and Petre, 184.

255 "took to brooding": Sobel (1994), 843–845.

255 "appeared to be foaming," "ignored the 'No Smoking' sign": Jack Anderson, "Ambassador Watson's Playboy Ways," *The Washington Post,* March 16, 1972; "Ambassador at Large," *Newsweek,* March 27, 1972, 47, 50.

256 "The most one could say": "Watson Said Report Exaggerated Drinking," *The New York Times,* March 29, 1972.

256 "people get drunk": "Nixon Dismissed Official's Intoxication," *Houston Chronicle,* March 2, 2002; "Maney," *Man,* pp. 439–440.

256 article in the *New York Times* reporting the resignation: "President Accepts Resignation of Watson as Envoy to France," *New York Times,* August 30, 1972.

257 "no real power or authority": Sobel (1994), 845.

257 "sturdy blue sixty-eight foot ketch": Watson and Petre, 403.

257 "the sun never set": Foy.

257 "You must come home," "stand by helplessly," "I was in no state," "Hard feelings had darkened": Watson and Petre, 405.

Chapter 25: Denouement for Tom

259 "Are you all right?" "merry guy who loved to play," "Dad never had a heart attack": Watson and Petre, 392.

260 "In the late 1960s," "compellingly superior product": Baldwin and Clark, 211–212.

261 "Whereas, plaintiff has concluded": *United States v. International Business Machines Corp.,* Civil Action No. 69 Civ. 200 (S.D.N.Y. 1974) (dismissal filed January 8, 1982).

261 worked on the case around the clock, "more than 760 million documents": Carroll, 57.

262 "It depressed me to see IBM," "sorts of code words," "mealy-mouthing," "I wanted IBM to be the best": Watson and Petre, 386.

262 "constant punch, punch": Watson and Petre, 390.

263 "Why don't you get out," "secret list of adventures": Watson and Petre, 393.

263 "I hope this is the biggest get-well card": Watson and Petre, 394.

264 "I hardly felt as if I'd given up": Watson and Petre, 399.

264 "He didn't make heroic moves": Watson and Petre, 395.

264 "had to contend with the fact": Watson and Petre, 399.

264 "I'm sure he expected," "Act like a beggar": Watson and Petre, 400.

Chapter 26: Denouement for IBM

265 IBM PC would have ranked: Chandler (2001), 138.

266 more than half the chief information officers: Carroll, 64.

266 "the most successful capitalist": Max Ways, "The Hall of Fame for Business Leadership—1976," *Fortune,* January 1976, 122.

266 "controlled explosion that was IBM": Watson (1987).

267 "Every morning at Armonk you could see him arrive": Carroll, 329.

269 "Dear Vendor": Carroll, 42.

Epilogue

273 "understand how precariously close IBM came": Gerstner, 66.

273 "microchips with chocolate chips": Gerstner, 81.

273 "There's been a lot of speculation": Gerstner, 68.

274 "difficult, boring, and painful": Gerstner, 64.

274 "all about execution": Gerstner, 71.

275 "You could argue that a lot of them represented": Gerstner, 72.

276 products were not launched: Gerstner, 186.

276 "It was well known throughout business circles," "It was one of the easiest decisions," "Dress according to the circumstances": Gerstner, 184–185.

277 "As I sat in my pew": Gerstner, 102.

Bibliographical Essay

This book is an interpretive essay. I have attempted to look at what is already known about the Watsons and IBM in a new way. The bibliographical essay is designed to list and describe the principal sources upon which I have relied.

The most important source for *The Watson Dynasty* is Thomas J. Watson Jr. and Peter Petre, *Father, Son and Co.: My Life at IBM and Beyond* (New York: Bantam, 1990). This is a lengthy book, 449 pages with a lot of print per page. It provides fine-grained detail not only about Tom Watson Jr.'s professional life but also about his family life. More important, it provides information about how he felt, about the turmoil within him, and the fighting—with his father, his rivals, his neighbors in Greenwich, and his wife—in which he was constantly engaged. Part of Watson wanted fights. Part of him wanted peace. The second part always made way for the first.

I have studied *Father, Son and Co.* and used it with great care. The book provides more information about the inner life and insecurities of a great American business leader than any other ever published. It also contains inaccuracies, omissions, and passages which are simply incomprehensible.

Most of the inaccuracies do not really matter in the big picture, but they do disturb the reader. Here is one example. In discussing the New York World's Fair, Watson (and Petre) write: "The opera stars Grace Moore and Laurence Tibbett sang, and the Philadelphia

Orchestra played Bach, Sibelius—and the IBM Symphony" (p. 84). Grace Moore did not sing on that occasion. Lily Pons did. The headline in the *New York Times* on May 14, 1940, page 20, was "Lily Pons, Tibbett Thrill Fair Crowd." Why mention this? Because Watson Sr. attended the Metropolitan Opera often, tone-deaf though he was. Lily Pons, according to Dad's most recent biographer, Kevin Maney, "was the opera star whom Watson adored."

Opera is an acquired taste. Steuben County, New York, is not Milan. Watson did not grow up with people singing the melodies to great arias all around him. The fact that he "adored" Lily Pons, one of the great performers of her era, of whom there is today an enchanting portrait in the Metropolitan Opera House, leads me to believe that all those nights he attended the opera were not merely for the purpose of being seen there. My guess is that he enjoyed himself. It certainly speaks well of him that he could tell the difference between Lily Pons and Grace Moore.

A small point. But there are other inaccuracies which trouble the reader.

The omissions are more worrisome. Where is Watson's younger sister Helen in his autobiography? The treatment of his brother, Dick, is downright frightening in its honesty. Perhaps no place else in the autobiography are the costs of business greatness and the dangers of a family firm made so clear. Nowhere, however, does Watson mention Dick's alcoholism.

One example of an incomprehensible passage is the caption to a photograph of Watson with Al Williams. The caption is: "My happiest years at IBM were the early 1960s, after Al Williams became president." But it was during the Williams presidency that the System/360 was announced in 1964 and that the crises following it took place.

Thus the book is vital but must be used with caution.

Also essential for the Watson family are Thomas Graham Belden and Marva Robins Belden, *The Lengthening Shadow: The Life of Thomas J. Watson* (Boston: Little, Brown, 1962) and William

Rodgers, *THINK: A Biography of the Watsons and IBM* (New York: Stein and Day, 1969). The most recent biography of Watson Sr. and a book which deserves to be consulted is Kevin Maney, *The Maverick and His Machine: Thomas Watson, Sr., and the Making of IBM* (Hoboken, N.J.: Wiley, 2003). See also the chapter on Watson Sr. in Richard S. Tedlow, *Giants of Enterprise: Seven Business Innovators and the Empires They Built* (New York: HarperBusiness, 2001) and the accompanying footnotes. And see my forthcoming review essay on the books by Watson and Petre, Maney, and Gerstner in the *Business History Review.*

Other sources for Watson's early years and the surroundings in which he spent his youth include local history, such as John H. Martin and Phyllis G. Martin, *The Lands of Painted Post* (Corning, N.Y.: Bookmarks, 1993); Steuben County Bicentennial Commission and historians of the county, *Steuben County: The First 200 Years, a Pictorial History* (Virginia Beach, Va.: Donning, 2002); Thomas P. Dimitroff and Lois S. Janes, *History of the Corning–Painted Post Area: 200 Years in Painted Post Country* (Corning, N.Y.: Bookmarks, 1991); W. B. Thrall, *Pioneer History and Atlas of Steuben County, N.Y.* (Perry, N.Y.: W. B. Thrall, 1942); and Lillian Adams, *Lillian's Hornby: Life in Hornby, N.Y., in the 1800s, Places—Pioneers—Genealogy* (Knoxville, Tenn.: Tennessee Valley Publishing, 2000).

For New York State preceding Watson's birth, see Whitney R. Cross, *The Burned-Over District: The Social and Intellectual History of Enthusiastic Religion in Western New York, 1800–1850* (Ithaca, N.Y.: Cornell University Press, 1950). A recent volume which will become the standard history of New York State is Milton M. Klein, ed., *The Empire State: A History of New York* (Ithaca, N.Y.: Cornell University Press, 2001). See the outstanding bibliographical essay, pp. 737–815. See also Irene D. Neu, *Erastus Corning: Merchant and Financier, 1794–1872* (Ithaca, N.Y.: Cornell University Press, 1960).

For the history of salesmanship in the late nineteenth and early twentieth centuries in the United States, see Walter A. Friedman, *Birth of a Salesman: The Transformation of Selling in America* (Cambridge,

Mass.: Harvard University Press, 2004). See also Timothy B. Spears, *100 Years on the Road: The Traveling Salesman in American Culture* (New Haven, Conn.: Yale University Press, 1995). For the history of the cash register and the biography of John H. Patterson, I relied upon Richard L. Crandall and Sam Robins, *The Incorruptible Cashier: The Formation of an Industry, 1876–1890*, vol. 1 (New York: Vestal Press, 1988); Samuel Crowther, *John H. Patterson: Pioneer in Industrial Welfare* (Garden City, N.Y.: Garden City Publishing, 1926), pp. 166–67; Walter A. Friedman, "John H. Patterson and the Sales Strategy of the National Cash Register Company, 1884 to 1922," *Business History Review*, vol. 72, no. 4 (winter 1998), pp. 552–84; Kenneth Brevoort and Howard P. Marvel, "Successful Monopolization through Predation: The National Cash Register Company," viewed on March 1, 2003, at http://economics.sbs.ohiostate.edu/hmarvel/ncr.pdf; Judith Sealander, *Grand Plans: Business Progressivism and Social Change in Ohio's Miami Valley* (Lexington, Ky.: University Press of Kentucky, 1988); and Roy W. Johnson and Russell W. Lynch, *The Sales Strategy of John H. Patterson* (Chicago: Dartnell, 1932).

For the early history of data processing, see Geoffrey D. Austrian, *Herman Hollerith: Forgotten Giant of Information Processing* (New York: Columbia University Press, 1982) and James W. Cortada, *Before the Computer: IBM, NCR, Burroughs, and Remington Rand and the Industry They Created* (Princeton, N.J.: Princeton University Press, 1993). See also Cortada's useful *Historical Dictionary of Data Processing: Biographies* (New York: Greenwich, 1987).

For the history of computing after World War II, see Paul E. Ceruzzi, *A History of Modern Computing* (Cambridge, Mass.: MIT Press, 1999) and also a book by the world's leading business historian, Alfred D. Chandler Jr., *Inventing the Electronic Century: The Epic Story of the Consumer Electronics and Computer Industries* (New York: Free Press, 2001).

For the antitrust case, the books to consult are Franklin M. Fisher, James W. McKie, and Richard B. Mancke, *IBM and the U.S. Data Processing Industry: An Economic History* (New York: Praeger,

1983) and Franklin M. Fisher, John J. McGowan, and Joen E. Greenwood, *Folded, Spindled, and Mutilated: Economic Analysis and U.S. v. IBM* (Cambridge, Mass.: MIT Press, 1983).

For an understanding of IBM in general and the 360 specifically, the sole-authored and coauthored works by Emerson W. Pugh are invaluable. See Emerson W. Pugh, *Memories That Shaped an Industry: Decisions Leading to IBM System/360* (Cambridge, Mass.: MIT Press, 1984); Emerson W. Pugh, *Building IBM: Shaping an Industry and Its Technology* (Cambridge, Mass.: MIT Press, 1995); Charles J. Bashe, Lyle R. Johnson, John H. Palmer, and Emerson W. Pugh, *IBM's Early Computers* (Cambridge, Mass.: MIT Press, 1986); and Emerson W. Pugh, Lyle R. Johnson, and John H. Palmer, *IBM's 360 and Early 370 Systems* (Cambridge, Mass.: MIT Press, 1991). A unique perspective on the 360 is provided in Carliss Y. Baldwin and Kim B. Clark, *Design Rules: The Power of Modularity*, vol. 1 (Cambridge, Mass.: MIT Press, 2000). See also the classic by Frederick P. Brooks Jr., *The Mythical Man-Month: Essays on Software Engineering* (Boston: Addison-Wesley, 1995).

For the decline of IBM, see Paul Carroll, *Big Blues: The Unmaking of IBM* (New York: Crown, 1993). For IBM's rebirth, see Louis V. Gerstner Jr., *Who Says Elephants Can't Dance? Inside IBM's Historic Turnaround* (New York: HarperBusiness, 2002).

I also made extensive use of articles in newspapers, in general-circulation periodicals, including the *Saturday Evening Post* and especially *Fortune,* and in academic journals such as the *Business History Review* and the *Annals of the History of Computing.*

ENUMERATION OF SOURCES

Books

Adams, Lillian, *Lillian's Hornby: Life in Hornby NY in the 1800s, Places—Pioneers—Genealogy.* (Knoxville, Tenn.: Tennessee Valley Publishing, 2000.)

Allyn, Stanley C., *My Half Century with NCR*. (New York: McGraw-Hill, 1967.) A useful memoir by a former CEO of NCR.

Ambrose, Stephen E., *Eisenhower: Soldier and President*. (New York: Simon and Schuster, 1990.) Some brief information on Watson Sr. and Eisenhower.

Amonette, Ruth Leach, *Among Equals: A Memoir*. (Berkeley, Calif.: Creative Arts Book Company, 1999.) A very interesting book about a pioneering female executive at IBM.

Applebaum, Stanley, *The New York World's Fair, 1939/1940*. (New York: Dover Publications, 1977.) As the title suggests—material on the world's fair.

Austrian, Geoffrey D., *Herman Hollerith: Forgotten Giant of Information Processing*. (New York: Columbia University Press, 1982.)

Baldwin, Carliss Y., and Kim B. Clark, *Design Rules: The Power of Modularity, vol.I*. (Cambridge, Mass.: MIT Press, 2000.)

Bashe, Charles J., Lyle R. Johnson, John H. Palmer, and Emerson W. Pugh, *IBM's Early Computers*. (Cambridge, Mass.: MIT Press, 1986.)

Belden, Thomas Graham, and Marva Robins Belden, *The Lengthening Shadow: The Life of Thomas J. Watson*. (Boston: Little, Brown, 1962.)

Bell, C. Gordon, and Allen Newell, *Computer Structures: Readings and Examples*. (New York: McGraw-Hill, 1971.)

Bernstein, Irving, *The Turbulent Years: A History of the American Worker, 1933–1941*. (Boston: Houghton Mifflin, 1970.) An excellent narrative of the kind of labor troubles IBM did not experience.

Black, Edwin, *IBM and the Holocaust: The Strategic Alliance between Nazi Germany and America's Most Powerful Corporation*. (New York: Crown, 2001.) This controversial book should be supplemented by its review by Professor Henry A. Turner in the *Business History Review* 75 (Autumn 2001), pp. 636–39.

Brayer, Elizabeth, *George Eastman: A Biography*. (Baltimore, Md.: Johns Hopkins University Press, 1996.) The standard biography, full of very interesting material.

Brooks, Frederick P. Jr., *The Mythical Man-Month: Essays on Software Engineering*. (Boston: Addison-Wesley, 1995.)

Bruchey, Stuart, *Robert Oliver: Merchant of Baltimore*. (Baltimore, Md.: Johns Hopkins University Press, 1956.) A useful biography of an American merchant prior to the age of big business.

Campbell-Kelly, Martin, and William Aspray, *Computer: A History of the Information Machine.* (New York: Basic Books, 1996.)

Carroll, Paul, *Big Blues: The Unmaking of IBM.* (New York: Crown, 1993.)

Ceruzzi, Paul E., *A History of Modern Computing.* (Cambridge: MIT Press, 1999.)

Chandler, Alfred D. Jr., *The Visible Hand: The Managerial Revolution in American Business.* (Cambridge, Mass.: Harvard University Press, 1977.) The essential work by the world's leading business historian.

———. *Scale and Scope: The Dynamics of Industrial Capitalism.* (Cambridge, Mass.: Harvard University Press, 1990.) Uniquely valuable comparative history.

———. *Inventing the Electronic Century: The Epic Story of the Consumer Electronics and Computer Industries.* (New York: Free Press, 2001.)

Chandler, Alfred D. Jr., and Richard S. Tedlow, *The Coming of Managerial Capitalism: A Casebook on the History of American Economic Institutions.* (Homewood, Ill.: Irwin, 1985.)

Chandler, Alfred D. Jr., Thomas K. McCraw, and Richard S. Tedlow, *Management, Past and Present: A Casebook on the History of American Business.* (Cincinnati, Ohio: South-Western, 1996.)

Chernow, Ron, *Titan: The Life of John D. Rockefeller, Sr.* (New York: Random House, 1998.) Very useful, and full of interesting details.

Chesler, Ellen, *Woman of Valor: Margaret Sanger and the Birth Control Movement in America.* (New York: Simon and Schuster, 1992.) Useful for enriching an understanding of events in Steuben County.

Christensen, Clayton M., *The Innovator's Dilemma: When New Technologies Cause Great Firms to Fail.* (Boston: Harvard Business School Press, 1997.) An important thesis on the nature and problems of innovation.

Cortada, James W., *Historical Dictionary of Data Processing: Biographies.* (New York: Greenwich, 1987.)

———. *Before the Computer: IBM, NCR, Burroughs, and Remington Rand and the Industry They Created.* (Princeton: Princeton University Press, 1993.)

Crandall, Richard L., and Sam Robins, *The Incorruptible Cashier: The Formation of an Industry, 1876–1890,* vol. 1. (New York: Vestal Press, 1988.)

Critchlow, Donald T., *Studebaker: The Life and Death of an American Corporation.* (Bloomington, Ind.: Indiana University Press, 1996.) A good history of a company that attempted to make a transition from carriage maker to carmaker.

Cross, Whitney R., *The Burned-over District: The Social and Intellectual History of Enthusiastic Religion in Western New York, 1800–1850.* (New York: Cornell University Press, 1950.)

Crowther, Samuel, *John H. Patterson: Pioneer in Industrial Welfare.* (Garden City, NY: Garden City Publishing, 1926), pp. 166–167.

Dassbach, Carl H. A., *Global Enterprises and the World Economy: Ford, General Motors, and IBM, the Emergence of the Transnational Enterprise.* (New York: Garland Publishing, 1989.)

Dimitroff, Thomas P., and Lois S. Janes, *History of the Corning-Painted Post Area: 200 Years in Painted Post Country.* (Corning, N.Y.: Bookmarks, 1991).

Doctorow, E. L., *Ragtime.* (New York: Bantam, 1976.) An interesting novel which sheds light on American big-business executives.

Drandell, Milton, *IBM: The Other Side, 101 Former Employees Look Back.* (San Luis Obispo, Calif.: Quail Press, 1990.)

Drucker, Peter F., "Thomas Watson's Principles of Modern Management." In *Fifty Who Made the Difference.* (New York: Villard Books, 1984.) A useful essay by a very well-known author.

Dyer, Davis, and David Gross, *The Generations of Corning: The Life and Times of a Global Corporation.* (New York: Oxford University Press, 2001.) Useful for the history of Corning in Steuben County.

Eckert, W. J., *Punched Card Methods in Scientific Computation.* (New York: Thomas J. Watson Astronomical Computing Bureau, Columbia University, 1940.)

Engelbourg, Saul, *International Business Machines: A Business History.* (New York: Arno, 1976.) Reprinted doctoral dissertation.

Fisher, Franklin M., John J. McGowan, and Joen E. Greenwood, *Folded, Spindled, and Mutilated: Economic Analysis and U.S. v. IBM.* (Cambridge, Mass.: MIT Press, 1983.)

Fisher, Franklin M., James W. McKie, and Richard B. Mancke, *IBM and the U.S. Data Processing Industry: An Economic History.* (New York: Praeger, 1983.)

Fishman, Katharine Davis, *The Computer Establishment.* (New York: Harper & Row, 1981.)

Flamm, Kenneth, *Creating the Computer: Government, Industry, and High Technology.* (Washington, D.C.: Brookings Institution, 1988.)

Flink, James J., *The Automobile Age*. (Cambridge, Mass.: MIT Press, 1988.)

Flint, Charles R., *Memoirs of an Active Life: Men, and Ships, and Sealing Wax*. (New York: Putnam, 1923.) Not as useful as one would wish.

Foreman-Peck, James, *A History of the World Economy: International Economic Relations Since 1850*, 2d ed. (New York: Harvester Wheatsheaf, 1995.) An authoritative source, suggested to me by my colleague, Professor Geoffrey G. Jones.

Foster, Lawrence G., *Robert Wood Johnson: The Gentleman Rebel*. (State College, Pa.: Lillian Press, 1999.) An excellent biography of the man and of the company, Johnson & Johnson, in which his impact is still felt.

Foy, Nancy, *The Sun Never Sets on IBM*. (New York: Morrow, 1975.) Great title.

Friedman, Walter A., *Birth of a Salesman: The Transformation of Selling in America*. (Cambridge, Mass.: Harvard University Press, 2004.)

Garr, Doug, *IBM Redux: Lou Gerstner and the Business Turnaround of the Decade*. (New York: HarperBusiness, 2000.)

Gelernter, David, *1939: The Lost World of the Fair*. (New York: Free Press, 1995.) A rather strange but thought-provoking book.

Gerstner, Louis V., *Who Says Elephants Can't Dance? Inside IBM's Historic Turnaround*. (New York: HarperBusiness, 2002.) Vital for understanding IBM's recovery in the 1990s.

Grant, Richard H. Jr., and Teri E. Denlinger, *Freewheeling: 80 Years of Observations by the Patriarch of Reynolds and Reynolds*. (Dayton, Ohio: Landfall Press, 1994.) A useful letter from Watson Sr. is reproduced.

Gregory, Frances W., and Irene D. Neu, "The American Industrial Elite in the 1870s: Their Social Origins." In *Men in Business: Essays in the History of Entrepreneurship*, ed. William Miller. (Cambridge, Mass.: Harvard University Press, 1952.) The standard source on the subject after 1952.

Grove, Andrew S., *Physics and Technology of Semiconductor Devices*. (New York: John Wiley and Sons, 1967.) A very important text of the time.

———. *High Output Management*. (New York: Random House, 1983.) Exceptionally interesting.

———. *One-on-One with Andy Grove: How to Manage Your Boss, Yourself, and Your Coworkers*. (New York: Penguin, 1988.) Very witty.

———. *Only the Paranoid Survive: How to Exploit the Crisis Points that Challenge Every Company and Career*. (New York: Currency Doubleday, 1996.) Essential reading for anyone interested in management.

Harrington, Bates, *How 'tis Done: A Thorough Ventilation of the Numerous Schemes Conducted by Wandering Canvassers Together with the Various*

Advertising Dodges for the Swindling of the Public. (Chicago: Fidelity Publishing Company, 1879.) The subtitle says it all.

Harrison, Helen A., *Dawn of a New Day: The New York World's Fair, 1939/1940.* (New York: New York University Press, 1980.)

Hofstadter, Richard, *Anti-Intellectualism in American Life.* (New York: Knopf, 1963.) A Pulitzer Prize-winning study.

Hounshell, David A., *From the American System to Mass Production, 1800–1932: The Development of Manufacturing Technology in the United States.* (Baltimore, Md.: The Johns Hopkins University Press, 1984.) Essential for understanding Ford.

Howard, Donald, *Chaucer: His Life, His Work, His World.* (New York: Fawcett Columbine, 1987.)

International Business Machines Corporation, Annual Reports. (New York, N.Y., and Armonk, N.Y.: IBM, 1912–2002.)

———. *The Electric Tabulating and Accounting Machine Method.* (New York: IBM, 1923.)

———. *Managerial Accounting by Machine Methods.* (New York: IBM, 1934.)

———. *Machine Methods of Accounting: A Manual of the Basic Principles of Operation and Use of International Electric Bookkeeping and Accounting Machines.* (New York: IBM, 1936.)

———. *Thirty Years of Management Briefings, 1958 to 1988.* (Armonk, N.Y.: IBM, 1988.)

———. *IBM Highlights, 1885–1969.* (Armonk, N.Y.: IBM, 2001.)

Johnson, Paul E., *A Shopkeeper's Millennium: Society and Revivals in Rochester, New York, 1815–1837.* (New York: Hill and Wang, 1978.) Important for understanding New York State.

Johnson, Roy W., and Russell W. Lynch, *The Sales Strategy of John H. Patterson.* (Chicago: Dartnell, 1932.)

Josephson, Matthew, *The Robber Barons: The Great American Capitalists, 1861–1901.* (New York: Harcourt, Brace, 1934.) If only this book were as good as its title. . . .

Kaplan, Justin, *Mr. Clemens and Mark Twain: A Biography. (New York: Simon and Schuster, 1966.)* Useful for understanding Twain's relationship with H. H. Rogers.

Kennedy, David M., *Birth Control in America: The Career of Margaret Sanger.* (New Haven, Conn.: Yale University Press, 1970.) Should be used with Chesler's book.

Khurana, Rakesh, *Searching for a Corporate Savior: The International Quest for Charismatic CEOs*. (Princeton, N.J.: Princeton University Press, 2002.)

Kirkland, Edward C., *Industry Comes of Age*. (Chicago: Quadrangle, 1967.) A standard study.

Klein, Milton M., ed., *The Empire State: A History of New York*. (Ithaca, N.Y.: Cornell University Press, 2001.)

Leslie, Stuart W., *Boss Kettering*. (New York: Columbia University Press, 1983.)

Little, Arthur D., Inc., *The Electronic Data Processing Industry: Present Equipment, Technological Trends, Potential Market*. (New York: White, Weld, 1956.)

Livesay, Harold C., *Andrew Carnegie and the Rise of Big Business*, 2nd ed. (New York: Longman, 2000.)

Manes, Stephen, *Gates*. (New York: Touchstone Books, 1994.)

Maney, Kevin, *The Maverick and His Machine: Thomas Watson, Sr. and the Making of IBM*. (Hoboken, N.J.: Wiley, 2003.)

Marchand, Roland, *Creating the Corporate Soul: The Rise of Public Relations and Corporate Imagery in American Big Business*. (Berkeley, Calif.: The University of California Press, 1998.) Outstanding.

Marcosson, Isaac F., *Colonel Deeds: Industrial Builder*. (New York: Dodd, Mead, 1947.)

————. *Wherever Men Trade: The Romance of the Cash Register*. (New York: Dodd, Mead, 1948.)

Martin, John, and Phyllis G. Martin, *The Lands of Painted Post*. (Corning, N.Y.: Bookmarks, 1993.)

Mayer, Martin, *Madison Avenue, U.S.A*. (New York: Harper & Brothers, 1958.)

McCraw, Thomas K., *American Business, 1920–2000: How It Worked*. (Wheeling, Ill.: Harlan Davidson, 2000.) An exceptionally useful survey of history.

McKelvey, Blake. *Rochester, The Water-Power City, 1812–1854*. (Cambridge, Mass.: Harvard University Press, 1945.) This, like McKelvey's other books, is useful for understanding western New York State.

————. *Rochester, The Flower City, 1855–1890*. (Cambridge, Mass.: Harvard University Press, 1949.)

————. *Rochester: The Quest for Quality, 1890–1925*. (Cambridge, Mass.: Harvard University Press, 1956.)

————. *Rochester on the Genesee: The Growth of a City*. (Syracuse, N.Y.: Syracuse University Press, 1973.)

Miller, Arthur, *Death of a Salesman*. (New York: Penguin Books, 1998.) The classic.

Mills, D. Quinn, and G. Bruce Ferizen, *Broken Promises: An Unconventional View of What Went Wrong at IBM*. (Boston: Harvard Business School Press, 1996.)

Mowry, George E., *The Era of Theodore Roosevelt*. (New York: Harper, 1958.) A useful survey.

Mulford, Uri, *Pioneer Days and Later Times in Corning and Vicinity, 1789–1920*. (Corning, N.Y.: Uri Mulford, 1922.)

Neu, Irene D., *Erastus Corning: Merchant and Financier, 1794–1872*. (New York: Cornell University Press, 1960).

Olegario, Rowena. "IBM and the Two Thomas J. Watsons." In *Creating Modern Capitalism: How Entrepreneurs, Companies, and Countries Triumphed in Three Industrial Revolutions*, ed. Thomas K. McCraw. (Cambridge, Mass.: Harvard University Press, 1997.) An excellent case study.

Pugh, Emerson W., *Memories That Shaped an Industry: Decisions Leading to IBM System/360*. (Cambridge, Mass.: MIT Press, 1984.)

———. *Building IBM: Shaping an Industry and Its Technology*. (Cambridge, Mass.: MIT Press, 1995.)

Pugh, Emerson W., Lyle R. Johnson, and John H. Palmer, *IBM's 360 and Early 370 Systems*. (Cambridge, Mass.: MIT Press, 1991.)

Rodgers, William, *THINK: A Biography of the Watsons and IBM*. (New York: Stein and Day, 1969.)

Sackett, Beatrice Wasson, "The Wasson–Watson Genealogy." Revised by Jeannette Stowell Cammen and Matthew Michel Paul Cammen, n.p., 1988.

Sealander, Judith, *Grand Plans: Business Progressivism and Social Change in Ohio's Miami Valley, 1890–1929*. (Lexington, Ky.: University Press of Kentucky, 1988.) Very useful for the history of Dayton and its environs.

Simmons, William W., with Richard B. Elsberry, *Inside IBM: The Watson Years*. (Bryn Mawr, Pa.: Dorrance, 1988.) An informative memoir.

Sklar, Martin J., *The Corporate Reconstruction of American Capitalism, 1890–1916: The Market, the Law, and Politics*. (Cambridge, England: Cambridge University Press, 1988.) Comprehensive and meets the highest standards of scholarship. Vital for understanding its period.

Sloan, Alfred P. Jr., *Adventures of a White Collar Man*. (New York: Doubleday, Doran, 1941.)

———. *My Years with General Motors.* (Garden City, N.Y.: Doubleday, 1972.) This book became a classic.

Sobel, Robert, "Arthur Kittridge Watson" in *Dictionary of American Biography,* supplement nine. (New York: Scribner's, 1994.)

———. *IBM: Colossus in Transition.* (New York: Quadrangle, 1981.)

———. *Thomas Watson, Sr.: IBM and the Computer Revolution.* (Washington, D.C.: Beardbooks, 2000.)

Sorensen, Charles E., with Samuel T. Williamson, *My Forty Years With Ford.* (New York: Norton, 1956.)

Spears, Timothy B., *100 Years on the Road: The Traveling Salesman in American Culture.* (New Haven, Conn.: Yale University Press, 1995.)

Steuben County Bicentennial Commission and historians of the county, *Steuben County: The First 200 Years, a Pictorial History.* (Virginia Beach, Va.: The Donning Company, 2002.)

Stevenson, Howard H., *New Business Ventures and the Entrepreneur,* 5th ed. (Boston: McGraw-Hill, 1999.)

Tedlow, Richard S., *New and Improved: The Story of Mass Marketing in America.* (Boston: Harvard Business School Press, 1996.)

———. *Giants of Enterprise: Seven Business Innovators and the Empires They Built.* (New York: HarperBusiness, 2001.)

Thrall, W. B., *Pioneer History & Atlas of Steuben County N.Y.* (Perry, N.Y.: W. B. Thrall, 1942.)

Tolstoy, Leo, *The Death of Ivan Ilyich.* (Toronto: Bantam, 1981.) The name of the author speaks for itself.

Twenty Years on the Road, or The Trials and Tribulations of a Commercial Traveler. (Philadelphia: Baker and Hayes, 1884.)

Wall, Joseph Frazier, *Andrew Carnegie.* (New York: Oxford University Press, 1970.) A great book, and essential for understanding Carnegie.

Walton, Sam, with John Huey, *Sam Walton, Made in America: My Story.* (New York: Doubleday, 1992.) Very useful.

Watson, Thomas J., *Men—Minutes—Money: A Collection of Excerpts from Talks and Messages Delivered and Written at Various Times.* (New York: International Business Machines, 1934.) Not a man afraid to repeat himself.

———. *"As a Man Thinks . . ." Thomas J. Watson, The Man and His Philosophy of Life as Expressed in His Editorials.* (New York: n. p., 1954.)

Watson, Thomas J., Jr., *A Business and Its Beliefs: The Ideas That Helped Build IBM.* (New York: McGraw-Hill, 1963.)

Watson, Thomas J., Jr., and Peter Petre, *Father, Son & Co.: My Life at IBM and Beyond.* (New York: Bantam, 1990.)

Wiebe, Robert H., *Businessmen and Reform: A Study of the Progressive Movement.* (Chicago: Quadrangle, 1962.) An authoritative monograph.

————. *The Search for Order, 1877–1920.* (Westport, Conn.: Greenwood Press, 1980.) An authoritative synthesis.

Wolfskill, George, *The Revolt of the Conservatives: A History of the American Liberty League, 1934–1940.* (Boston: Houghton Mifflin, 1962.) Useful for understanding the kind of man Watson was not.

Articles

Akera, Atushi, "IBM's Early Adaptation to Cold War Markets: Cuthbert Hurd and His Applied Science Field Men." *Business History Review,* vol. 76, no. 4 (winter 2002), pp. 767–802.

"Ambassador at Large," *Newsweek,* March 27, 1972, pp. 47, 50.

Anderson, Jack, "Ambassador Watson's Playboy Ways." *Washington Post,* March 16, 1972, p. G7. This is the article about Dick Watson.

Aron, Joel D., "Discussion of SPREAD Report, June 23, 1982," *Annals of the History of Computing,* vol.5, no.1 (January 1983).

Breckenridge, Gerald, "Salesman No. 1," *Saturday Evening Post* (May 24, 1941).

————. "Market-Maker: IBM's Watson Proves He's Still Salesman No. 1," *Saturday Evening Post* (May 31, 1941).

Brevoort, Kenneth, and Howard P. Marvel, "Successful Monopolization Through Predation: The National Cash Register Company," viewed on March 1, 2003 at http://ecenomics.sbs.ohio-state.edu/hmarvel/ncr.pdf.

Christensen, Clayton M., Michael Raynor, and Matt Verlinden, "Skate to Where the Money Will Be." *Harvard Business Review* (November 2001).

Evans, Bob O., "Introduction to SPREAD Report," *Annals of the History of Computing,* vol.5, no.1 (January 1983).

Friedman, Walter A., "John H. Patterson and the Sales Strategy of the National Cash Register Company, 1884 to 1922," *Business History Review,* vol. 72, no. 4 (winter 1998), pp. 552–584.

Friedman, Walter A., and Richard S. Tedlow, "Statistical Portraits of

American Business Elites: A Review Essay," *Business History* (forthcoming).

May, George S., "Hugh Chalmers." In *Encyclopedia of American Business History and Biography: The Automobile Industry, 1896–1920*, ed. George S. May. (New York: Bruccoli Clark Layman and Facts on File, 1990).

Simon, Herbert A., "The Steam Engine and the Computer: What Makes Technology Revolutionary," *EDUCOM Bulletin* (spring 1987). Extremely thought-provoking.

Turner, Henry A., Review of Edwin Black's "IBM and the Holocaust: The Strategic Alliance between Nazi Germany and America's Most Powerful Corporation." *Business History Review* 75 (autumn 2001), pp. 636–39.

Usselman, Steven W., "IBM and Its Imitators: Organizational Capabilities and the Emergence of the International Computer Industry." *Business and Economic History*, vol. 22, no. 2 (winter 1993), pp. 1–35.

———. "Computer and Communications Technology." In Stanley I. Kutler, Editor in Chief, *Encyclopedia of the United States in the Twentieth Century*, vol. II. (New York: Scribner's, 1996.)

Watson, Thomas J. Jr., "The Greatest Capitalist in History," *Fortune*, (August 31, 1987).

Wise, T. A., "IBM's $5,000,000,000 Gamble," *Fortune* (September 1966).

———. "The Rocky Road to the Marketplace," *Fortune* (October 1966).

Zaleznik, Abraham, "Managers and Leaders: Are They Different?" *Harvard Business Review*, vol. 55 (1977).

Court Documents

Additional Brief for Plaintiff in Error Thomas J. Watson, on Certain Questions, 6th Circuit (Cincinnati), Records and Briefs, Case 2571, Records of the U.S. Court of Appeals, Record Group 276, National Archives and Records Administration—Great Lakes Region (Chicago).

Brief for the Plaintiffs in Error, 6th Circuit (Cincinnati), Records and Briefs, Case 2571, Records of the U.S. Court of Appeals, Record Group 276, National Archives and Records Administration—Great Lakes Region (Chicago).

Brief for the United States Upon the Facts, 6th Circuit (Cincinnati), Records and Briefs, Case 2571, Records of the U.S. Court of Appeals, Record

Group 276, National Archives and Records Administration—Great Lakes Region (Chicago).

Decrees and Judgments in Federal Anti-Trust Cases, July 2, 1890—January 1, 1918. Compiled by Roger Shale. (Washington, D.C.: Government Printing Office, 1918.)

Transcript of Record, Vols. 1 & 2, 6th Circuit (Cincinnati), Records and Briefs, Case 2571, Records of the U.S. Court of Appeals, Record Group 276, National Archives and Records Administration—Great Lakes Region (Chicago).

United States v Patterson et al. (District Court, S.D. Ohio, W.D., February 3, 1913), 205 *Federal Reporter,* 301.

Periodicals Consulted

Annals of the History of Computing
Business History Review
Business Week
Corning Journal
Corning Leader
Datamation
Dun's Review
Forbes
Fortune
Life
New York Times
Newsweek
Saturday Evening Post
Sports Illustrated
Think (New York: IBM)
Time
Wall Street Journal
Washington Post

Reference Sources

American Men and Women of Science. (New York: Bowker.)
Current Biography. (New York: H. W. Wilson.)

Dictionary of American Biography. (New York: Scribner's.)

Encyclopedia of American Biography. (New York: American Historical Company, 1957.)

Garraty, John A., and Mark C. Carnes. *American National Biography.* (New York: Oxford University Press, 1999.)

Ingham, John N. *Biographical Dictionary of American Business Leaders.* (Westport, Conn.: Greenwood Press, 1983.)

Moody's Industrial Manual. (New York: Moody's Investors Service.)

National Cyclopaedia of American Biography. (New York: J. T. White.)

Trow's New York City Directory. (New York: J. F. Trow.)

Who Was Who in America. (Chicago: Marquis Who's Who.)

Who's Who in America. (Chicago: Marquis Who's Who.)

Databases

ABI/ProQuest

Biography and Genealogy Master Index

Compustat

CRSP

Datastream

Factiva

LEXIS-NEXIS Academic Universe

Local historians in Corning, N.Y.; Greenwich, Conn.; New Canaan, Conn.; and Short Hills, N.J., contributed their assistance.

Principal Sources by Chapter

This book has drawn on many sources. In this section, I list the most important sources by chapter. These sources are the places to go if you would like more information about specific points.

Prologue
Gerstner (2002)

Chapter 1: Defining Moments
For the New York World's Fair: Applebaum (1977), Gelernter (1995). For LaGuardia and Germany: Marchand (1998), *Guide Book* (1939). Watson quotation: *Men* (1934). For Drucker's comment: Drucker (1984). For Young Tom's comments: Watson and Petre (1990). IBM songs: Rodgers (1969). See also contemporary articles in the *New York Times* (hereafter, *NYT*).

Chapter 2: The Early Years of the "Man of Men"
For Watson's background: *THINK* magazine (1956), Rodgers (1969), the Steuben County local histories, Cross (1950), Klein (2001), Neu (1960), Belden and Belden (1962). For Watson Sr.'s father: Belden and Belden (1962) and Rodgers (1969). This chapter as a whole relies heavily on the Belden account.

Chapter 3: Watson and National Cash
For big business: Chandler (1977). For Watson and Range:

Belden and Belden (1962). For salesmanship: Friedman (forthcoming) and Spears (1995). This chapter relies on the Beldens and Rodgers for Watson's education as a salesman. For Watson's sisters and his household: Belden and Belden (1962). For Patterson: Crowther (1926) is the principal source. See also: Friedman (1998), Belden and Belden (1962), Rodgers (1969), Johnson and Lynch (1932), Marcosson (1948), Crandall and Robins (1998), Watson and Petre (1990), and Tedlow (2001). For Watson's aggressive sales tactics: Belden and Belden (1962). For Watson and the second-hand cash register scam: Belden and Belden (1962), Tedlow (2001). For Patterson's purchase of NCR: Crowther (1926). For the *Primer* and the "Do's" and "Don'ts": Crowther (1926) and Tedlow (2001). For Patterson's sales harangues: Crowther (1926). For Watson's original estrangement from and reconciliation with Patterson: Rodgers (1969) and Tedlow (2001), with accompanying footnotes.

Chapter 4: *Crime and Punishment*

For the spirit of the times: Kirkland (1961), Sklar (1988), Wiebe (1962 and 1980), Miller (1952), Josephson, unavoidably (1934), and Friedman and Tedlow (forthcoming). For the Asher quote: Tedlow (1996). For the trial: see *United States vs. Patterson et al* (1913) and other legal records cited above in "Court Documents." Belden and Belden (1962) was once again very useful in setting the stage for the trial from Watson's point of view and in illustrating how Watson managed himself during the trial as well as after it. The book is also the source for the issue of the fairness of the prosecution and much of the material on Watson's success prior to the case and for his budding relationship with his bride-to-be. For the Revson quote: Tedlow (2001).

Chapter 5: *High Water and Hell*

For Dayton in 1913: Sealander (1988). For Patterson and the flood: Belden and Belden (1962). For the Watson/Kittredge marriage: Rodgers (1969). For the Patterson sales system Crowther

(1926) and Johnson and Lynch (1932). For the 1913 Convention: Belden and Belden (1962) and Rodgers (1969). For Patterson's peculiarities: Friedman (1998). For the photograph of Patterson: Johnson and Lynch (1932). For the comparison between NCR and IBM: Rodgers (1969). For the conclusion of the antitrust case: consult the legal documents cited above.

Chapter 6: *Down and Out*

For Watson's feelings about being fired and his subsequent job offers: Watson and Petre (1990). For Flint: Flint (1923). For the early years of CTR, once again Belden and Belden (1962), especially for Watson's early experiences, including his encounter with the board of directors and salary negotiations. Engelbourg (1976), Austrian (1982), Cortada (1993), and Pugh (1995). For the Watson family: Watson and Petre (1990).

Chapter 7: *Terrible Tommy Watson*

Watson and Petre (1990).

Chapter 8: *Thomas J. Watson Sr. in 1893 and Thomas J. Watson Jr. in 1933*

Belden and Belden (1962), Watson and Petre (1990).

Chapter 9: *The Searing Insight*

For Carnegie: Wall (1970), Livesay (2000), Tedlow (2001). For Eastman: Brayer (1996), Tedlow (2001). For Ford: Hounshell (1984), Tedlow (1996), Tedlow (2001). For Watson's improvements in CTR's products: Belden and Belden (1962). For James E. Burke and Tylenol: Foster (1999). For Watson and the future in 1932: Pugh (1995).

Chapter 10: *The Watson Way*

For the 1925 speech: Watson (1934). For the Rodgers quote: Kaplan (1966). For THINK: Belden and Belden (1962), Rodgers

(1969) and Watson and Petre (1990). For songs: Rodgers (1969). For IBM Conventions: Rodgers (1969) is exceptionally insightful.

Chapter 11: The Big Payoff

For the investment in IBM: Breckenridge (May 24, 1941). For working under Watson: Belden and Belden (1962). For IBM sales training: Breckenridge (May 24, 1941). For the silver dollar anecdote: Mayer (1958). For hiring salesmen during the depression: Watson and Petre (1990). For IBM's policy on salaries during World War II: Pugh (1995). For the importance of the punched card business: *Fortune* (January, 1940) and Belden and Belden (1962). For the Hyatt quote: Sloan (1941).

Chapter 12: High Time to Grow Up

Watson and Petre (1990), Black (2001) supplemented by Turner (2001) and Tedlow (2001).

Chapter 13: Watson at War

Watson and Petre (1990).

Chapter 14: Father, Son and Charley Kirk

Watson and Petre (1990). For Kirk's obituary: *NYT* (June 18, 1947).

Chapter 15: God Damn You, Old Man!

Watson and Petre (1990).

Chapter 16: Siblings: A Brief Introduction

For "My Joy": Rodgers (1969). For nineteenth-century liberalism: Wall (1970). For Dick Watson's position in the family: Watson and Petre (1990). For Watson and women at IBM: Pugh (1995) and Amonette (1999). For world markets in the 1950s and 1960s: Foreman-Peck (1995). For IBM World Trade: *Fortune* (November, 1960). For Dick as "almost equal": Foy (1975).

Chapter 17: *Awakening the Electronic Brain*

For Watson and World War II: Pugh (1995). For the punched card: Pugh (1995) and Belden and Belden (1962). For Watson and magnetic tape: Watson and Petre (1990). For Herbert Simon on invention: Simon (Spring, 1987). For Watson and nomenclature: Pugh (1995). For IBM's start in computers: Pugh (1995). For the Hurd, McDowell, and Dunwell quotes: Fisher, McKie, and Mancke (1983). For statistics on horses: Flink (1988). For carriage builders: Critchlow (1996). For Watson Sr. ceding the computer business to his son: Pugh (1995), Watson and Petre (1990).

Chapter 18: *Death of a Salesman*

For the train trip and the last speech: Watson and Petre (1990). For *NYT* articles on Sr.'s death: June 20, 1956 and June 22,1956. For Watson and Eastman: Brayer (1996) and Watson (1934).

Chapter 19: *On His Own*

For the *Fortune* article: September, 1956. For Williamsburg: Watson and Petre (1990). For IBM organization charts: Pugh, Johnson, and Palmer (1991). For UNIVAC's threat: Pugh, Johnson, and Palmer (1991). For Learson: Bashe, Johnson, Palmer, and Pugh (1986), Pugh, Johnson, and Palmer (1991); and Watson and Petre (1990).

Chapter 20: *The New Thomas Watson's New IBM*

For Andy Grove's views on assignment of executives: Grove (1988). For Watson's penchant for "sharp, scratchy . . . guys": Watson and Petre (1990). For Walton: Walton with Huey (1992) and Tedlow (2001). For Grove: Grove (2001). For Sloan: Sloan (1963). For DuPont: Chandler (1962). For Watson's tension at home: Watson and Petre (1990).

Chapter 21: *Threats from Without and from Within*

Consulting Report: Little (1956). For computers in the 1950s:

Baldwin and Clark (2000). For GM's product policy: Chandler and Tedlow (1985). For Evans and SPREAD: Evans (1983). For biographical information on Evans: Cortada (1987). For the complaints of IBM's customers: Baldwin and Clark (2000).

Chapter 22: The System/360

For the Model T: Hounshell (1984) and Sorenson with Williamson (1956). For *Fortune*'s view of the 360: (September 1966). For the Watson family on the eve of the 360: Watson and Petre (1990) and Maney (2003). For Watson Sr.'s aggressive management during World War II: Maney (2003). For Brooks and his disagreement with Evans: Pugh, Johnson, and Palmer (1991). For Brooks's law: Brooks (2003). For Brooks's biography: Cortada (1987). For Haanstra's "rear guard action": Baldwin and Clark (2000). For Haanstra's fate: Pugh, Johnson, and Palmer (1991) and Baldwin and Clark (2000). For the SPREAD Report: *Annals of the History of Computing* (January, 1983). For succession planning at IBM: Watson and Petre (1990).

Chapter 23: The Destruction of Dick Watson

For the 360 in April of 1964: Pugh, Johnson, and Palmer (1991). For the "horse race" between Dick and Learson: Watson and Petre (1990). For the disinterested view of Dick's inexperience: Pugh, Johnson, and Palmer (1991). For 360 sales: Pugh, Johnson, and Palmer (1991). For Dick's failure: Watson and Petre (1990).

Chapter 24: Denouement for Dick and for Jane

For Dick's "brooding": Sobel in Jackson (1994). For Dick's drinking: Anderson in the *Washington Post* (March 16, 1972), *Newsweek* (March 27, 1972), *Houston Chronicle* (March 2, 2002), and Maney (2003). For Dick's situation on his return to IBM's board: Sobel in Jackson (1994). For Dick's death and funeral: Watson and Petre (1990).

Chapter 25: *Denouement for Tom*

For the heart attack: Watson and Petre (1990). For the success of the 360: Baldwin and Clark (2000). For the impact of the lawsuit, including the twenty-seven hours of billing in one day and the number of documents involved: Carroll (1993). For Watson's departure from IBM: Watson and Petre (1990).

Chapter 26: *Denouement for IBM*

For IBM PC sales: Chandler (2001). For IBM's ubiquity in the 1970s: Carroll (1993). For Watson as history's greatest capitalist: *Fortune* (August 31, 1987). For the "song" about Akers: Carroll (1993). For the search for an IBM CEO: Carroll (1993) and Gerstner (2002).

Epilogue

Gerstner (2002). The phrase "physics and technology of semiconductor devices" is from the title of a book by Andy Grove (1967).

Acknowledgments

Adrian Zackheim suggested the idea for *The Watson Dynasty* to me when he was the associate publisher and editor in chief of HarperInformation. Adrian left that position in 2001 to become the publisher of Portfolio, the first dedicated business book imprint within Penguin Group (USA) Inc. He felt that the history of the Watsons and IBM combined the story of the growth of a great company with the drama of the conflicts within a family in a way that was unique but from which, nevertheless, there was a lot to learn for all of us. He was very enthusiastic about this idea. I was skeptical. He was right, and I was wrong.

My agent, Helen Rees, negotiated the contract with Harper-Business, which had successfully handled my previous book, *Giants of Enterprise: Seven Business Innovators and the Empires They Built.* Helen has not only been a business partner, she has been a friend and a cheerleader.

At HarperBusiness, I have had the pleasure of working with Marion Maneker as editor of *The Watson Dynasty.* Marion quickly understood that this book took on a life of its own. He understood what I wanted to do from the beginning and offered innumerable suggestions for the improvement of the manuscript.

At the Harvard Business School, my debts are numerous. I must first express my gratitude to Dean Kim B. Clark, who has been consistent in his support of the business history enterprise at the school and has helped turn that enterprise into something really special in the academic world. Kim's coauthor and my friend and colleague, Professor Carliss Y. Baldwin, shared with me her remarkable grasp of the business and technical issues surrounding the creation of the IBM System/360, which proved to be a turning point in the history of the company and the industry.

Professor Rowena Olegario, now at Vanderbilt University, wrote a case on "IBM and the Two Thomas J. Watsons" which I have taught to hundreds of Harvard Business School students. I am grateful to her and to them for what I have learned from their discussions of this case.

Kim Bettcher, Ph.D., has worked with me on my research for five years. He provided a great deal of information which has enriched *The Watson Dynasty*. Also of vital importance in obtaining information has been the team of business information analysts at the Baker Library of the Harvard Business School, especially Sarah C. Eriksen, Jeffrey Cronin, Kathleen Ryan, and Chris Allen. I believe this group is the best of its kind in the world.

The preparation of the manuscript was managed by Christopher Albanese, Aimee Hamel, and Darcy Weber; and I am grateful to them all.

My college classmate, Reed E. Hundt, offered critical insights into how best to position this book to maximize its impact. A senior adviser at McKinsey, member of the board of Intel, and former chairman of the Federal Communications Commission, Reed has a knowledge of the business world which an academician like myself does not; and that knowledge enriched this book.

My greatest debt is to my wife, Joyce. Joyce is a psychiatrist, and most of the psychological insight in the book comes from her. During the writing of this book, Joyce has been dying of ovarian cancer. The book was completed because of her loving generosity in the face of a situation which cannot be described. It has to be experienced to be understood.

INDEX